THE BODY, CHILDHOOD AND SOCIETY

D1104669

Also by Alan Prout

THEORIZING CHILDHOOD (*with Allison James and Chris Jenks*)

CONSTRUCTING AND RECONSTRUCTING CHILDHOOD (*editor with Allison James*)

The Body, Childhood and Society

Edited by

Alan Prout
Reader in Sociology
University of Hull
and
Director
ESRC Children 5–16 Research Programme

Consultant Editor: Jo Campling

First published in Great Britain 2000 by
MACMILLAN PRESS LTD
Houndmills, Basingstoke, Hampshire RG21 6XS and London
Companies and representatives throughout the world

A catalogue record for this book is available from the British Library.

ISBN 0–333–65948–1 hardcover
ISBN 0–333–65949–X paperback

 First published in the United States of America 2000 by
ST. MARTIN'S PRESS, INC.,
Scholarly and Reference Division,
175 Fifth Avenue, New York, N.Y. 10010

ISBN 0–312–22144–4

Library of Congress Cataloging-in-Publication Data
The body, childhood and society / edited by Alan Prout.
p.   cm.
Includes bibliographical references and index.
ISBN 0–312–22144–4 (cloth)
1. Children.   2. Body, Human—Social aspects.   I. Prout, Alan.
HQ767.9.B63   1999
305.23—dc21   98–49901
                                                                  CIP

This book is printed on paper suitable for recycling and made from fully managed and sustained forest sources.

10   9   8   7   6   5   4   3   2   1
09   08   07   06   05   04   03   02   01   00

Printed and bound in Great Britain by
Antony Rowe Ltd, Chippenham, Wiltshire

To Pia whose idea this book first was

Contents

Acknowledgements

I am grateful to Jo Campling for her invaluable guidance through the publishing process, to Sue Hodgson for her help in preparing the manuscript, and to all the contributors for their sociological imaginations and their patience.

Notes on the Contributors

Pia Haudrup Christensen is Research Fellow and Associate Director of the Centre for the Social Study of Childhood, University of Hull, and an associate researcher with the University of Southern Denmark.

Ronnie Frankenberg is Professor Emeritus in Sociology and Anthropology, teaching and researching at both Keele and Brunel Universities.

Allison James is Reader in the School of Comparative and Applied Social Sciences, University of Hull and Director of the Centre for the Social Study of Childhood.

Nick Lee is a lecturer in the Department of Sociology and Social Anthropology at Keele University.

Kathryn Backett-Milburn is a sociologist based in the Department of Public Health Sciences at the University of Edinburgh Medical School.

Bernard Place did his doctoral research at the University of Hull and does nursing research at St Thomas's Hospital, London.

Shirley Prendergast teaches and does research at the Department of Sociology, Anglia Polytechnic University.

Alan Prout is Reader in the School of Comparative and Applied Social Sciences, University of Hull and Director of the ESRC Children 5–16 Research Programme.

Brenda Simpson is a graduate student at the Centre for the Social Study of Childhood, University of Hull.

1 Childhood Bodies: Construction, Agency and Hybridity

Alan Prout

INTRODUCTION

Childhood and the body are topics which have both seen an enormous growth of sociological interest in recent years. Both have been reconstituted as legitimate topics of sociological enquiry, that is as properly belonging to the 'social' sphere and in need liberation from their previous confinement to the 'natural'. In both cases a substantial and still growing literature has been produced to this end. In general, however, these developments have occurred on separate tracks, with remarkably little contact between the two fields and only occasional cross-reference. This volume takes a step towards remedying this mutual neglect by bringing together a series of papers and research reports by sociologists and anthropologists who have investigated their intersection.

In this introductory chapter I review some of the theoretical issues that underlie this enterprise, commenting on their debate as they emerge in this volume. The first theme of my discussion is the parallel emergence of social constructionism in the literatures of childhood and the body – a synchrony that makes their isolation from each other all the more remarkable and in need of remedy. Looking at them together has reinforced the need to examine critically the value of social constructionism as a theoretical orientation. Whilst it undoubtedly provided a necessary, useful and even essential counterpoint to biological reductionism, helping to create a conceptual space within which to think about the non-biological correlates of both the body and childhood, social constructionism has proved too narrow in its focus. The nub of the issue is the manner in which social constructionist accounts of childhood and the body tend to exclude (or at least de-emphasize) the possibility that social life has a material as well as a discursive (or representational)

1

component. In contrast, the chapters in this volume show, in various ways, the possibility of apprehending childhood bodies as both material and representational entities.

The second theme is that of children's agency in the interpretation, negotiation and utilization of their bodies. It derives directly from the recent sociology of childhood and its concern to reconstitute children as social actors. Entailing a shift in emphasis from seeing children as the outcomes of society, this balances a former emphasis on the socialization of children by highlighting the ways in which children are also agents, participants shaping, as well as being shaped by, society. That this possibility has been muted in sociological engagements with childhood for so long is testimony to how strongly adult-centric a discipline it has been (for exegesis of this point, see James and Prout, 1990; Mayall, 1994). Elementary though this point is, it has yet to be fully absorbed by mainstream sociology. It therefore remains an essential starting point for empirical enquiry, one paid particular attention in the early chapters of this volume. What emerges strongly from these discussions is that children's understanding of the body cannot be treated as an imperfect or incomplete version of the adult. Rather, children understand and perform their bodies in ways often different from adults; entering into their world is thus an essential step in an adequate sociology of childhood bodies.

The final theme, which in some ways is an extension of the first, emerges towards the end of the volume. Here we find contributors drawing on the sociology of translation in order to unravel some of the ways in which children's (or for that matter, adults') bodies are inextricably interwoven with other aspects of the material environment – artefacts, machines and technologies. Children's bodies emerge as hybrid entities. They are inseparable from, produced in, represented by and performed through their connections with other material objects (including the medical monitoring equipment, video cameras and musical instruments that feature in the analyses of the final chapters). This line of enquiry feeds back into the question of children's agency by reconstituting it less as an essential attribute of children and more as an effect of the connections made between a heterogeneous array of materials, including bodies, representations and technologies.

CONSTRUCTING CHILDHOOD BODIES: DISCOURSE AND MATERIALITY

As noted above, the 1980s saw a significant change of direction in the sociology of childhood. The balancing of structural determinations with a concern for children's agency was accompanied by an embrace of social constructionism. Whilst biological immaturity was conceded as a human universal, childhood was hailed as a social and cultural phenomenon marked by spatial and historical variability. The move to social constructionism therefore entailed making a radical disjunction between society and biology. Not surprisingly this new thinking gave little attention to the body, although a current of uneasiness about it is detectable in some social constructionist writings. For example, Prout and James (1990) in proposing the study of childhood as social construction, acknowledged that the (material) body should be understood as at least a limit or constraint on the possibilities of the social construction of childhood. This posed questions about the extent to which childhood as discursive construct could be understood independently of childhood as a stage of biological growth, and about the weight that should be given to each. These worries, however, remained marginal to a discussion that was predominantly concerned to establish childhood as 'social' rather than 'natural'. As was also the case for studies of the body, social constructionism became something of an orthodoxy in the new sociology of childhood. The reason for its attraction was much the same in both cases: it seemed to provide the most secure defence against attempts to read social relations as epiphenomena of nature. For those intent on seeing either childhood or the body (or both) as part of culture not nature this seemed a congenial position to occupy.

In fact, as Brian Turner (1984, 1992) has suggested, sociological treatments of the body have been plagued by a tendency to fall into either biological or cultural reductionism: divided between what he terms 'foundationalist' and 'anti-foundationalist' approaches. Foundationalists take the view that the body is a real, material entity, which is connected with but different from the many different frameworks of meaning in which it is variously represented in human cultures. At its most basic, foundationalists assume that there is something constant (but perhaps changing) which functions independently of the social context within which it is found. The body (and its processes of change) form an entity that is experienced and lived. What is prioritized in this perspective, therefore, is largely phenomenological. The task of sociologists is to document and analyse how the body is experienced and interpreted by different actors in different social and cultural contexts. Anti-foundationalists, however, are unwilling to make a distinction between the body and its representations. In an extreme form anti-foundationalists might argue in an entirely idealist fashion: that there is no material body – only our perceptions, constructions or understandings. Less extreme, but also less consistent, is the view that even if the materiality of the body is conceded we only have access to it through discourses of various kinds. It is these discourses, or ways of representing the body, that structure and shape our experiences of it and the meanings we give to it. In this view, then, the task of social scientists is to analyse these representations and uncover the social processes through which they are made and have their effects.

The problem is that, as Turner argues, it is not possible to be simultaneously and consistently foundationalist and anti-foundationalist, because each position is defined in opposition to the other. Turner's suggested way out of this problem is methodological eclecticism: that is to say, he suggests accepting the intellectual legitimacy of both approaches, using each as and when it is appropriate and seeing them as in some way different but complementary. Whilst this allows empirical flexibility and diversity of approach, it is not theoretically coherent: different and irreconcilable assumptions are being made about the material character of the body. In taking up this point, Shilling suggests that Turner fails in his ambition to synthesize foundationalist and anti-foundationalist approaches and argues (in effect though not quite in these terms) that this is because his method is additive rather than relational. Turner, he correctly observes, attempts to 'combine foundationalist and anti-foundationalist frameworks without altering any of their basic parameters' (Shilling, 1993: 103). Consequently, he does not examine the *relationships* between the body in nature and the body in society.

Shilling attempts to synthesize the two approaches, and in so doing develops a position that is of great potential importance for studies of childhood. The essence of his suggestion is that the human body is socially and biologically unfinished at birth. Over the life course – and childhood would seem to be a crucial stage – it changes through processes that are simultaneously biological and social. Drawing on a very wide range of social theory he suggests two basic elements of a framework. The first, that the mind–body relationship has to be seen in the wider context of the culture–nature relationship, is drawn from both anthropological and feminist analyses. Important among the former is the theory of symbol and metaphor developed by Lakoff and Johnson (1980). They argue that there is a close, but not one-to-one, relationship between mind and body as a result of the mind being located in and dependent on bodily mechanisms for the perception of the natural world. We exist, for example, in a world where gravity creates phenomena of motion as 'up' or 'down' and human thought incorporates, draws on and elaborates this phenomenon. Feminist writers have also, though to different degrees, pointed to irreducible biological differences between the sexes which shape experience differently for men and women. Whilst some feminist analyses tend towards biological reductionism (often with an inversion of male claims to superiority), others look to an interaction between biological and social processes in which natural differences are transformed or distorted into social ones (Chernin, 1983; Orbach, 1988). In these accounts the body is not only shaped by social relations, but also enters into their construction as both as resource and a constraint.

The theme of the body as socially and biologically unfinished reconnects what social constructionism separated. It draws attention to how the body and society work on each other – a theme that emerges throughout the chapters of this volume. James, for example, shows how material differences in size and weight present children with a series of problems which must be negotiated by working representational transformations that can render them nearer to or further from the bodily appearances of their peers. Similarly, Prendergast shows how girls manage bodily changes at menarche in home and school settings which render menstruation a shameful secret. Christensen and Milburn show how children's bodies are the targets of parental practices at home which protect and nourish them, whilst Simpson describes how teachers attempt to regulate the appearance and time/space trajectories of their bodies in school.

The multifaceted character of these practices, at one and the same time biological and social, can be contrasted with the analysis of children's bodies in a social constructionist account such as Armstrong's (1983, 1987). His interest in childhood bodies derives from the important role that he argues childhood as a changing cultural construction has played in the constitution of twentieth-century medicine. He strongly contests the claim that there is a biology outside social life to which we might refer when trying to

understand the enterprise of biomedicine. Instead the body is understood not as an underlying reality but as a form of knowledge shaped
by the social circumstances of its construction. Knowledge of the
body is, therefore, not to be understood as a more or less accurate
representation of some underlying reality, but as a way of looking
and representing which is sustained and is sustaining of social practices (1987: 66). The body is a perception, construction, invention,
classification or representation that is endlessly perceived anew,
reconstructed, reinvented, reclassified and represented. It is from
this perspective that Armstrong traces the development of paedi-
atrics as a distinct medical discipline, at first as a speciality concerned
with the diseases of children, but later in its attempt to claim a
concern with the health and development of children as a whole,
producing on the way an array of different children: 'Nervous children, delicate children, neuropathic children, maladjusted children,
difficult children, oversensitive children and unstable children...'
(1983: 15)

Enlightening though this account is of how medicine created
categories of children, the body remains remarkably incorporeal.
Armstrong's body is, in Terence Turner's terms, an 'anti-body', one
which:

> ... has no flesh; ... is begotten out of discourse by power...
> the desires that comprise it illusory subjectivity are themselves
> the predicates of external discourses rather than the products or
> metaphorical expressions of any internal life of its own. (Turner,
> 1994: 36)

The contributors to this book do not neglect or underestimate how
powerful discursive formations can be in shaping how children's
bodies are perceived, understood, worked upon and produced.
Christensen's account of the manner in which notions of children's
essential vulnerability enter into adult understandings of even the
most commonplace of accidents or mishaps in the school playground
illustrates this well. However, because the contributors engage with
multiple components of children's lives, confining their attention
to only one of these, that is discourse, would be unsatisfactory.

CHILDREN AS AGENTS

The second theme of this volume concerns what has been a central preoccupation of the recent sociology of childhood: the effort to document not only how children are shaped by society but also how they shape it. Recent critiques (see, for example, James and Prout, 1990; Mayall, 1994; Qvortrup et al., 1994; Hutchby and Moran-Ellis, 1998; James, Jenks and Prout, 1998) have argued that the concept of socialization renders children passive; they become outcomes of social processes but not actors participating within them. Although not entirely uniform in their approach (see James, Jenks and Prout, 1998), recent sociological engagements with childhood have set out to make children's agency more visible. As Alanen (1997) notes:

Children are treated as speaking, knowing and experiencing subjects, as social actors actively involved in the social worlds they live in, and as interactive agents who engage with people, ideologies and institutions and through this engagement forge a place for themselves in their own social worlds.

This shift has undoubtedly had many positive effects, theoretically guiding studies which, because they have allowed conceptual autonomy to children, have noticed aspects of their agency previously rendered invisible. Whilst, like all social actors, children can be seen as shaped and constrained by the circumstances of their lives, they also shape them and are enabled by them. They are limited by the conditions of their social lives, but also find ways of creatively managing, negotiating and extending the possibilities.

Whilst the anti-foundationalist view of children's bodies speaks to the role of professions such as medicine and their role in the creation of frameworks through which the body is understood, it has little to say about the childhood body in these terms. On the contrary the person with a body is generally construed quite passively: acted upon, regulated, disciplined and determined. This may be thought a problem for any account of the body, but it poses a particularly sharp problem in the study of childhood. For a countervailing view we have to turn to those, including many of the contributors to this book, who have placed the lived worlds of childhood more centrally. Working within a framework that rejects the passive view of children that is implicit in socialization theory, their accounts are usually accomplished through the use of intensive ethnographic immersion in the detail of children's lives. In an earlier example of such work, James (1993) deals with how children create and enact categories of significant difference, especially bodily difference at home and in school. She notes that bodily differences (of height, weight, etc.) have been employed to create 'the child' as an Othered category in Western cultures. Cultural stereotypes about what constitutes a normally developing body for a child assume, she argues, great importance for both parents and children themselves. Deviations from these normative notions can create intense anxiety. Amongst children themselves, experience of the body, and especially of bodily differences, function as important signifiers for social identity. In her ethnography James noted five aspects of the body that seemed to have particular significance for the children she studied: height, shape, appearance, gender and performance. Each of these acted as a flexible and shifting resource for children's interactions and emergent identities and relationships.

Although cultural stereotypes about each of the five features mentioned by James played a role, children did not simply passively absorb them. Rather they actively apprehended and used them in experiencing not only their own body, but also its relationship to other bodies and the meanings that were forged from these encounters. One reason for this was that children have to come to terms not only with their own constantly changing bodies and those of their peers, but also with the changing institutional contexts within which meaning is given to these changes. For example, James reports how in the later stages of nursery school children came to think of themselves as 'big'; their apprehension of the difference between themselves and children just entering the nursery plus the significance of the impending transition to primary school signalled this identity. But once they had made the transition and were at the outset of their career in primary school they were catapulted back into being small again. This relativity produced, therefore, a fluidity about the relationship between size and status, which produced what James identifies as a typical 'edginess' amongst the children about body meanings. The body became a crucial resource for making and breaking identity precisely because it was unstable.

It is somewhat surprising that Shilling devotes little attention to childhood. It would after all appear to be a time when work on and by the body is relatively intense. Childhood *per se*, however, appear in relation to only two substantive topics: Norbert Elias's account of the 'civilizing process', that is the long-term historical trend towards individuals practising internalized control and restraint over forms of behaviour concerned with bodily functions such as eating, copulating and defecating; and Bourdieu's account of the transmission of class habitus. From the point of view of the sociology of childhood both Elias and Bourdieu are deficient, or at best ambiguous, in their assumptions about childhood socialization. Both treat children as passively and gradually accreting or accumulating embodied dispositions in the transition to the full sociality of adulthood. There is little (or only equivocal) recognition of the possibility that children actively appropriate and transform as well as absorb. Nor is there a sense that childhood and growing up are full of reversals, transformations and inversions rather than being a progression to an ever closer copy of adulthood. In short, what is missing is a sense of children as being as well becoming, childhood as staged and children as active, creative performers (see also, for example, Bluebond-Langner et al., 1991).

In this volume several contributors show how children are actively engaged in work on and with the body. James revisits her earlier ethnography, re-emphasizing the active role of children, but now placing this in temporal perspective, suggesting how children negotiate and renegotiate identities. In the process of growing up, bodily changes create new possibilities; children cannot control bodily changes, but through skilful handling can use them as flexible resources for translation into identity. Backett-Milburn shows how middle-class children and parents translate, and thereby partially transform, official discourses of health into everyday practices. Whilst adhering to the rhetoric of health promotion, officially sanctioned behaviour is also practically contested, subverted and renegotiated in families according to countervailing pressures and interests. The chapter shows that far from being docile in the face of officially distributed norms, children (as well as parents) are actively involved in negotiating their meaning and in resisting or modifying their implementation. Simpson also emphasizes the body as a site of contestation, this time in schools. Arguing that rhetorics of children's safety displace attention from the body as a site of disciplinary and regulatory regimes, she suggests that teachers, in attempting to produce docile bodies, are met with resistance from children. Both boys and girls, in taking up the idiom of the body, engage in sometimes subtly pitched activities which subvert this aim.

Prendergast and Christensen illustrate how the body and society are inextricably woven at particular moments of the life course. Prendergast shows how the body is shaped by and is shaping of feminine identity as girls experience menarche. She examines how adolescent girls on the cusp of womanhood live a present which in its social and material arrangements emphasizes the shame and secrecy of menstruation. Through this they gaze into a future when their body is rendered problematic and at the same time are able to remember a childhood past when the relationship between gender and identity could be flexible and open. As she has pointed out:

> The issue of embodiment as a cultural process surfaces most poignantly at key points in the life cycle: the trajectory of the body is given symbolic and moral value: bodily forms are paradigmatic of social transition . . . Each stage requires that we adjust to and attend to our body, or that of others, in an appropriate and special way . . .' (Prendergast, 1992: 1)

The possibility that childhood is created through, even perhaps requires, certain kinds of bodily performance is directly addressed by Christensen. She shows not only their creative activity but also that contemporary children inhabit a highly staged world – 'childhood' – which is marked off from the rest of society. As such it stands in a paradoxical relationship to the adult world and cannot to be taken as an incomplete or faulty version of it. In her theoretical discussion Christensen raises important questions about 'vulnerability' as one of the central defining features of this contemporary childhood. Rather than accepting children's vulnerability as simply a fact of nature, she proposes the need for investigation into the components of this vulnerability. She suggests that whilst children, like many others, may at times be vulnerable, there is a push towards its use as a master identity for children. Ideologically children are separated from adults, rendered as objects of concern, help and intervention, and minimized in their capacity for dealing with their problems. At the same time their actual experiences, those that they experience as vulnerability, are not much listened to by adults.

In a finely observed ethnography of a Danish primary school she shows that in everyday accidents children's attempt to observe their own bodily processes is often immediately apprehended by adults as a call for help. In response they generally tried to teach the

children to make less fuss, sometimes by telling them so and sometimes by ignoring their complaints. Observation of the children
showed that they often drew attention to bodily experiences in very
dramatic ways, often with the request from others to 'Look!' For
the children, however, this demand was not one for medical attention, first aid or help of any kind. Rather the children were drawing
on a wider practice, engaged in during all kinds of games, play and
other activities, of asking others to share their experience of the
body. In her interactions with the children she, as an adult, came
to learn to share in the act of looking rather than reprimand the
child for over-dramatizing or even to give help in a leap to the
assumption of vulnerability.

THE HYBRID BODY

Work of this kind, although not formally based upon it, shows how
the notion of the body as socially and biologically unfinished might
be worked through in relation to children – provided that children's interpretative activity as social beings is also appreciated.
Children's bodies then appear in a variety of roles: in the construction of social relations, meanings and experiences between
children themselves and with adults; as a products of and resources
for agency, action and interaction; and as sites for socialization
through embodiment. By emphasizing the relationship between the
body and society they begin to undermine the notion that it is possible
to understand social relations as if the body were able to be abstracted
from them.

Rather, what emerges is an account of children as hybrids of
culture and nature, a vision that accords well with Latour's notion
that social life can only be properly understood as inescapably impure,
constituted in and through 'heterogeneous networks'. These are,
as he puts it 'simultaneously real, like nature, narrated, like discourse and collective, like society' (Latour, 1993: 6). Latour's point
is that this complexity must be confronted, not avoided. When childhood bodies (or other entities) are thought of as purely discursive,
as social constructionism tends to do, then the account given is
bound at best to be seriously incomplete and at worst misleadingly
reductionist. Both the object of analysis (in this case, childhood
bodies) and our notion of the social are diminished in ways no less
consequential than those commissioned by biological reductionism.

The chapters of this book demonstrate this. Whatever the topic or the theoretical interest of the authors, their detailed concern with the lives of their research subjects shows the interplay of representations and materialities. Sometimes the discursive practices highlighted by social constructionism, for example the ways in which the body is represented or classified, are paramount. But at other moments practices that are material ones, for example diet, exercise and disciplinary regimes, which materially shape the body, are. Heterogeneity is the rule, although the combinations are multiple and the practices of combining the different components of social life highly variable.

Contained in Latour's position is a refusal to accept a settled and given distinction between nature and culture. Recognition that the body and childhood are simultaneously products of both follows from this. That sociological discourse often finds it difficult to comprehend such simultaneities results from its tendency to delineate the content of social life as that which is not nature. In this perspective the body must be conceded to the biological sciences because if a line has to be drawn it appears *prima facie* as part of nature. Similarly, when childhood was thought of as a biological phenomenon it was not much attended to in sociology, although it was appropriated to the degree that socialization, that is becoming social, was understood precisely as a transition from nature to culture. The concept of socialization therefore rested on a view of children as social only in so far as they gradually ceased being natural. Ironically, social constructionist visions of childhood made the disjunction between culture and nature even sharper.

However, once social life is recognized as heterogeneous, no *a priori* parcelling out of entities (people, bodies, minds, artefacts, animals, plants, etc.) into culture or nature is thinkable. Amongst these both the body and childhood can be comprehended as complex entities in which a medley of culture and nature is given as a condition of possibility. This is analytically more challenging than starting with a stable and given division between the natural and the cultural. It requires the close but open-ended empirical investigation which childhood bodies are given in this book, an examination which shows them to be the product of exactly such combinations. The implications of this move, however, exceed either the body or childhood. It takes us towards an appreciation of all those other entities which issue from the imbrications of culture and nature. The social becomes a construction not only of and by humans (whether adults or children), not only of and by bodies (not to mention minds), but also of and by technologies.

Prendergast explicitly attends to such a source of hybridity by pointing to the importance of material objects and artefacts in the creation of meaning around menarche. Arguing that culturally organized embarrassment, negativity and secrecy about menstruation is not only learned attitudinally but is embodied in posture and corporeal demeanour, she shows the ways in which shame is transmitted through forms of discourse (for example, teasing and name-calling), social interaction (for example, by boys publicly tipping out the contents of a girl's bag to reveal tampons) *and* in the material organization of school life (for example, inadequate, unhygienic and inaccessible toilets). Frankenberg, in his detailed analysis of Jane Campion's film *The Piano*, similarly points to the shifting alliances between people and things, in his case fictional nineteenth-century individuals of varying statuses, including a child, and the eponymous Piano. In an analysis enriched by a viewing of the film or a reading of the film script, he suggests that the film-maker is able to combine past, present and future in ways much more difficult to accomplish than in the conventional ethnographic narrative.

Such insights underline the necessity of moving beyond the relationship between body and society *per se* and locating this in the dense, networked heterogeneity that is social life. A highly pertinent example of this approach is found in the work of Bernard Place (1994 and this volume). He shows how different approaches to the body might be integrated by looking at the processes surrounding the intensive combination of children's bodies with medical technologies. The ethnographic location he chose was the modern hospital, specifically a paediatric intensive care unit. He points out that in this particular location the human body is perforated, cannulated, intubated and catheterized before being connected to sets of technological artefacts which enable detailed examination of the functioning of the heart, kidneys, brain, lungs and other organs. Such artefacts generate sets of symbols (traces, numbers and images) which are manipulated by the doctors and nurses. In the process of connection to these artefacts the body is ordered, externalized, and its boundary extended. The body becomes circumscribed by both corporeal (human) and non-corporeal (technological) elements, becoming in Place's term 'technomorphic'.

In this setting the nurses and doctors, as well as the parents and child patients, are concerned to maintain the integrity of the body.

But what is the body in these circumstances? On the basis of his participant observation Place makes a distinction between what he calls 'child data' (what is happening within the corporeal body) and 'data child' (the visible manifestation of that corporeality through its connection to the surrounding technological artefacts). The co-incidence of the two cannot be taken for granted and it is argued that the conditions whereby they are held together is accomplished minute by minute. He argues that the work of the intensive care unit entails maintaining an association between 'child data' and 'data child'.

CHILDHOOD BODIES AS TRANSLATIONS

Place's insights give a fresh perspective on Turner's central divide between foundational and non-foundational views; the body and its representations are not mutually exclusive but mutually dependent, embedded in heterogeneous networks. These concerns are well developed within one strand of the social study of science and technology (see, for example, Latour and Woolgar, 1986; and Latour 1993). Sometimes called the sociology of translation (or actor-network theory), this literature is concerned with the materials from which social life is produced and the practices by which these are ordered and patterned. Being substantively interested in science and technology, its object constantly undermines a sharp distinction between culture and nature by focusing on the network of mediation between them. The sociology of translation has much in common with forms of sociology that emphasize the relational, constructed and processual character of social life. At the same time it is quite distinct in one crucial and radical respect: it rejects the assumption that society is constructed through human action and meaning alone. In this feature it is sharply different from social constructionism. It remains constructivist, but in a radically generalized way; and it restates materialist sociology, but in a way which places the material in relation to the other elements that constitute society. In fact 'society' is seen as produced in and through patterned networks of heterogeneous materials; it is made up through a wide variety of shifting associations (and dissociations) between human *and* non-human entities. Indeed, so ubiquitous are associations between humans and the rest of the material world that all entities are to be seen as hybrids – what Latour (1993) has termed 'quasi-objects' and 'quasi-subjects' – where the boundary between the human and the non-human is shifting, negotiated and empirical.

In this view social life cannot, therefore, be reduced either to the 'purely' human (adult or child) or to the 'purely' anything. As a general rule (but subject always to detailed empirical examination) we can say that no entity alone determines the ordering that results from their combination. Sociological approaches that try to make one kind of entity do all the explanatory work result in some form of reductionism – in the way Turner indicates that foundational and non-foundational approaches to the body have a tendency to do. Like all phenomena, the sociology of translation would see children and bodies as constructed not only from human minds and their interactions, not only from human bodies and their interactions, but also through an unending mutually constituting interaction of a vast array of material and non-material resources.

Analysis focuses on the 'translations' – the network of mediation – between these different entities. It is concerned to trace the processes by which these heterogeneous entities mutually enrol, constitute and order each other, processes which always involve something being retained, something being added and something being taken away. Bodies are included – but alongside aspects of the natural and material environment, including their orchestration and hybridization into artefacts of many different types. All of these are to be seen as a priori equal (or symmetrical) actants in the creation of society – or more properly 'the networks of the social'. This approach would place childhoods and bodies in relation to not only symbolic but also material culture. What produces them is not simply biological events, not only the phenomenology of bodily experience, and not merely structures of symbolic and discursive meaning – although all of these are important – but also the patterns of material organization and their modes of ordering. Examining childhood bodies in this view becomes a matter of tracing through the means, the varied array of materials and practices involved in their construction and maintenance – and in some circumstances their unravelling and disintegration.

CHILDHOOD AND AGENCY REVISITED

I suggested above that recent developments in the sociology of childhood have emphasized children as social actors. This theoretical possibility has allowed new questions to be asked in empirical studies which have rendered children's agency visible. This empirical vigour is, however, matched by a weakness: the 'agency' in 'children's agency' remains inadequately theorized. Whilst instances of children's agency are readily found and the limits on it beginning to be specified (see, for example, Mayall, 1996) there is a tendency to leave matters at the level of discovery and description. Whilst the excitement of registering and mapping the hitherto unnoticed is understandable, it is open to the criticism that it treats children's agency in an essentialist way. It is valorized, but treated as a given but previously overlooked attribute of children. Instead, I suggest, we need to decentre agency, asking how it is that children sometimes exercise it, that is bring about some effect in the relationships in which they are embedded, whilst on other occasions they do not. The observation that children can exercise agency should be a point of analytical embarkation not a terminus.

In this volume Lee makes an analysis of the type I am advocating in relation to the introduction of video testimony by children in abuse cases. He argues that the introduction of this practice in English courts is not well explained by a general cultural shift in the appreciation of children's capacity as witnesses. Rather there was a dual shift in the mediations between children and courts. On the one hand, medical claims to speak for children's bodies were diminished through the (at least partial) discrediting of the anal dilation reflex test during in the Cleveland Enquiry into child abuse accusations. At the same time, technologies were brought into play which helped to overcome long-standing legal objections to children as proper witnesses, objections which he argues are only one instance of a general procedure used to test the credibility of all witnesses. In creating a new alliance between child and device, video testimony arrangements constitute children as proper witnesses and construct them as speaking subjects in this setting.

In my view Lee, although right to be suspicious of general cultural change as an explanation of the events he describes, underestimates the discursive component. Discussions in social work, law and more broadly around children's rights had perhaps a greater role to play than he suggests. Nevertheless, the changes he describes came about only when practical means for their implementation (a technology of video cameras and recording) were coupled with discourses of childhood. The general theoretical point underlying this example is derived from the sociology of translation: agency is an effect brought about by the assembly of heterogeneous materials. It is produced through the connections between an empirically diverse set of resources: discursive, biological, technological, and so on. In this sense children's agency is in principle amenable to analysis in exactly the same way as the agency of adults. What is required is detailed examination of the network of connections, the materials and the means of their translation, through which children's agency is (or is not) produced.

CONCLUSION

Recent attempts to constitute childhood as a sociological topic emphasized it as a social phenomenon in at least two ways: by pointing to the social construction of childhood as a discursive formation and by enquiry into the active and creative capacities of children to shape their lives. As with the body, the turn to social constructionism in the sociological study of childhood seemed to wrestle their object away from the assumption that it belongs to the sphere of nature rather than culture. In both cases, however, the attempt to render all things 'social' was problematic. In the sociology of the body it led to theoretical inconsistencies in assumptions about the status of the material body. In addressing these Shilling argued, through his notion of the body unfinished, for an interaction between the body and society and a more open boundary between nature and culture.

In the sociology of childhood, the body was at first approached with caution but it became clear that a move similar to Shilling's was necessary. The literature which emerged made sense in terms of the weakening of the culture/nature divide but with some significant modification in the attention to children's own creative activity. In its empirical detail this work revealed the connection between children as social actors and the body and, though emergently, their heterogeneous composition.

The chapters in this volume demonstrate that attention to children's bodies, and how these act, are experienced and constructed, is important to the project of understanding children as social actors. In pursuing it they track the shift from seeing children as outcomes to viewing them as agents, take in both the corporeal and the representational aspects of body and broaden the picture to take in extensions to the body through artefacts. Although not always the stated intention of the different authors, this work points towards the heterogeneous character of the social and the need to be empirically open to the multitude of hybridities that this may entail. It is a way of looking at children and bodies which traverses many settings, in this volume schools, hospitals, households and courts, and requires the sort of enquiry into the varieties of material and symbolic work done on and by children's bodies that the contributors to this book have made. In reviewing this work I suggest that the issue is not whether there is a material body as distinct from representations – because this could be accepted as a taken-for-granted feature of the heterogeneous social, a position reconciling the different versions of the body that permeate sociology. Neither is it contentious to include children as active creators of social life rather than passive products of society; viewed from the sociology of translation all entities are seen as having this potential – although the extent to which they perform it and the means of its enactment are the stuff of empirical enquiry. Rather analysis concerns the different, often conflicting and contested, attempts, including those by children themselves, to 'speak for' this body, to translate it and enrol it in social action.

2 Embodied Being(s): Understanding the Self and the Body in Childhood

Allison James

INTRODUCTION

Though so commonplace as to be unremarkable, the school photograph offers us a splendid iconography of childhood and the child's body. In British primary schools of the 1950s and 1960s, three sometimes four rows of children are lined up to face the camera. In the back rows the children stand tall: backs straight, with arms hanging down by their sides or, just occasionally, with hands clasped together. The front row kneels or sits crossed legged, hands in laps. Bearing smiles and half-smiles, bodies are visually uniform, if not in accordance with school rules of dress, certainly with that era's fashion for children's clothes and hair styles. Here is a class of children, barely differentiated members of a group, united by a common age, fixed at a particular point in time (see also Prendergast, this volume). Though now often displaced by portraits of the child (occasionally accompanied by a sibling, reflection of perhaps the growing recognition of children's agency and an increasing sense of individualism), now in colour, the school photograph of the 1990s none the less continues to offer us a redolent image of childhood: still wearing the badge of school membership, with a uniformed body, hair brushed and newly washed face, the child poses, its stilled body presenting us, quite literally, with a picture of the school(ed) child: of a body tamed, ordered and controlled.

And yet if such photographs are placed side by side, year upon year, subtle changes are evident in those bodies: the same faces, some new ones maybe, but each year bodies have become fatter, thinner, taller, tidier or indeed more unruly; hair is longer, shorter, worn in plaits, or hanging loose. Thus, a child's development is

19

charted for us through these summer photographs, as a staged and
phased progression to maturity.

In my own school photographs of the 1950s and early 1960s there
is, however, one constant: being tall for my age, in each photograph I am in the centre of the back row of children. In those
days, as often now, artistic style favoured a pictorial pyramidic symmetry so that I am in the middle of the photograph, sometimes
head and shoulders above the other children, who in decreasing
size sequence are placed on either side of me. Here, then, is a
picture not only of a static and controlled child's body, but also of
its simultaneous potential for change and growth over time.[1]

Taking these potent images of childhood as a starting point, this
chapter explores the ways in which bodily change is used as a marker
of child identity. First it considers how the temporality of childhood has been and continues to be mapped onto the body of the
child and offers a theoretical account of that process of embodiment; second, using ethnographic data, it suggests how an approach
which begins from a theory of embodiment offers us greater insight
into the meanings, for children, of bodily change and of the passing
of time during childhood.

That childhood is shaped through particular envisionings of time,
as both nostalgic cultural and personal pasts and as visions of individual and collective futures has been variously noted (James and
Prout, 1990; Jenks, 1994) and the impact of temporal routines upon
children's own and everyday activities remarked (James, Jenks and
Prout, 1998). But the exact ways in which the passage of time in
the life course is experienced by children has received consider-
ably less attention, with Solberg's (1990) account of the impact of
conceptions of age upon children's social experience and activities
being one of the few studies available. That it is the body that facili-
tates this passage of time in the life course for children seems, for
the most part, to have remained unremarked, despite the fact that
it is children's rapidly changing bodies which provide unique and
potent iconic symbols for the passing of time, in a diversity of arenas
from great literature through to TV advertisements.[2] There is a
paucity of sociological and anthropological research which explores
how children understand and experience their embodiment of time.
Indeed, it would seem that only in studies of children for whom
time threatens to be cut short (that is studies of children with terminal
illnesses) is this given any prominence (Bluebond-Langner, 1978).

This is a curious omission for, as this chapter will demonstrate, children's bodies (and minds)[3] have been and continue to be the medium through which the passage of time in the early part of an individual's life course is charted and judged. Particularly apparent in the health, welfare and educational fields, it is a view which extends both into the privacy of the family home to shape parenting practices and into the social world of the school to contextualize children's own social relations. It would be surprising, then, if children's understanding and experiencing of their bodies did not reflect this insistent attention to bodily change which they encounter in their everyday lives. But we know little, as yet, of children's experiential understanding of their bodies, a reflection of not only the ways in which sociological work has addressed the body but also the ways in which it has, until recently, dealt with the agency of the child (James and Prout, 1990). In Shilling's (1993) terms both have been 'absent presences' within sociological research; both have been assumed, rather than critically conceptualized.

CHILDHOOD: GROWTH AND THE EMBODIMENT OF TIME

As Shilling (1993) and Csordas (1994) have observed, the recent upsurge of interest in the phenomena of the body reveals two opposing traditions and one rather large lacuna. Traditionally, the study of the body begins either from the view that the body is a natural entity, providing what Shilling calls the 'biological *base* on which arises the superstructure of society' or, alternatively, from a largely social constructionist view, that the 'body is the outcome of social forces and relations', the product of particular discourses (1993: 16). Thus, the naturalistic perspective holds that:

> the capabilities and constraints of human bodies define individuals, and generate the social, political and economic relations which characterise national and international patterns of living. Inequalities in material wealth legal rights and political power ... are given, or at the very least legitimised, by the determining power of the biological body. (Shilling, 1993: 41)

Within this view, for example, sexual difference is taken to be a given feature of bodies and held to account for the 'natural' propensity of women for mothering and of men for dominance, these bodily differences providing justification for gendered social and political inequality. A mainstay of sociobiology and medical models of the body, the naturalistic approach is, none the less, also to be found within contemporary sociological theorizing. In particular, feminism finds in the 'naturalistic' model a powerful set of arguments for celebrating women's identities and, in its sociological variant, feminist work on eating disorders (Chernin, 1983) and reproduction (O'Brien, 1989) begins from a naturalistic perception of the body to explore the ways in which social differences and gender inequalities arise from the particularities of women's biology.[4] Within anthropology, on the other hand, naturalistic views of the body take on the more descriptive task of demonstrating cultural variation in discussions of 'the cultural meaning [to] be distilled from the treatment of body products such as blood, semen, sweat, tears, faeces, urine and saliva' (Csordas, 1994: 5).

Social constructionist accounts of the body, in contrast, reject such materialism, preferring to focus instead on the ways in which perceptions of the body are constrained and shaped by society. At their most extreme and most controversial – the work of Foucault (1979) is a good example – they view the body as simply a product of discourses of power, to the extent that it sometimes disappears altogether as a material entity. As Grimshaw (1993) notes, such a view denies autonomous agency to bodies, failing most importantly to differentiate between male and female bodies (see also McNay, 1994). Less radical formulations see the body as a receptor of cultural meanings, as reflecting or representing sets of social relations. Thus Featherstone's (1982) body is a product of consumer culture, Turner's (1984) the outcome of complex historical and social processes, and Mauss's (1950) and later Bourdieu's (1984) a clear indication of the varied and unconscious workings of culture, a visible and immediately apparent demonstration of cultural difference.[5]

What none of these perspectives offers, however, is an adequate account of the agency of the body. In their focused concentration on the study of the *body*, these approaches simply take the fact of *embodiment* for granted and do not problematize the experiencing body (Csordas 1994: 6). Indeed, they often register a strong ambivalence towards an appreciation of the theoretically productive links to be forged between the very materiality of the biological body and the social experience of embodiment, or what Turner (1994) calls 'bodiliness'. But, as Lyon and Barbalet (1994) note, such an approach has great sociological potential for, although the body is a subject of (and subject to) social power . . . it is not merely a passive recipient of society's mould, and therefore external to it. The human capacity for social agency, to collectively and individually contribute to the making of the social world comes precisely from the person's lived experience of embodiment. Persons do not simply experience their bodies as external objects of their possession or even as an intermediary environment which surrounds their being. Persons experience themselves simultaneously *in* and *as* their bodies. (Lyon and Barbalet, 1994: 54)

With respect to the study of children, embodiment, or more precisely this neglect of an appreciation of the embodied nature of human action, takes on a particular poignancy. First, if, as Shilling argues, the body is 'unfinished' at birth and is only 'completed' through action in society, then it is during childhood, marked as it is by rapid bodily change, that this process of 'finishing' the body (embodiment) should be particularly well revealed (see also Prout, this volume). Second, precisely because, as noted, the child's body is characterized by accelerated biological change, children's embodiment will be markedly different from that of adults, with perhaps only a comparable rapidity being experienced at the very end of the life course (Hockey and James, 1993). Third, as this chapter will argue, that childhood is commonly envisaged as the literal embodiment of change over time – the phrase 'when you grow up' makes this quite explicit – means that a focus on children's experience of embodiment as the experience of changing bodies should be central to any account of children's social action. Hitherto, however, for the most part childhood bodily change has been interpreted solely from within a naturalistic frame, children's identities as children being understood as a 'natural' outcome of their bodily difference from adults.[6]

However, just as historians such as Duroche (1990) have now established that the 'natural' differences between male and female bodies represent a particular view of the body's biology (until the eighteenth century the body was seen as generic, its female version regarded as but a different arrangement of the male body) so, too, historians of childhood are beginning to document the ways in which views of the child's body and the child's physiology have both changed over time. Steedman (1995), for example, argues that it was the nineteenth century that fixed childhood, not just as a category of experience, but also as a time span . . . [through] the development of mass schooling, and its grouping of children together by age cohort. In the same period the practices of child psychology, developmental linguistics and anthropometry provided clearer pictures of what children were like, and how they should be expected to look at certain ages (Steedman, 1995: 7).

Indeed, it could be argued that during this period ideas of child growth and development became a trope around which a whole variety of social, political and educational ideologies and reforms were woven, with the peculiarity of the child's changing physiology becoming seen as the very embodiment of time passing, giving visible material form to the notion of the biological clock:

> The building up of scientific evidence about physical growth in childhood described an actual progress in individual lives, which increased in symbolic importance during the nineteenth century, whereby that which is traversed is, in the end, left behind and abandoned, as the child grows up and goes away. In this way childhood as it has been culturally described is always about that which is temporary and impermanent, always describes a loss in adult life, a state that is recognised too late. Children are quite precisely a physiological chronology, a history, as they make their way through the stages of growth. (Steedman, 1992: 37)

Thus, during the nineteenth century not only was the rapidly developing conceptual space of childhood being shored up by a variety of philanthropic and political reforms[7] but, increasingly, an understanding of the child's body became central to this endeavour. Progressed and popularized through contemporary physiology, the child's body was seen as one characterized by change and growth, a process of biological development which was increasingly in need of measurement and monitoring (Armstrong, 1983). To grow up as an adult was to outgrow (or, more precisely, to grow out of) the body of a child and, as Armstrong has shown, the charting and surveying of the child population gradually began to define certain limits of normality for that child-like body. Elsewhere, drawing on the work of the Labour Party activist Margaret McMillan, Steedman shows how, for working-class children of the period, the fact of their retarded growth, measured against such visions of normality, took on great political and social significance and established the grounds for the welfarist policies of the later twentieth century: [8]

[Child physiology] structured around the idea of growth and development . . . allowed for comparisons to be made between children, and, most important of all as a basis for a social policy on childhood, it rooted mental life in the material body and the material conditions of life. In this way, working-class children could be seen as having been robbed of natural development, their potential for health and growth lying dormant in their half-starved bodies. (1992: 25)

And, McMillan believed, through a purposive and healthy education – open-air schools offered fresh air and exercise – the children of the poor could be rescued from deprivation and restored 'to become agents of a new social future' (Steedman, 1992: 35).

This explicit linking of the welfare of children's bodies to the future welfare of the nation was a consistent feature of nineteenth-century social and political thought and bears witness to the growing perception of the temporality of childhood and the temporary, but none the less critical, nature of the child's body: it was a body that needed to be nurtured in the present, its changes and development monitored, to ensure the well-being of the future adult it would become. Thus, though the life course had long been conceived in terms of a sequence of stages from birth to death – the seven ages of man depicted by Shakespeare, for example – the time of childhood became increasingly refined and, through this classificatory process, more discreet child identities and bodies were defined. While the beginning of the nineteenth century saw 'infancy' (the first of the seven ages of man) being merely divided into two, the years from 7 to 14 forming a new period of 'Puerita' (Steedman, 1995), by the early twentieth century definitions of infant mortality had led to the 'sub-division of the first year of life into smaller analysable components' which, by the mid-1950s, saw deaths for children under one year of age being distinguished as follows: stillbirths, perinatal, neonatal and infant deaths (Armstrong, 1983a: 214). Thus, the history of the firming up of the conceptual space of childhood is, in part, a history of the firming up of the child's body as the embodiment of time.

Against this background, then, any account of childhood and the body must include an appreciation of the ways in which ideas of growth and change over time are inscribed upon and through the child's body. But such a social constructionist view presents only one side of the picture: children themselves have to live with their changing biology, a biology that both shapes what they are and what they can do and one that, at the same time, invites particular perceptions of what, as children, they should be and should do. Thus, an approach to childhood and the body which takes the notion of embodiment seriously would be one which takes account of both the materiality and experiential subjectivity of the body in the same moment that it also acknowledges the body as an objectified entity within the social world. It is an approach that sees the body as neither simply the product of social relations nor a determinant of them:

> The shapes, sizes and meanings of the body are not given at birth and neither is the body's future experience of well being: the body is an entity which can be 'completed' only through human labour. (Shilling, 1993: 124–5)

It is to children's labour with and as their bodies that the next section turns its attention.

CHILDREN AND THE EMBODIMENT OF CHILDHOOD

In outlining the historical shaping of perceptions of children's bodies it is clear that one consequence was very material indeed. The explosion of health, welfare and educational reforms, which were the culmination of this rapid nineteenth-century interest in children's bodies, led, by the early twentieth century, to physiological changes in those bodies: for example, to declining infant mortality from 148 per 1,000 live births in 1841–5 to 50 in 1941–5 (Woodroffe et al., 1993); to a decline in the incidence of tuberculosis from the 1930s following the discovery of the importance of vitamins and fresh air (Bryder, 1992); to an increase in weight and size according to age, a direct result of state interventions to improve food provision, housing and sanitation for the children of the poor and, through education policy, to encourage physical exercise within the curriculum (Mayall, 1996: 25–6). Here, then, is a clear indication of the necessity for a perspective on childhood and the body which explores the different facets of the notion of embodiment for it was, presumably, children's (and their parents') active engagement with these changing health practices, combined with a more general improvement in the social and economic conditions of their everyday lives, that contributed to the changing physiology of children's bodies. Increases in children's height and weight and a decline in chronic sickness did not occur as a somehow 'natural' follow-on from increased knowledge about nutrition or better housing. Nor was this simply a matter of seeing children differently. Rather, as Steedman (1990: 1992) and Urwin and Sharland (1992) have shown, it was the active participation of parents (and their children) in new theories of childrearing and parentcraft, their acceptance of a particular envisioning of the importance of child health and their willingness to defer to or be the beneficiaries of reformist social policies which combined to effect a change in childhood morbidity through physiological change in children's bodies.

The concept of embodiment emphasizes, then, the situated agency of the body and a view of the body as not divorced from the conscious, thinking and intentional mind. Following Csordas, it provides a perspective on the body in which 'the body might be understood as a seat of subjectivity . . . [and] . . . in which mind/subject/culture are deployed in parallel' (1994: 9). For an understanding of childhood and the body such a definition is particularly instructive: as I shall demonstrate, it allows us to explore children's developing self-consciousness about their identities both as individuals and as members of the cultural category 'children'. Drawing on ethnographic fieldwork, conducted during 1988–90 among English school children aged between 4 and 9,[9] the following account illustrates the workings of the mind, body and culture in childhood.

A first observation to be made is that in Western cultures such as Britain the category of 'child' is, as indicated above, largely predicated upon the very peculiarity of children's physiology. Thus, as I have argued at length elsewhere (James, 1993; 1995) bodily stereotypes of 'the normal child', historically derived and ultimately contingent, provide a measure of any individual child's conformity to that category of child. But, while parents may monitor their child's development in terms of percentile growth charts and advice about childhood norms from medical practitioners (James, 1993), it is through their more mundane, everyday actions and social interactions with each other that children develop both a consciousness of the self as an individual and as an individual child. And, for those whose bodies differ from the norm, there is, in addition, the potential for an emerging acute self-consciousness:

> Through noting and remarking upon differences between one body and another and through having their own bodies singled out,

children learn to distinguish between anybody's body and their own and between normal and different bodies. (James, 1995: 66)

Underpinning this process of constant comparison, which takes place across the desks in the classroom as much as it does in the secret recesses of the playground, are, of course, the rapid physiological changes which children's bodies are experiencing and, of these, the increasing height of the body receives the closest of scrutinies:

achieving and fulfilling the status of a child is ... understood by children to be accomplished partly through abandoning the status of infant and one very eloquent statement of being a normal child lies in possessing a body which is child sized. Thus, children whose bodies are smaller than those of their contemporaries may gradually become self-conscious of their difference through a dawning recognition of their own body's failure to conform. (James, 1995: 70)

But why should this bodily difference make the difference that it does? Why is it important to know, as the children were always keen to tell me, who is the smallest – indeed the 'tiniest' – in the class?

One clue can be found through examining some further aspects of the notion of embodiment. Lyon and Barbalet (1994) argue that the concept of embodiment draws attention not only to the active agency of the individual body but to the body as intercommunicative, as belonging to the wider, institutional 'social body':

The body in society can ... be seen as an ordered aggregation of particular and specific types of relationships between individual bodies or, rather, the relevant aspects of individual bodies. (1994: 56)

Thus, children experience their bodies not just as individuals, but as school children and as playmates, social statuses and social relationships which create awareness of the variety of childhood bodies. These highlight, therefore, not just the particular body a particular child *has* but the particular body a child *is* among other bodies. In the school, structured as it is around age-classes, these same aged bodies may be smaller, bigger or of equivalent size, with each variation providing a differential reference point for the child's own bodily sense of self. It is in the classroom and the playground, then, that children get to know their place as a pupil amongst other pupils and a child amongst other children.[10]

That the height of the body should facilitate the embedding of individual child bodies within the wider social body of children at school stems from the particular way in which a child's changing physiology is culturally held to account. Not only does height register the present social status of the child – for example, as a 6 or 7-year-old who is the same as or different from other 6 or 7-year-olds – but it also provides a literal yardstick for a child's status as a future adult: an appropriately growing body provides comforting assurance of the steady progression towards adulthood. Small bodies are reminders of the stage of infancy, not long ago relinquished, or signs of a body which may not achieve an adult size. Thus, while the phrase 'growing up' is taken by adults to refer to concepts of age and associated degrees of social maturity, young children may also literalize its meaning. This provides apt illustration of Lyon and Barbalet's definition of embodiment: 'I am my body' (1994: 56).

> CAROL: (after comparing her height with Lorna) I'm bigger.
> ALLISON: Would you like to be tall?
> CAROL: Yeah ... I want to be fifteen.

> ARTHUR: Your birthday is before mine.
> GEORGE: Yeah, I'll be six and I'll be bigger than you then.

Quite literally, children's experience of embodiment is the experience of the embodiment of time.

Growing taller is, however, a somatic change over which children have little or no control, a factor that would seem to detract from the emphasis on agency which the concept of embodiment necessarily entails. However, as I shall explore below, through the adoption of particular bodily strategies children may alter the perceived shape and appearance of their own and other people's bodies. Even those children whose bodies are not tall enough may develop sufficient dexterity in manipulating how their body size is read by others to be able to gain salvation from the potential social stigma or exclusion which having a small body threatens to bring. Thus Jerry, very small for his age, bespectacled and bookish, gambled daringly with his body. One afternoon, self-deprecatingly, he described himself to the other, more laddish boys as a 'titchy little boring person' and thus forestalled their use of his body as a target for ridicule. It was a successful strategy. Despite visible evidence to the contrary, the other boys were both embarrassed by and admiring of his daring. Too quickly, and in some confusion, they loudly refused his admission of difference and temporarily welcomed him into their game.

In Jerry's actions, then, can be seen a first glimpse of the mental and physical labour of embodiment which, to use Shilling's formulation, involves children in working to 'finish' their bodies. These bodies, which are neither 'given' nor static, are bodies characterized by rapid physiological change, and children anxiously watch over the form and direction those changes take. Thus, as I have remarked elsewhere (James, 1993), the showing of cuts, bruises and abrasions to adult caretakers may be not so much a demand for sympathy but more a request for acknowledgement and reassurance of the normality of bodily change itself.

But more conclusive evidence still of the importance of bodily change for children can be found in their attitudes towards the altering shape and outline of their bodies. Although undoubtedly revealing how specific cultural ideas about the body shape styles bodily behaviour among children, children's thoughts on body shape also provide eloquent testimony of the experience of embodiment as an active subjectivity. As in the adult population fat bodies are often derided by children, with ethnographic data revealing widespread acceptance of the cultural stereotype that fatness is an unacceptable body shape (De Jong, 1980), a stereotype that persists despite the growing conflictual evidence of increasing incidence of obesity within both adult and child populations *and* an emphasis on the desirability of young, thin and fit bodies (Featherstone, 1982). But, I would argue, for children this is far from the passive intoning of a received cultural stereotype. More complexly, it is instead illustrative of how children understand, experience and use their changing bodies and how, through monitoring physiological body change, children can be seen to be engaged in particular forms of body work.

That bodies are 'worked on' has been recognized by Featherstone (1982) in his account of the maintenance regimes which adults employ to keep their bodies in line with contemporary images of a fit and healthy body. Children, too, clearly learn to work on their bodies, in this way with much of their early socialization devoted to such an activity: children learn that their bodies must be washed, nourished, exercised and rested (see Milburn, this volume). However, beyond this, as this chapter goes on to explore, they learn to perform a rather different kind of body work centred on the momentary and changing presentation of the body – its actions and its appearances. Though clearly drawing on those early adult lessons about body preservation and maintenance, this kind of body work in contrast takes place largely among the social body of children.

Casual conversations with children produced, for example, a number of common observations about fat bodies: 'fat people are funny' or 'fat people are horrid', and it was a received wisdom among the children that 'fat people eat too much' and that a particularly fat child had the body shape that he did 'because he's greedy and eats three bars of chocolate a day'.

However, thinness was equally no guarantee of freedom from critique: thin children risked being derided for being too 'skinny' and being nicknamed 'skinnyman', a negative body image also experienced by those children suffering from cystic fibrosis (Burton, 1975) and leukaemia (Bluebond-Langner et al., 1991). It would appear, then, that to be culturally acceptable a body must fit somewhere between these extremes. But at what upper and lower limits – and every fat of child who is teased quickly gets to know such limits do exist – do children understand those boundaries to be set? And, perhaps more importantly, how do children get to know where those lines are drawn? The short answer is: through body work.

An initial kind of work involves children coming to understand and appreciate the relationship between the body and society. As noted elsewhere (James, 1993), children do not passively accept the stereotypes of body shape and size which they encounter, but, instead, seek plausible explanations for negative stereotyping from their own bodily encounters. Children told me, for example, that one of the reasons why being fat might be problematic was that 'you couldn't walk properly', 'you couldn't do your shoelaces up' and that 'you couldn't run fast'. That these explanations are both context-specific and offer a practical rationalization for the negative connotations of possessing a fat body is highly suggestive. It indicates that children's understanding of 'fatness' as a body characteristic is based on considered and careful observation of the body in its social context. It is this knowledge that is worked on.

Through their experience in the school classroom children get to know that an acceptable body must be both controlled and seen to be controllable: teachers exhort children to 'walk properly' just as often as they insist that they must 'sit up straight' and refrain from fidgeting. Fat bodies cannot walk tall and sit straight. The body must also be orderly: tying shoelaces (along with, in some schools, the knotting of a tie) is a skill taught in the first few weeks at school and both neatens the body's appearance as well as protects children from tripping up and scraping their knees. Fat bodies are untidy bodies. The body must also enable children to participate in the games that other children play: to be able to escape the chaser in games of Tig and Stuck in the Mud. Fat bodies get caught. Clearly, then, it is undesirable to have a fat body; through observation and personal experience a cultural wisdom receives local endorsement.

However, aside from these practicalities, experience teaches children that the body is also an eloquent expressive tool which can inform unknown others about the more personal, inner aspects of the self. The primary school children with whom I talked judged the fat bodies of others in moral terms, associating fatness with greed and, what is potentially more problematic for the fat child, with anti-social behaviour of a bullying kind. Despite visual evidence to the contrary, a character in a poem about bullying was described by one 6-year-old boy, for example, as a 'fat bully'. When I challenged the accuracy of his observation, he insisted emphatically that 'He *looks* like a fat pig!' That is to say, his depicted behaviour – acting anti-socially like those other children to whom the insult 'fat pig' would be applicable – is what makes him look *as if he were* fat. Thus, it was that in the stories the children wrote about a boy or girl who was friendless, their bodies were without exception grotesquely caricatured, for children 'know' (in their bones and from experience) that people who behave so badly as to have no friends must without doubt have fat or ugly bodies (James, 1993: 134–7).

Thus, if the body is a mirror for the self – the two examples here suggesting that tallness speaks to age and maturity, with fatness indicative of the absence of bodily control – then what is the experience of embodiment like for those children whose bodies are neither tall nor, as one girl poignantly described it, 'medium thin'? Clearly for some it leads to misery, as work on bullying has described (Tattum and Lane, 1989), but for the many others whose bodies do not quite fit within the unwritten and often unspoken frame of how bodies should be styled, a second kind of body work comes into play: negotiation.

An indication of what this body work entails is already apparent in Jerry's act of self-degradation. But in so boldly offering up his body for critique Jerry set out some very stark rules of engagement with the other boys. There was little room for movement. Other children, less brave, work more actively to negotiate a wider arena for damage limitation. Bodily negotiation is an *'as if'* activity: the body is worked on and with so that it appears other than it is. Through the styling of behaviour the body acts *'as if'* it were another kind of body, and is temporarily recast.[11]

A powerful illustration of this kind of body work can be found in the gendered differences between the use and appearance of girls' and boys' bodies. Among the children stereotypes of gender were clearly and frequently articulated: girls are weak, boys are strong, with these differences being firmly located in perceived different physiologies. I was told, for instance, that boys have big muscles which gives them the strength to enable them to run faster than girls. Big muscles are what make boys good fighters. However, the children were also aware that in the everydayness of playground encounters girls could often prove themselves to be strong and faster than boys, while some boys were weak and slow in games of chase. It is in the explanations offered by children for these apparent contradictions that a first inkling is achieved of how an *'as if'* bodily behaviour comes to be enacted.

Elaine was a tall girl with a dominant and powerful personality. The other children were cautious of her bad temper and few would dare to cross her in playground disputes. If it was her turn to be 'it' – the chaser – in games of Tig, and Elaine did not want that role, she would be excused and another child would take her place. Her friendships with other girls were extremely volatile:

> HELEN: Sometimes if you don't do it [what she wants], she blows her lid. She says: 'You don't have to be so selfish' and that. She's a bit all right, but sometimes she says, because she ain't got them [a particular pair of shoes] she says: 'Oh, they're horrible'.

That this atypical female social self – bold, assertive and dominating – was somehow reflected in an atypical female body is clear from her friend Claire's description:

> CLAIRE: . . . Say she's got a ring on and you went like that [squeezes her hand] really hard, it wouldn't hurt her a bit because she's . . . She comes from a tough family really, her dad was a boxer. That's

where she gets her tough hands. Well, they're soft but they are really hard. She's stronger than me. When we do weighing in maths she has like three kilos on her hand and does like weight lifting.

Like the bully who looked *as if* he should be fat, Elaine looks *as if* she has tough hands. Although her hands are in fact soft – as soft as any other girls hands, as soft as Claire's – the manner in which she uses her body makes them appear *as if* they are really hard: 'well, they're soft but they are really hard'. Thus Elaine, in Claire's view, is excused; she negotiates her way past the gender stereotypes which constrict her bodily behaviour by using her body – loud, aggressive behaviour – *as if* it were the body of a boy.

Through bodily negotiation appearances can indeed be made deceptive, something which the girls noted wryly about the failure of some boys to negotiate with their bodies successfully. Commenting on the behaviour of her male classmates Christine observed: 'They act tough. We know they are weak but they act tough. We see their weaknesses.' Such social weaknesses are literally visible upon the surfaces of the boys' bodies: in fights and argument their faces redden in the same moment as they vociferously deny being hurt and tears well up in their eyes.

It is clear then that children's body work relies, therefore, upon two kinds of seeing: first, looking at the bodies of others and interpreting the information gained to judge the status of one's own body and, second, making one's own body look or seem *'as if'* it were another kind of body. Thus it is that in the classroom, children who wish to gain favour from their teachers straighten their backs, fold their arms, look straight ahead and sit still: they present their bodies for view *'as if'* they were the bodies of those who are orderly and well behaved. These are the same bodies that in the playground must be made to look *as if* they can run fast, jump high, fight well, skip quickly or strut boastfully. Such looking is a constant activity for children and, as Christensen (1993) notes, is a central feature of children's wider social games and sickness episodes in which they invite others to share in their experiences of the body.

But for some children an additional labour may be involved: for children whose bodies are marked by the signs of illness or disease, or whose social skills are poor, the work of making and masking the body may become a more emotionally intense and intensive

activity. Though not a necessary outcome of disabling illness stig-
matizing of the body by others may occur and, if it does, such body
work becomes pressing. Pauline, having had severe eczema throughout her childhood, but now at 19 free from the condition, recalls
her attempts to negotiate her itchy, raw and bleeding body:

> PAULINE: Your self-confidence takes an awful lot of building up
> afterwards because even now when my hands are good they look
> a bit dry. I used to hide my hands. I didn't want anyone looking
> at them because they were not as smooth as anyone else's. I
> never used to like people asking me what I had done.

Tim, a fine athlete but an asthmatic, similarly has to be discreet
when taking his medication:

> TIM: Once I was having my popper [inhaler] and someone said:
> 'You're taking drugs and you shouldn't be taking them'. I said:
> 'It just makes me up to a normal person, it's not cheating'.

Although such strategies of concealment are common in the management of what Goffman (1968) terms a spoiled identity, they are
not the sole prerogative of the child with a chronic illness. They
are simply a more obtrusive reminder of the body work which all
children must learn to do to manage the looking over by others of
what their own bodies look like.

CONCLUSION

If, as I have suggested, childhood is the embodiment of time, the
work that children do with and to their bodies is work that enables
the changes which the physical body undergoes to be temporarily
halted and controlled. For particular moments in time, through
combining close and careful observation with considered action,
some children can make their bodies appear other than they are as
a conscious strategy of action to re-represent the self (Goffman,
1959). For other children this body work may take place at a more
implicit, even unconscious level, as they learn to 'fit in' and to ac-
commodate their bodies to the different stylistic demands of the
home, the school and the playground (James, 1986). However such
work is done, that their bodies are read by others 'as if' they were

of a different kind is testimony to the persuasive and successful re-presentations of the body which children achieve through this body work. And in the daily, successfully negotiation of the ever-changing nature of their bodies and of the self which it presents, children are exploring not only their present social relationships but also laying the groundwork for those future, more adult ones. Each new rendering of the body is a potentially new rendering of the self. Now confident in her adult status, Pauline recalls the intense body work of a childhood plagued by eczema:

> I didn't want to be treated differently. I think you can almost make yourself like a leper, cast yourself out if you want to. A lot of it is up to you. Self-help. What you think you can do. You have to know your limitations obviously but . . . you just have to give yourself a bit more time, to fit what you've got to do in.

In her reflections is writ large the embodied nature of social action in childhood: the body is an active agent of self-help through which alternative present and future possibilities for the self are engendered. To 'finish' the childish body successfully is, as Pauline describes it, to actively engage with and think through the material visibility of its form.

NOTES

1. Though clearly adult bodies also display subtle signs of time passing – the first grey hairs and lines of age upon the face being regarded as worrisome markers of mortality (James and Hockey, 1993) – the intense and rapid 'whole body' change which occurs during childhood contributes to the significance of the body in children's social relationships (see James, 1993).
2. See James and Prout (1990a) and Hockey and James (1993) for examples of this.
3. This distinction, though apparent in much of the historical and socio-logical literature, is not one that is maintained in the theoretical approach adopted here. The terms 'body' and 'bodies' are used not simply to refer to the material object but also, following Csordas et al. (1994) to the experiential subjective (mindful) experience of being a body (embodiment). Within this formulation the mind/body dualism of both naturalistic and representational approaches to the body are rejected (see below).

4. For an overview of these approaches, see Shilling (1993); Turner (1992).
5. See note 3. In the concept of 'habitus' Bourdieu reveals that his engagement with the agency of bodies takes the form of an unconscious, rather than active or reflexive habituating.
6. The work of Piaget in developmental psychology is the most obvious example. For a critical account, see Burman (1994).
7. For a discussion of childhood as a social construction, see Prout and James (1990).
8. A fuller account of the work of Margaret McMillan can be found in Steedman (1990).
9. For a full account of this fieldwork context, see James (1993).
10. Within the family a different process of recognition takes place. Here children experience their bodies not just as children but as sons or daughters. Family resemblances are sought in order to 'place' or 'locate' the child as a family member. As the son or daughter of particular parents, the child is said to have his/her 'mother's eyes', 'father's hair' or to 'get it (a body feature) from his/her parents'. In such a view the body becomes fragmented, detachable portions providing locating reference points for a child's social identity.
11. The use of the term 'as if' behaviour here is not meant to suggest that these forms of action are those of deliberate 'pretence' or 'imitation' as described in the literature on child development; see, for example, Vaihinger (1924); Sarbin (1966).

3 Childhood and the Cultural Constitution of Vulnerable Bodies[1]
Pia Haudrup Christensen

Adults like children when they behave and help cleaning or tidying up and do what they are told, but not if they cry and shout and hit the adults – but sometimes also if they [children] say something funny.

nine-year-old Danish boy

The only universal language in the world is a child's cry.

Save the Children Fund campaign

INTRODUCTION

This chapter is concerned with the cultural meanings of vulnerability in childhood. The implicit assumption of both research into and everyday practice around childhood is that children are vulnerable, and that during illness the child is particularly vulnerable and in need of adult care and therapy. Adults are therefore viewed as being in charge of, and having responsibility for, the child, and the child is positioned as the dependent and passive object. Whilst not wishing to make a general challenge to the idea that children may be vulnerable, or to the biological dimension of it, in this chapter I suggest that the construction of children as essentially vulnerable tends to exclude consideration of the cultural and social context in which vulnerability is constituted and to render children's own understandings of themselves and their bodily experiences as unimportant. I will suggest that a child's vulnerability is in part associated with the way in which people are perceived by themselves and by others. Understood in this way vulnerability is seen as a constructed status, in this instance embedded in cultural understandings of the child as a social person, of the child's body and conceptions of health and illness in childhood. I investigate perceptions of the vulnerability of children both by examining cultural perspectives on the child's body and by using fieldwork material gathered during an ethnographic study of childhood illness conducted among 6–13-year-old Danish school children in a district of Copenhagen.

The analysis focuses on the approaches of adults to everyday accidents and illnesses and shows how these may be contrasted to and questioned by the perspectives of children themselves. In these events the hierarchy between child and adult was routinely and starkly revealed. In the everyday life of both school and after-school centres, adults generally expected that children should be engaged in more or less genuinely active roles. In many situations adults encouraged children to take an outgoing and active part; for example they were expected to take part in manual work projects or were urged to take risks in competitive play or in football matches. Adults might likewise express their disapproval if children seemed disengaged or lacked what they called a 'fighting spirit'. Whilst girls were not pushed to participate or cheered for their actions to the same degree as boys, and they were not expected to display the same physical effort or strength,[2] this was a difference of degree not of kind (see also Prendergast, this volume). The overall expectation was that children, girls as well as boys, should be active and participatory. This general picture was, however, in marked contrast to the anticipated passive role of the child when illness or accidents occurred. These situations expressed a child's vulnerability and implied the positioning of an active, protecting and responsible adult in relation to a passive and unprotected child.

IMAGES OF VULNERABILITY IN CHILDHOOD

The social positioning of child and adult during episodes of childhood illness can be seen as a particular reflection of more ubiquitous images of children and childhood in Western cultural thinking. Anthropological studies have suggested the specificity of these by documenting how in different cultures children are thought of in terms of their vulnerability (Mead, 1955; 1962; Briggs, 1971; 1986; Stafford, 1995). Briggs' classic study of Canadian Inuit families, for example, paid particular attention to the cultural practices and social interactions of child and adult. She suggested that it was crucial for children to develop an understanding of the ambiguous but interlinked conceptual framework of vulnerability, caring and protection on the one hand, and of strength, power and killing on the other. This combination not only helped to secure their personal survival but also to sustain the existence of the community in a harsh environment. This concern formed a central part of childrearing practices as adults engaged in purposeful playing with the boundaries of weakness, danger and risk and engaged in almost brutal teasing in order to motivate articulated and independent understandings, abilities and strategic actions in children.

In contrast, most discussions within a Western cultural perspective, particularly those using a psychological approach, focus on understanding the child as dependent on others. However, even though studies may view 'vulnerability' as a basic quality of children or childhood, it is taken for granted and its analysis neglected or excluded from the core of theoretical discussions. The major concern has been with the dependence and independence of children, an emphasis motivated, I would suggest, by the dominant cultural ideal of the individual as autonomous, responsible and mature. Unlike vulnerablity, dependency has been subject to a certain amount of critical cultural analysis. Hockey and James (1993), for example, examine notions of dependency, providing an important account of the powerful influence of social and cultural ideas and practices in constructing dependence and independence in childhood and old age, suggesting how these processes are reflected and maintained at both extremes of the life course. The concept of vulnerability, however, has been employed as a general notion in relation to 'special needs' or preventive health programmes of psychologically vulnerable children (Anthony et al., 1978), with the aim of detecting sociocultural settings or factors in children's physical environments that may cause pathological conditions or developmental problems. In contrast, rather than taking the vulnerability of the child as given, as such arguments tend to do, I shall begin to unravel some of the ways in which childhood is constituted as essentially 'vulnerable' in much Western discourse, acting almost as a master identity for children.

That childhood is and should be a 'nice', protected world in which only problematic external forces from the environment or perhaps from malevolent adults sometimes intervene is an important component of the perception of Western childhood (Ennew, 1986). Children are constituted as essentially vulnerable beings who can only survive and develop successfully if intensely nurtured and protected by adults. This conception is expressed in two sets of ideas which form current notions of modern childhood and which as such are fundamental for the prevalent view of children in Western societies and for the structuration of childhood (Giddens, 1991: 20). One set of ideas separates children from adults and defines the ideal family as a nuclear unit, the appropriate context for socialization. The family as social institution thus becomes the locus for undertaking the proper development and sustenance of both child and parental health (Crawford, 1994). Within the family these perceptions imply the positioning of adults as responsible providers and carers of the child and the child 'as not yet part of society' receiving care, protection and training. The other set of ideas separates children from adults in production processes. The child has the status of a 'non-worker'; in fact, children (depending of their age) may formally be excluded from work. The child must not work and is not expected to do so, but has instead the right to play and learn.

This discourse of children and childhood is also linked to popular images and public pictures which inform us about the different sources and expressions of the cultural meanings of children. The process is particularly seen in fundraising campaigns addressed at protecting and saving children. American child survival programmes, which have great international influence, represent young children as worth saving because they are seemingly innocent and need to be protected. As such these campaigns have been criticized for separating out the health and well-being of the young child from that of her household and family (Nichter and Cartwright, 1991). Adolescents' and adults' perceptions and use of alcohol, cigarettes and medicines are, by implication, considered irredeemable, for these groups have grown up and have lost their innocence. Another example of the emphasis on the protection of children is provided by European campaigns that urge us to 'Adopt (or Support) a Child' in a developing country. These campaigns assert that the health of the local community will be improved through the sponsorship of a particular (and identifiable) child. The images of these campaigns are similar images to those of the 'Adopt a Whale' (or Dolphin) campaigns, which aim to safeguard the environmental health of the ocean. The fellowship between children and animals is expressed in the use of visual displays and vocabulary which reinforce the symbolic analogy, thus supporting understandings of children as 'endangered species'. The ambiguity constituted by images of children suffering, children as victims of wars or as victims of natural disasters is expressed by Patricia Holland (1992: 148):

Children are seen as archetypal victims: childhood is seen as weakness itself. As the children in the image reveal their vulnerability, we long to protect them and provide for their needs. Paradoxically, while we are moved by the image of a sorrowful child, we also welcome it, for it can arouse pleasurable emotions of tenderness, which in themselves confirm adult power.

THE CHILD AS 'THE SPIRIT OF LIFE'

One important aspect of the pictures in these campaigns to protect children is that the child is constituted as an agent or a catalyst by which the survival of the whole community is secured. However the child may not be constituted as being the central concern; rather, their image as the personified and vulnerable being attracts the attention of the (primarily) adult public. The campaigns attempt to provoke immediate emotional empathy with the suffering child to forward a central purpose and to justify 'rationally' based arguments, for example sustaining the basic needs of people or preventing disasters from taking on more universal dimensions. Thus the campaigns imply that the value of financially contributing to them is not achieved in *actually* 'saving a child' – thus substantiating that the instrumental value of children has been largely replaced by their symbolic value for adults (Scheper-Hughes, 1989). The images almost stereotype a 'universal truth' in their portrayal of children as essentially vulnerable, suffering and in need of help. The messages point to a set of cultural ideas about the 'charm of children' that sees them as embodying the 'spirit of life'. In these views the child represents the continuity but also the fragility of human life and its future symbolized in the fragility of the child's body as well as in images of their natural vitality. Strength and the capacity for survival are depicted, for example, in the image of a newborn infant's forceful and eager suckling, which demonstrates a determination to live but also characterizes children's (rapid) growth, development and activity.

A further set of values is expressed in the infant's purity and innocence, constituting him or her as a 'living symbol of the forever lost' values of adulthood. In Denmark the infant is praised for representing that which, in a sense, every one of us loses in growing up, that is 'the innocence of childhood'. This view is reflected through children as their increasingly complex nature is perceived to be associated with 'losing' their charm. The child represents continuity in their similarity to the images of adults just as their difference represents uniqueness and hope of another and 'better' future. The notion of continuity, and further that children are expected to survive adults, forms at the same time a challenge to adult control and power. This was illustrated in the following conversation, recorded in my fieldnotes, which I observed in my fieldwork:

A staff member of the after-school centre and a 12-year-old boy teased each other one afternoon. The adult said: 'You are a "silly-child"' and the child replied: 'Yes and you are a "silly adult".' After some banter back and forth the adult wanted to conclude saying triumphantly: 'OK, then, but I don't mind being a "silly-adult" because I am the one who makes the decisions. What do you want to be then?' The child concluded their conversation with the reply: 'I want to be a "silly-child" because I will live longer than you'.

The ambiguity of the relationship between the child and the adult has been almost poetically described as encapsulated in the notion of 'difference' (Jenks 1982: 9). Jenks writes:

The child is familiar to us and yet strange, she/he inhabits our world and yet seems to answer to another, she/he is essentially of ourselves and yet appears to display a different order of being.
  Thus the child cannot be imagined without considering the idea of 'adult' just as it is impossible to picture the adult and society without positing 'the child'.

In the perception of their otherness, that is the innocence of the child, as the symbol of new life but also in their sameness as being the continuation of oneself, the child symbolically defends and purifies the 'dark side' of adulthood. A child's naive, open and curious investigation of and interactions with the world represent a charm that fascinates the adult, who may recognize the imagination and fantasy that (as in romantic love) acknowledges the unboundedness of the world. This imagined world represents the simple, spontaneous, unconditional and infinite dimensions of social relations, unconstrained by conventional restrictions or limitations. Hence the symbolic value of the child incorporates notions of originality and 'not being spoilt', which are rarely associated with modern adult life.

Such modern life has been described as a social and cultural world constituted by a multiplicity of unsolved paradoxes, contradictions and experiences, where fragmentation and inconsistency are central traits (Giddens, 1991; Isern, 1993). In order to create sufficient degrees of integration and affinity to life and personal experience people devote themselves to a number of cultural practices in order to produce meaning. One example of such a practice is striving for the 'authentic' as a means of bridging the gaps and contradictions of the modern experience. I suggest that the symbolic value of children for adults reflects such attempts at re-establishing originality and authenticity in modern adult life. Thus different European and North American notions of children and childhood constitute a paradox. On the one hand, some perceptions ascribe to childhood a special meaning as a phase in human life surrounded by care, concern and affection, associated with endeavours providing for and protecting the child. On the other hand, these perceptions may not necessarily attribute value to childhood and the child in their own right, as children are being judged only in relation to an adult world.

THE BODY: SOMATIC AND INCARNATE: BOUNDED AND UNBOUNDED

From addressing notions of vulnerability in childhood represented in the collective imagery of children the following section will turn to investigating the understandings of these questions in relation to the child as body and self. In the process I draw specific attention to a view on the child's body which distinguishes between the exterior (or surface of the) body and the interior body in which the transformed surface of the child is seen as a sign of vulnerability. Different perspectives on the child's body are examined to indicate how they relate to adults and children's understandings of vulnerability.

The quote which opens this chapter illustrates how a nine-year-old boy acknowledged the importance of the (outer) appearance and the (inner) qualities of a child for adults:[3] 'behaving', 'doing what they are told', 'crying', 'shouting', 'hitting', and so on. Below I show how specific ideas about children's exterior bodies, their interior bodies and the relationship between them shaped adult approaches to children's everyday illness episodes and minor accidents. In particular children's vulnerability was understood and acted upon through what Frankenberg has termed the 'somatic' aspect of the body – an objectification of the body beyond subjective experience: 'revealed at a particular diagnostic instant . . . [a] partial, often technologically mediated, clinical view, restricted in time and space' (Frankenberg, 1990: 356).

Working in this mode adults were concerned, for example, to validate the 'objective reality' of an illness or injury (rather than its experience to the child) and localize it within a culturally dominant categorization of the body and its parts.

This approach contrasted with that of children themselves. Their perspective may usefully be thought of as based on the 'incarnate body':

a unity of past, present and future simultaneously experienced from inside and outside. . . . The perspective of the incarnate body lacks boundaries in both time and space and is permeable to the world. (Frankenberg, 1990: 358)

As I will suggest below this experience of the permeability, fluidity and extensibility of the body is transformed for children when adults attempt to translate the body incarnate into the somatic body, a process which routinely occurs during minor illnesses or everyday accidents. These translations objectify the body, fragment and classify its parts and constitute the exterior body as a shield – that is to say, a boundary between the child and the world.

The transformation of the child's bodily experience and conception is an important aspect of cultural learning because it relates to notions of the person as a unity. Clifford Geertz (1983: 59) has given the following description of the unity they are said to learn:

The Western conception of the person as a bounded, unique, more or less integrated motivational and cognitive universe, a dynamic centre of awareness, emotion, judgment, and action organized into a distinctive whole and set contrastively both against other such wholes and against its social and natural background.

Psychological and social assertiveness and physical boundedness are seen as characterizing a mature person, achieved in part through the 'toughening' of the body surface. However the exterior of the person must not harden so much that the person and his or her vitality suffocates and the surface inevitably cracks. Ideas of the consistency of personhood are reflected in understandings of a balance between the inner and the outer nature of the person, established in a responsive but well-defined and united outer appearance.

The contrast between the body as object and the body as lived subjectivity has led Battersby (1993) to suggest the importance of examining the 'unboundedness' of the body – the body in process, in continuous action and connection with other features of the social and natural world. Whilst Battersby makes these suggestions in relation to understanding gender differences, they also resonate with my fieldwork data, where children expressed their experience of self and body as inseparable. As an embodied experience illness was not experienced as distinct from their person. In the accounts of 6–7-year-old children, 'to be ill' was associated in a quite literal sense with another state of subjective being. They said: 'It doesn't feel very nice' or simply 'I did not feel well'. Illness episodes were sometimes described exclusively through a symptom, for example by saying 'I had a cough' or 'It hurts'. Often the youngest children stated that they had been ill without adding any further explanations of the condition. In their stories the children also emphasized the relationship between illness and their own or others' actions. For example a seven-year-old boy explained: 'When you are ill you lie in a bed and vomit in a bucket.' Another boy told me about how one of his friends had been hurt and in his story he emphasized the amount of blood the injury caused. When I asked him why it was bleeding, he said:

> 'It bleeds because you fall and hurt yourself or because some-body beats you.'

Rather than providing me with an account based on bodily functions, such as 'because the skin was cut', he, as the children typically did, emphasized his own actions and social interactions with others. In relation to illness children expressed these as disruptions to their everyday practices and routines, for example because of parental restrictions imposed on them as part of a therapy. Recovering and feeling well was again expressed in terms of social interaction. This was illustrated, for example, by Karen, a seven-year-old, who firmly stated that getting better means: 'To do as I usually do.'

In observations of everyday illness episodes or minor accidents at school and the after-school centres, it became apparent that children's concern was with the interruption of their body and their connections with the social and material world, not with, for example, the penetration of the body skin or naming the body part that hurt. They experienced the situations in which they were involved and the associated interactions as an integrated process. Thus children's accounts showed that experiencing vulnerability also related to the experience of losing their social position, activities and relationships and changes in their environment. This suggests that, from children's perspectives, they *are* their world and did not see themselves as separate from the part they take in processes and events and their experiences of them. Children, then, spoke from the perspective of the body incarnate, the body as experience, in action, involved with the environment as well as in interactions with others.

THE EXTERIOR AND INTERIOR BODY

Terence Turner (1980) has suggested that the surface of the body may be conceptualized as 'the social skin', a surface upon which the drama of socialization is inscribed. Bodily adornment, like body paint and clothing, becomes the language through which the social actor and cultural subject are constructed and expressed (Turner, 1980: 112). Here I take up this idea by suggesting that the surface of the child's body in European and North American cultural contexts presents a medium from which cultural understandings of the child and of the structural, mutually constituting position of child and adult can be read. In particular, the transformation of the exterior body exposes the opposing but still complementary values of vulnerability and protection. I will argue that, from an adult point of view, the transformed body surface of the injured child represents the child's vulnerability and the moral demands on adults to protect, be responsible for and care for children.[4]

Underlying the 'adult' perspective, I suggest, is an embedded cultural understanding of the child that designates an implicit distinction between the exterior and the interior body of the child, and a consequent compartmentalization of the complexity of children's nature into two parts. The first is a visible, exposed and specific outer nature of a child, and the second is the idea of a hidden, wild and vulnerable inner nature. The adult approach to the child mirrors this division, also taking two forms. One attends to the exterior body through observing, cleaning, clothing, grooming, touching, and so on. The aim of the other is to nurture the interior body with food and knowledge. That the adult focus tends to be on the child's exterior body may be, as I will return to below, because it provides a possible route to conceptualizing the 'inner' child. In this view the child's surface is particularly significant because, whilst adults engage in attending to the child's body, it becomes well defined for them, constituting the child's physical presence and existence, and at the same time the object of their love, affection or rejection. Adult emphasis on and constant engagement in discovering and understanding the child through the perspective of the exterior is exemplified in parental instructions to and monitoring of children's comportment, in the stories exchanged among adults about the children's appearance, behaviour, and talk, and in adults requests of the younger children to perform, sing, dance or repeat funny words in front of an audience.

There is, however, a complementary notion of the child's inner body, which is seen as a source of hidden information, emotions and bodily processes – that is, the motivated agent in the body which becomes the subject of control. The child is thought to develop from what are seen as primitive inarticulate functions to a complexity following acceptable cultural norms. Thus the child is acknowledged to be elusive and flexible, but capable of being modulated by the influence of adults. Attending to the surface of the child, that is to the child's exterior body, forms first a means of expressing love and adoration of the child. Second it serves as a means of formation and social control (Turner, 1992). However the surface of the body does not form the target of control in itself. Interventions, restrictions and modulations directed at the exterior body have a more subtle concern with disciplining the inner body.

The child's body as visible appearance, acted upon by others to establish an appropriate and acceptable surface, is distinguished from the interior processes of the body or the 'inner' child. The child who is cleaned and dressed exhibits the social status of its carers, and consequently the child may become a symbol of adult creation, and a moral statement of adult achievements. Children are seen as picturing their family (see also Milburn, this volume). They present the image of their family in their person. For example, one school nurse told me that she could always spot children who lived alone with their father because of the way they were dressed: 'The colours don't match and the clothes don't quite fit,' she said.

Taken further this meant that the pathology of a child could be established by professionals working with the children through their observations of his/her appearance and behaviour. The child reflected the pathology of the family and, in a circular argument, the pathology of the family could be established through the child's appearance and behaviour. Instances of the 'passive child', for example, could be detected by their exterior presentation: pale, inactive and unresponsive, described by professionals in a Danish idiom which can be translated as 'Just part of the wallpaper', an extreme form which communicates a shallow person, one who merely exists.

THE PROTECTIVE SHIELD

In adult estimation a child's skin is appreciated as the 'perfect' skin. Its softness and fine character represent values of purity and innocence. However, ideas of the openness and transcendence of the child's body are reflected in the assumption that through growing up the child develops a unified hardness of the body surface. In this perspective the body surface serves as the protective shield of the vulnerable interior of the child (cf. Scheper Hughes and Lock, 1987). Thus an intact exterior body is indicative of the wellbeing of the child. One important aspect of understanding the child as vulnerable is the extent to which the body surfaces are transformed through change, ageing and damage. This is illustrated in popular understandings of the 'stages' of childhood which are perceived to be particularly problematic in the sense of exposing visible representations of the child's conflictual and fragile state. In adolescence (the transitional phase from childhood to adulthood) the perception is that severe inner and outer conflictual processes take place. These battles are perceived by others through visible manifestations on the child's exterior body exposing troublesome transformations in their appearance and social behaviour. This signals what is seen as the young person caught in the tensions between an intruding complexity of adult life and status, and the immature competencies and understandings of the child. Whereas below I will argue that early childhood also takes on specific meaning from suffering displayed on the outside of the body, during growing up the reverse picture is presented. Suffering is understood in terms of concealed symptoms and interior illnesses. This is illustrated in the psychological emphasis on the effects in adult life of mental

distress and effects of social constraint in childhood, reflected in
the number of psychological therapies (as well as popular
understandings) that seek to offset the supposed effects of childhood
experiences and childhood relations. In this perspective the developmental process constitutes a shift in the perception of illness.
Being unhealthy is no longer concerned with the apparent con-
creteness and exterior reflection of childhood, but with the concealed
nature and subtle severity of the psychological and inner pathological
organic processes of adulthood.

In their everyday life the children in my study[5] continually displayed their vulnerability as they stumbled or were hurt in other
ways, such as in childhood diseases like measles or chickenpox.
This may reinforce for adults the importance of the child developing a hard surface through their constant observation of 'the inside
leaking out'. The diffuseness of the inner body is reflected and
established on the surface through blood, crying and screaming. It
may also be indicated by fever. Adults explained that 'Children
often get a high temperature without being ill'. They believed that
children, in infancy and early childhood, may be more affected by
a virus, developing a high fever but for a relatively short period in
comparison with older children and adults. Biologically (from the
point of view of the somatic body) this can be explained in terms
of the immaturity of their immune defence system and temperature
regulation centre. However *the experience* of this situation for a
child, that is understood from the point of view of the body incarnate, is still one of illness, which seriously affects their lives for a
time. For adults on the other hand *the length of time* a child was
affected by a high temperature was the crucial factor in indicating
its severity.

During the fieldwork I was struck by such differences, and sometimes even discrepancies, between adults' and children's perceptions
of vulnerability. These divergent perspectives were illustrated by
the approaches taken to a minor accident of a child in school. In
these situations teachers generally reacted immediately. They were
alarmed and greatly concerned, especially when a child was bleeding. In contrast the injured child (and also sometimes other children
attending) were often deeply engaged with quite other matters –
for example, in investigating the blood and establishing the amount
of it. Often this was done without showing any signs of fright or
repulsion. In other situations, however, children appeared to exag-
gerate and magnify the scale of their injury. Maria, a ten-year-old,

dramatically said 'Look, I'm bleeding!' whilst presenting a drip of blood the size of a pin head on her finger. And in a football match Suzanne jumped about, pointing to a foot which looked quite normal and declared 'Oh look! My toe is all blue and swollen.' As I have shown in another paper (Christensen, 1993), the most frequent and characteristic reaction to such claims amongst other children was precisely 'to look'. A child's claim of 'a swollen toe' was not met with judgement or correction from other children. This response was in marked contrast to adults, who would meet such dramatic expressions of children with disapproval. They would correct them by pointing out that the toe looked quite normal and would jokingly minimize the importance of the cut by suggesting there was little or no blood.

This suggests that even though different but very visible signs are displayed on the surface of the child's body they take their meaning for adults from the complexity of the child's inner nature. Whilst the inside of the body spreading to the exterior of the body signals severity, the manifestations may be instrumentally and symbolically 'wiped off'. An adult washed blood from a wound, drying tears at the same time as calming the child, saying: 'Shh, shh, stop crying' or 'Stop now! Don't make a fuss'. During this process the adult investigates the severity of what has happened and through re-examining the damaged surface the event may be re-established as 'innocent'. These indicators thus establish the diffuseness of the child at the same time as establishing the innocence and unproblematic aspects of their nature. In my fieldwork I frequently observed that after everyday accidents, adults cleaned wounds and covered them with a plaster or bandage to sustain the healing process. The adults acted to produce a protective shield. The plaster acted as substitute skin protecting the broken surface of the child, aimed at re-establishing it, and thus toughening and hardening the surface of the body.

CONCEPTUALIZING THE CHILD'S BODY IN ILLNESS

During childhood adults figuratively form and provide a shield in embracing, covering and guarding the child's small body with their own when the child is confronted with dangers or is scared or feeling shy. In growing up, the child's body surface has to harden to take over this protective role, that is to become its own shelter and even possibly to provide protection for others. In European and North American cultures, experience and awareness of the body surface are encouraged and acknowledged as being essential for the child to develop a sense and awareness of self. It thus forms a part of a child's enculturation to distinguish and define her exterior body. In infancy different professional techniques are used to assess children's acquisition of self-awareness. These assessments are mainly based on observing the child observing (showing signs of acknowledging) her own body exterior. In this context developmental psychological assessments attend to the child's experience of and mastery of her exterior body. An example of such an approach is the 'mirror image' experiments (Lewis and Brooks, 1978). These experiments show that not until a child is about 18 months old is he able to recognize that he is looking at his own face in a mirror. Thus through such processes the child's experience of his body exterior constitutes a measurable sign of the child's sense of self.

Developmental psychologists have theorized the formation of identity in similar terms:

> The sense of self emerges gradually over the first two years. In the first month, infants have no awareness of their bodies as theirs. To them, for example, their hands are interesting objects that appear and disappear: two-months-olds, in effect, 'discover' their hands each time they catch sight of them, become fascinated with their movements, then 'lose' them as they slip out of view. Even eight-month-olds often don't seem to know where their bodies end and someone else's body begins, as can be seen when a child at this age grabs a toy in another child's hand and reacts with surprise when the toy 'resists'. By age one, however most infants would be quite aware that the other child is a distinct person, whom they might well hit if the coveted toy is not immediately forthcoming. (Berger, 1983: 147)

Such professional discourses draw on the everday convention that 'subjective states – sensations, feelings and emotions – cannot be found, recognized or discovered in bodies but are attributed to them on the basis of certain observable manifestations that warrant such attribution' (Vendler, 1984: 201). However, this approach neglects the child's subjective experience of its body. The child's subjective experience of self and of its body cannot be reduced to its observable state. That adults set out to comprehend the child's body experiences by reading off signs on the surface of the child's body posed particular problems for both parents, teachers and other professionals working with children in the setting I studied. The 'otherness' of a child was illustrated for adults in children's unexpected behaviours, sudden movements, unarticulated screaming or ambiguous reactions. Furthermore both parents and professionals expressed the idea that their own vulnerability was reflected in their experiences of a child getting hurt. Sometimes adults felt trapped by having to take action, in relation to their assumed responsibility for, and their protection of, children. The accounts of adults confirmed their uncertainty as to whether the significant meanings of a child's complaints or an unusual condition could easily be read off from the exterior of the child's body. A child's cry or expressions of pain might in some situations leave adults worried and puzzled about the invisible nature of the child's illness experience. One way of dealing with this problem was to exclude certain conditions and explicitly define the effect of an illness or accident in order to be able to establish its severity. Illness for adults had preferably to be specified as a set of distinct factors related to certain parts of the body, thus indicating its clear effects, and which treatment might be applied.

The somatic body implied here designated the child as a unity, but paradoxically so – through the differentiation of the body to its parts. An example of this process is seen in a game whose aim is that a child experiences and learns about her body. In nurseries, and between parents and very young children, the game considers naming and pointing out different parts of the child's body (or the adult's body). 'Where are your knees . . . your tummy . . . your chest and your nose, and where is mine?' It is an amusing game in which both successfully finding and correcting mistakes is appreciated by both adults and children. In addition to the pleasure that arises for both children and adults from the game, it has the purpose of the child playfully learning how the body appears from an adult's point of view. During illness too, naming parts of the body exterior is an important tool in the communication between child and adult. The child is requested by adults specifically to localize her complaint by pointing to a particular place on the body.

The naming of the body parts serves as part of the process of cultural learning of the object body or the body somatic (Frankenberg, 1990; 1994). Even though naming is emphasized as a tool, it is one that is problematic in relation to understanding the body images of younger children. A general practitioner in consultation with an ill child referred with amusement to how children under the age of seven years may on request localize their pain to their tummy and then, when asked to localize their pain further, would inevitably point to their 'belly button', despite the fact that the pain might subsequently be designated by doctors to a completely different part of their body. Another example will make this point clear. When an adult asks a crying child 'Where have you hurt yourself?' the youngest children reply by saying 'on the swing' or 'in the sandpit' or 'on the chair'. Answers like these were surprising to adults for they were asking for further guidance from the child to locate the specific part of the *body* that was injured. The child's reply referred to the experience of hitting the chair or falling in the sandpit or to the event of being hit by another child or having fallen. Following this argument from the child's point of view, she does not hurt her knee or elbow, the experience of pain *is* striking the sandpit. There is an integrated experience of playing in and then striking the sandbox, experiencing its texture, the unexpected alteration of the situation and the body in pain. The child feels her body as a subjective experience and does not have an 'outsider's view' of her body as an object. Rather, the body is incarnate and unbounded. However, the adult approach emphasizes the vulnerability of the child's body, placing it in the interior body although it is manifested in transformations of the exterior body.

In some way this does not allow adults to attribute to children the experience of 'real' suffering. This may be illustrated by the following two statements of childhood illness contrasted in the Open University text 'Birth to Old Age' (1985). The first example is from a medical textbook:

> Chickenpox is a common and highly infectious disease but it is usually mild in childhood. (Hull and Johnston 1981: 78)

This statement made by a paediatrician can be contrasted to a child's account of their illness experience. The child explained:

> My last illness was chicken pox and it was dreadful. The first two days were the worst. I did not just have chicken pox but was ill as well. I felt very lazy and was asleep all day and I would not eat. I think chicken pox is the worst illness I have ever had . . . it was dreadful and I hope I never have it again. (quoted in Bartram, 1965)

In my own study the issue of how adults' generally attributed suffering to children is illustrated in the following account. A school nurse told me:

> I want children to know that I help them. Because if they know that I am able to help with a small problem (for example, a wound on the knee) then they know that they can always come to me for help when they get bigger problems (for example, more complex psychological or social problems).

Thus children's everyday problems were in general thought of in terms of being simple, straightforward, concrete and visible to adults. The problems of an older child or adult, however, were associated with an enveloped and complex nature. The older child was seen as in and between more diverse social interactions and contexts. This was taken as implying experiences of a more complex nature, which were also considered as problems of the inner body that are symptomatic of emotional distress or other psychological tensions.

CONCLUSION

In this chapter I have shown how shifting the perspective from the child's body as object to the child's body as subjective lived experience opens a theoretical space for understanding the body as unbounded: the body as process and the experience of the body as constituted by continuous activity and (inter)action. During the fieldwork I found that the children, in particular the oldest children (10–12 year olds), who participated in the study were engaged in creating conceptual linkages between 'the incarnate body' and 'the somatic body'. Let me illustrate this with an extract from a conversation I had with Thomas (11 years old), Benjamin (11 years old) and Dan (10 years old).

> THOMAS: I know a boy called Michael from 7th (grade). He has such a strange disease of the liver. If he drinks a beer by accident, he will lose half a year of his life.
> PIA: How do you mean, half a year??
> THOMAS: He won't live as long if he drinks beer. Anyway, he doesn't drink beer or anything.

BENJAMIN: Orh yes! If he drinks 100 beers then he loses 50 years just like that (The boys burst into laughter)

THOMAS: It's the liver, that collects all that alcohol-something. The liver cleans the blood, right – and alcohol in the blood it will first reach the liver, then it goes up to the kidneys.

BENJAMIN (points to the right side of his tummy and asks): The liver it's that one, isn't it?

THOMAS: Yes, it looks like a sausage, it sits right here (he points to a particular point on his own tummy on the right, under his chest). That's the one that causes a stitch.

PIA: Where is it placed? In that side? (I point out again the place that Thomas just marked)

THOMAS: I am not quite sure . . .

BENJAMIN: It's placed here, right in the middle!

DAN: No, its placed here on your side, here (Dan taps his finger on an exact point on the right side under his chest).

THOMAS (insistently): The liver is placed over here!

DAN: Yes, that's it!! The liver is placed on your side and then there is such a small green one, that sticks on it, and if you run too much and the little green one starts to shake, then you get a stitch.

PIA: The little green one – Do you know what it is called?

BEN: How do you do, so it doesn't shake?

PIA: It's the gallbladder.

DAN: No!! The *gallbladder* that's the one [you see] when you pee.

PIA: The gallbladder, that's the little green one.

BENJAMIN: How do you do then so it doesn't shake? What about people who runs a marathon?

DAN: They are probably used to run.

BEN: Yes, but there is also something about, that you have to breathe in, in a particular way. You have to breathe in through your nose and then blow out through the mouth, I think. (Benjamin begins to practice according to his own instructions. Dan joins in with him and they practise for some time keeping in rhythm).

With this final example I will summarize some of my most important arguments. The three boys are engaged in a *collective bricolage* of their experiences, informations and biological knowledge which they discussed during our conversation and of which they tried to create a mutual understanding. They tried in particular to create an understanding of their experience, that 'when you run too much you get a stitch' (the incarnate body) by combining this experience with their knowledge about the different separate parts of the body and in particular the function of organs such as 'the liver' and 'the gallbladder' (the somatic body). In their conversation the body is central partly through using it to localize, mark and unite their different understandings, and partly in their final practical exercise and testing whether a particular way of breathing will work. Thus the body is in itself a project for investigation and a medium for deepened understanding.

The examination of vulnerability, I suggest, is useful for understanding not only illness in childhood, or other episodes where children may be injured, but also for understanding some basic conceptions of modern childhood itself. Children's vulnerablity may be partly associated with their biological being, but it is also a construction of the way in which children perceive themselves and are perceived by others. It is embedded in cultural understandings of the child as a social person, of the child's body and conceptions of health and illness. The cultural performance of (child) vulnerability and (adult) protection is accentuated when children's body surfaces are transformed. I do not wish to argue that this perspective forms any exclusive stance in adults' understanding of children. On the contrary it exists alongside other perspectives of children and their bodies held by adults and by children themselves. In this chapter, however, I have outlined how it forms an element of the cultural learning of children and I suggest further that this perspective may usefully be employed to further understanding of how the life course is culturally constituted in terms of frailty and strength.

The dissonances revealed in the communication between children and adults were an important element of the differences between their approaches to the everyday episodes I have been discussing. Vendler (1984: 201) has suggested that in order to bridge the gap in understanding between a person's subjective states and exterior manifestations a solution must be found in the interpreter's own experiences. In a recent paper, Hastrup addressed this point further, adding 'Solidarity is not achieved by inquiry but by imagination, the imaginative ability to see strange people as fellow sufferers' (Hastrup, 1993).

In this chapter I have suggested that adults attempting to understand children's experiences by translating them into those of adults themselves highlight particular problems in the interpretation of childhood illness. These problems may not be constituted from the adults' own experiences, but could be seen as arising from, in Hastrup's terms, the limitations of adults' imaginative abilities. However, this may be too easy. An anthropological understanding of children must be achieved by replacing adults' images of children as social persons and of their vulnerability and instead firmly contextualizing children in their own social worlds.

A statement by the founder of the international charity Save the Children Fund, used in a recent campaign, is that 'The only universal language in the world is a child's cry'. This quotation addresses the issue of children's suffering as an unarguable and recognizable global truth. Yet, as Putnam has pointed out, 'for a particular proposition to be "true", that is generally acceptable to others, it must display a degree of coherence with experience' (Putnam 1981: 49, cited in Hastrup, 1993). The child's cry, as any other behaviour, is given meaning within its particular social and cultural context. The understanding of vulnerability seen in a child's cry or through another expressive process poses a problem when it is interpreted through the knowledge and images of adults. Anthropological understanding of vulnerability must be achieved within the context of children's relations and social interactions, those between children and adults and it must be related to the child's position in the social structures and cultural frameworks which mediate their experiences.

ACKNOWLEDGEMENTS

I wish to acknowledge the Health Insurance Foundation (Sygekassernes Helsefond) and The Danish Research Council for the Humanities who funded the research project on which this chapter is based.

NOTES

1. An earlier version of this chapter was presented at the RAI seminar 'The Anthropology of Children', January 1994, held at the Pauling Centre for Human Sciences, Oxford.
2. A study of English primary school children showed similarly that girls were expected to take a more passive role in physical activities and were seen as being of a more fragile constitution than boys by teachers

and mothers. These distinctions were discussed by adults in terms of a child's 'wetness' (Prout, 1986).

3. A recent study has addressed the powerful role of images of the exterior body for children. This study conducted in England showed that younger school children constituted understanding of social identity as being reflected in the body appearance, shape, size and behaviour of another person (James, 1993).

4. Elsewhere I have shown how the moral demands of adults to take care of and be responsible for children implied that adults actively intervene and claim control during the everyday episodes of illness and minor accidents of children (Christensen, 1993).

5. The work presented here derives from a one-year ethnographic study of the cultural performance of childhood illness in Denmark. The aim of this chapter on the basis of this work is to sketch some more general ideas pervading European conceptions of the child's body and of vulnerability in childhood, ideas common to popular and scientific understanding.

The study was conducted in a state school and two associated after-school centres in Vanløse, a district of Copenhagen. Vanløse has a population of about 36,000 and may be considered to be a typical Danish middle-class area: skilled workers, teachers, nurses, clerical workers, small businessmen and professionals such as doctors, lawyers and architects. Few people are unemployed or receive social security. The school was one of the four schools that serviced the local area of Vanløse.

The research was carried out among 6–13-year-old children in different situations and contexts of their everyday life. The methodology consisted of both general ethnographic participant observation and more purposeful data production such as interviews, focus group discussions and children's essays. A combination of approaches was taken to examine issues such as health, illness, peer relations, play and games. These data from the children were supplemented by interview with parents, teachers, health workers and members of the staff in the two centres. This chapter draws in particular on data from 6–9-year-old children, their families, teachers and other professionals.

4 Regulation and Resistance: Children's Embodiment during the Primary–Secondary School Transition
Brenda Simpson

INTRODUCTION

This chapter is based on the results of fieldwork undertaken during the latter part of 1996 in two schools in northern England. Ethnographic methods were used to observe a cohort of pupils and understand their experiences as they transferred from a primary to a secondary school. The original intention was to study the experiences of children with Special Educational Needs[1] and the ways, if any, in which these differed from those of other children. As the fieldwork progressed, however, it became obvious that during the transition all children were subject to needs of one kind or another, especially with reference to the body. This chapter explores the importance of the body to all children in the power relations that are played out within schools.

A school is a locus of discipline, control and power, some manifestations of which are more obvious and clear-cut than others. In the everyday life of the school, the most overt display of power is that of teaching staff in relation to pupils, but, beneath the surface of school life, many other power relationships are apparent. Pupils, for example, possess the ability to resist their teachers and also to wield different forms of power over their peers; boys dominate girls and *vice versa*; and hierarchies of autonomy exist between pupils in varying age sets. 'Parent power' is a much-used catchphrase in the current educational arena, and both national and local government agencies possess overarching powers to determine such fundamental issues as general educational policies and individual school budgets.

What may not be immediately obvious, however, is the centrality of the body and bodily discourses to the power relations played out within schools.

Shilling (1993), following Goffman (1968), argues convincingly that, because visible bodies are enmeshed in webs of communication irrespective of individual intentions, certain professionals, including teachers, are required to be experts in body management. In their book, *Body Language for Competent Teachers*, Neill and Caswell (1993) claim that:

> Nonverbal skills are invaluable for teachers in 'getting the message across' to classes and understanding the messages pupils are sending – messages of interest or messages of confrontation, which are first expressed non-verbally. With increasing interest in classroom competence, teachers need to understand the use of gesture, posture, facial expression and tone of voice. These have become especially important for effective teachers in a climate where respect has to be earned rather than coming automatically with the job. (1993: preface)

They then go on to delineate the ways in which teachers may effectively use 'gesture, posture, facial expression and tone of voice' to establish a good relationship with pupils, and to determine the nonverbal messages they are receiving from pupils. Strategies and exercises are suggested to enable teachers to decipher the 'meanings' behind pupils' body language, and to counteract any possible challenges to their own authority. In one scenario, two boys arrive late for a lesson and arrive in a dishevelled state, with their ties undone, shirt tails out and chewing gum. The teacher is advised to subject the pupils to a series of 'status-reducing exercises' – insisting they stand up straight, remove their hands from their pockets, fasten their ties and maintain eye contact; in other words, maintain an appropriate bodily demeanour. The teacher is assured that utilizing these strategies will demonstrate that s/he holds the power to do such things, and 'in the process, strips the pupil of his assumed power' (1993: 23). Thus, the classroom is shown to be the site of a complicated power struggle in which the body constitutes an undeniably potent weapon.

By outlining such a power struggle, Neill and Caswell emphasize the importance to teachers of gaining control over pupils' 'unruly' bodies. Foucault (1977) also highlights the necessity of 'docile bodies' to the smooth and efficient management of institutions such as schools. By tracing the transition at the end of the eighteenth century from the public spectacle of theatrical torture to the use of power through imprisonment, Foucault outlines the transfer from the 'liturgy of punishment' of the body to control of the mind. Power reached out to regulate throughout a variety of institutions such as the prison, the asylum and the school, through the auspices of the 'disciplinary gaze'. As banishment was superseded by confinement, Jeremy Bentham's panopticon represented the symbol of the all-seeing completeness of power and surveillance, and increasing surveillance within schools has facilitated not only greater disciplinary control over pupils, their movement around school, and the manner in which they spend their time at school, but has also extended outwards in an ever-widening arc which expedites greater surveillance of their lives outside school. Disciplinary mechanisms seep out from their institutional space and begin to encroach on non-institutional spaces and populations. Foucault, for example, points to the church school which, under the guise of a concern with the training of children, began to gather information on parents, their lifestyles and their morals (Smart, 1985).

The gathering of this information originated ostensibly with a concern for children's health. Outlining a 'political anatomy' of the body, Armstrong (1983) describes the manner in which children's bodies came increasingly under the auspices of the medical gaze. Following Foucault's arguments concerning changes in the ways in which the body was treated as an object and target for power, Armstrong argues that bodily activities were temporally ordered by devices such as the timetable, which regulated cycles of repetition in institutions such as schools. Techniques of surveillance, such as tests, ensured that bodies were individualized and thus rendered manipulable. Discipline, and therefore power, evolved during the relationship between 'an individualized body and a disembodied gaze' (1983: 4). Disciplinary power remains invisible whilst those individuals who come under its sway are rendered visible. However, the body of the child, which had become the focus of the panoptic vision and a concern of medical discourse towards the end of the nineteenth century, was also subjected at the same time to various moral and pedagogic attentions, through the introduction of compulsory education.

The school was an opportune environment in which to exercise surveillance over the child and, simultaneously, to examine actual bodies, and the school medical service was established in Britain in 1908 (Armstrong, 1983). Service was provided through two separate clinics, one for treatment and the other for inspection. Under the auspices of the treatment centre, children's bodies were examined, illnesses diagnosed and appropriate treatment provided, whilst the inspection clinic screened all school children for incipient diseases, organized visits to children's homes by school nurses, and functioned as a co-ordination centre, where children's records were established, maintained and updated. In addition, inspection clinics evolved into assessment as well as diagnostic centres, purporting to offer, within a medical discourse, explanations for educational failure. Thus the link between systems of medical and educational surveillance were forged.

FORMS OF DISCIPLINE WITHIN SCHOOLS

The underlying intent of the school curriculum, which orders the spatial and temporal lives of children, is to ensure that schools are inhabited by 'docile bodies'. According to Lyon and Barbalet, the body, although a subject of social power, is not simply a passive recipient of society's mould, and therefore external to it. The individual capacity for social agency emanates from the lived experience of embodiment, 'persons experience themselves simultaneously *in* and *as* their bodies' (1994: 54). Childhood is seen as a period of control and passivity, during which the child's body is 'finished' and admitted into adult society, and society's expectation of the education system is that of transforming children from natural to cultured individuals, from primitive to 'civilized' beings (Elias, 1978; 1982).

Within the schools themselves, an integral part of the contemporary surveillance of pupils is the pastoral system, a regime founded on the ideology of 'caring for the pupil', who may experience personal problems and/or difficulties either at school or at home. None the less, although the system does undoubtedly provide the basis for dealing effectively with the problems a pupil may experience, individuals such as educational psychologists, social workers, welfare workers and health professionals augment disciplinary control over pupils through detailed knowledge of them obtained by surveillance, which includes personal files and home visits (see also James, 1998). In relation to the body more specifically, school rules dictate how students should comport themselves, and a considerable number of these rules revolve around notions of spatiality and embodiment. Part of the control exercised within schools is aimed at maintaining the correct use of space, and directing pupils to appropriate spaces at designated times.

The timetable or 'time–space path' (Gordon, 1996) is utilized to determine the location of any particular pupil at any one time, and to order the movement of cohorts of pupils through the school building from one classroom/lesson to the next. Rules and practices that constitute the 'curriculum of the body' (Lesko, 1988) detail what kind of embodiment is acceptable (you must not run, you must not chew gum, etc.) The importance of bodily comportment and movement within schools has been demonstrated by Gilborn, in relation to Afro-Caribbean pupils, who affected 'a particular style of walking (with seemingly exaggerated swinging of the shoulders and a spring in the step)' (1990: 27). The style appeared to be exclusive to Afro-Caribbean males, and was always deemed to be 'inappropriate' by (white) members of the teaching staff and, although it did not specifically contravene school rules, often led to criticism of pupils who adopted it. Pupils would be exhorted to 'get a move on', 'stand up straight' and 'walk properly', although the style of walking was perceived by the pupils concerned as simply a 'good feeling'. Gilborn is unable to determine whether the teachers' negative connotation of the style of walking was either a response to, or a catalyst for, its use as a form of resistance. Nevertheless, it can be seen that the manner in which pupils comport themselves can be perceived by school staff as oppositional, and as a threat to their own authority, even where this may not be the intended consequence of the pupils concerned.

This theoretical background will now be utilized to explore the experiences of pupils observed during fieldwork at the two schools involved in the transition. The primary school is referred to as Littlefields School, and the secondary as Greatfields School, and reference is made to different factions identified by pupils themselves, i.e. 'Hard Boys' and 'Boffin Boys' and 'Hard Girls' and 'Boffin Girls'. 'Boffin' types were perceived as studious pupils, whereas 'Hard' types were identified as rebellious and nonconformist.

DISCIPLINE AT LITTLEFIELDS AND GREATFIELDS SCHOOLS

From the first day at the secondary school, pupils were made aware of the need for bodily control and compliance. During their first assembly, their Year Co-ordinator reiterated the rules that they should follow at all times:

> You should stand in quiet orderly lines outside form rooms and act in a responsible manner, enter in *civilized* single file, sit sensibly on chairs with all four legs on the ground and sit in silence while the register is taken.

Whether or not the term 'civilized' is used intentionally, or even knowingly, the underlying concept of children being 'tamed' and 'made sensible' is pervasive. As they progressed to each new lesson, pupils were presented with another set of rules, all of which formed part of the school's policy of Assertive Discipline (Canter and Canter, 1976), and which related to aspects of bodily self-control, e.g.

1. Obey instructions/follow directions.
2. No shouting out or speaking without permission.
3. Keep your hands, feet and objects to yourself.
4. Stay in your seat unless you have permission to move.
5. No chewing.

Along with each set of rules was a list of negative and positive sanctions which would follow if pupils either contravened or adhered to these guidelines. Failure to conform resulted in a predetermined set of consequences, i.e.

First transgression	A warning
Second transgression	Name on the board and five minutes' detention
Third transgression	Ten minutes detention'
Fourth transgression	Sent out, parents contacted, twenty minutes' detention
Fifth transgression	Sent to foyer, dealt with by senior management, forty minutes' detention

Further transgressions led to pupils being placed 'on report', which entailed the use of different coloured report cards relating to the severity of the misbehaviour and which were presented to each teacher for their comments at the end of the lesson. On the other hand, those pupils who adhered to the rules received in their diaries at the end of the lesson a different 'good behaviour' stamp for each subject area, which when totalled eventually led to such rewards as raffles or 'free lessons' when pupils were allowed to play games or watch a videotape of their own choice.

It was evident during observation that much of the behaviour expected in both schools was conveyed to pupils at morning assemblies, which often took the form of moral discourses which focused on aspects of embodiment and spatiality. At the primary school, whole school assemblies were held four times a week. Great emphasis was placed on the manner that children entered and left the hall. They were expected to enter and stand quietly, and wait to be told to sit down, after which they should sit still and wait to be addressed with their eyes facing to the front. When the assembly had ended, children were required to stand quietly, and wait in lines until it was their turn to leave. The service itself began with the singing of a hymn, after which the children were addressed usually by either the Headteacher or the Deputy Headteacher. These 'sermons' generally took the form of a story with a moral ending, a fable illustrating the triumph of good over evil, or occasionally short playlets acted out by a group of the children themselves. One such playlet was in two scenes, the first depicting the correct way to behave during lunchtime, with children sitting and 'eating' properly and holding a conversation, and the second showing the 'wrong' way to conduct themselves, shouting, pushing each other around and eating in an uncouth manner.

During these assemblies, personal safety in relation to the body was constantly emphasized, such as the inadvisability of playing near electricity pylons and the need to exercise caution when crossing the road. Misdemeanours relating to school uniform were also addressed. Similar messages about the propriety of behaviour and appearance were conveyed during the assemblies at Greatfields School. Again, the emphasis was on entering in a silent, well-behaved manner, sitting quietly during the assembly, and leaving the hall in silence. Occasionally, pupils were instructed to sit down, then stand up again and repeat the procedure if they were considered not to have performed it in a suitable manner. As at the junior school, the main reason given for most of the rules and regulations was a concern for the health and safety of pupils' bodies. The Headteacher stressed that many areas of the school presented hazards for pupils, especially science laboratories which housed dangerous chemicals, corridors in which pupils were at risk of being crushed, and staircases and stairwells which presented many problems caused mainly by the pupils themselves, either by dropping heavy bags from the top landings, which could kill another pupil, or by spitting down the stairwells, which could cause other pupils to slip. They would see notices around the school informing them of which pupils were allowed to go into which areas. This was said by teachers to alleviate the possibility that pupils would be crushed because of the sheer volume of numbers. They were urged to obey these notices at all times for, as the Headteacher claimed, if there was an accident, he 'would have to send for the caretaker to clean you off the floor'.

Children's bodies were perceived as 'dangerous' and troublesome agents which must be controlled, especially in interstitial areas such as corridors and staircases where surveillance is of necessity enforced to a lesser degree than more formal areas such as classrooms. It can be seen from the above that, because of their inability to resort to *corporal* punishment[2] to control children, school staff are forced to utilize a real or supposed concern with the welfare of pupils' actual *bodies* to enforce discipline. One aspect of this concern with children's bodies may involve enforcing discipline by appealing to their 'better natures'. For example, on one occasion, two boys had been sent to the Headteacher after they had persisted in dropping their bags from the top floor of the staircase, and in their absence, their form tutor informed their classmates that:

> Throwing bags down is dangerous, as a bag weighing one and a half pounds dropped down forty feet would be doing 120 miles per hour at the bottom. If anyone was hit on the head it would be extremely dangerous. . . . If you break the rules, you will get grassed up [reported] so fast it will make your eyes water. People grass you up because it's their safety that's in question. It's foolish to expect to get away with it and [the Headteacher] has laid it on the line clearly, it's not just teachers being killjoys.

By using the pupils' own terms of reference, and pointing out that such constraints were for their own safety and not simply idle whims on the part of teaching staff, the form tutor was appealing to the pupils' sense of fair play and attempting to make the rules appear reasonable in their eyes. Here can be seen what Jenks has outlined as the shift in Western society's thinking from the image of the 'Dionysian child', whose innately wilful and demonic nature must be tamed, to that of the 'Appollonian child', who possesses a 'natural goodness and clarity of vision that we might 'idolize' or even 'worship' as the source of *all that is best in human nature*' (1996: 73, emphasis added). What Jenks refers to as the Dionysian child evokes images of original sin, of the child whose evil and potentially destructive nature must be curbed by a programme of strict parental and educational moral guidance. Successful socialization of this wilful child involves a battle of wills to ensure control and conformity. The Appollonian child, on the other hand, is all sweetness and light and, rather than striving to ensure the conformity of such a child, individuality is celebrated. Consequently, children in the latter image, in contemporary Western educational settings, are not beaten into submission, but 'encouraged, enabled and facilitated'.

Nowhere is there a greater need for 'docile bodies' than in the school setting and, during observation in the classroom, my fieldnotes point to the numerous occasions on which pupils are exhorted to 'sit up and sit still, eyes to the front, button your mouths, pin back your ears, engage your brains, calm down and listen'. Time and space are utilized in the control of unruly bodies. At both schools, children were warned that if they misbehaved, wasted time and failed to finish their work during the allotted time-span, they would be kept inside during break or lunch periods, in their 'own' time, to complete assignments or to write out lines as a punishment. At the primary school, pupils who transgressed during lessons by shouting out answers rather than raising their hands moved from their desks to sit on the carpet area in the corner of the classroom, whilst teachers at the secondary school moved children who were misbehaving to the front of the room, or in the case of serious or repeated episodes of bad behaviour, outside the classroom altogether. During a physical education lesson, two boys who were fighting were made to stand in opposite corners of the gymnasium with their faces to the wall. Okely (1978) describes how the pupils in her study received 'punishment by exposure'. Girls with the 'right' attitude to authority were rewarded by being allowed to merge into the group, whilst those who transgressed received a 'disobedience' or 'late' mark, the reason for which was read out in front of the whole school, and emblazoned on the notice board for all to see.

Those discovered to be talking whilst lining up for the dining room were made to stand in the main passage with their backs to the rest of the school, but conspicuous to all. Docile bodies, then, are permitted to remain invisible, whereas bodies that do not conform are made visible by being placed out of 'normal' time and space by members of staff.

It was evident during fieldwork that, apart from their actual behaviour during lessons and breaks, great emphasis was placed on pupils' actual embodiment and self-presentation. Both schools operated a well-defined dress policy, which included such items as jewellery, and attempted deviations from the policy were dealt with promptly. Pupils at the junior school were reprimanded for incorrect clothing, although they were never sent home, while at the secondary school, unsuitable clothing was tolerated only on the basis that school wear was being laundered and the clothing worn was temporary for that day. This was expected to be accompanied by a note from the parent, and a form was issued to the pupil to present to members of staff who queried their clothing. Emphasis was placed on the fact that shirts must be tucked into trousers or skirts at all times, and this was one rule which many boys encountered difficulty in adhering to, especially after break and lunchtime periods when they had been playing football in the playground. Pupils at both schools were expected not to wear make-up or nail varnish, and only small stud earrings were allowed. Hair braids and plastic 'friendship bands' were not to be worn. Children's bodies, then, were expected to conform both visibly and behaviourally.

TRANSITIONAL EMBODIMENT

A particular feature of children's embodiment during the transition from primary to secondary school was an emphasis by teachers on stereotypes of children as identified through bodily size and ability. James (1993) discusses the way in which children are the subject of such remarks as 'Haven't you grown?', 'Aren't you a big girl?', etc. and that,

> The stereotypical import of such statements is clear: the bigger one is, the better one is and the more social – literally the more personable – one becomes. The received emphasis for children is clear. It stresses the importance of the growth and development

of the physical body in the present for future social identities. (1993: 110)

Teachers at the primary school often remarked to the children about to transfer to the secondary school that 'You're not little babies now, so there's no need to fiddle' or complained that 'You're acting like a class of nursery children', and these remarks were reflected in the children's perceived ability to perform tasks that would be expected of them following the transfer. During a maths lesson, pupils were chastized for using expressions such as 'share' instead of 'divide'. Teachers commented: 'Share is for well down the school. Can we start to use the proper word now?' Whilst colouring a map, children were exhorted to make their colouring neat as teachers claimed that some of their work was 'no better than infants' colouring'. One child was repeatedly told that he should join up his writing as he was a Year Six pupil now, and another who claimed she was unable to complete a particular task was told, 'Don't say that, young lady, you won't be able to say that at the Comp. [comprehensive school]'. The spectre of the secondary school was present throughout the children's final term at the primary school. They were admonished to learn their tables, as knowledge of these would be vital at the new school, as would the practice of completing homework on time, and the ability to spell correctly. Children were about to enter a new space, which presented the new threat of visibility if the body refused to behave correctly.

After the transition to the 'new' school, staff continued to reinforce the notion that pupils had now assumed the identity of 'secondary school pupils' and should have left their 'childish' ways behind at the old school. During one of their first lessons, the teacher remarked that one rule which they might have difficulty adhering to was the one that required them to remain in their seats, as they had probably been used to walking around the classroom at their primary schools. However, he stressed that they were 'bigger now', so this should not prove to be too difficult. The notion of physical size was used to denote increased self-control on the children's part, whereas in fact a mere six weeks had elapsed since they had left the primary school. Misbehaviour was often ascribed to the fact that they had not successfully relinquished their previous 'primary school' identity, and had perhaps not yet achieved the requisite amount of control over their bodies. Once when they insisted on chatting during a lesson, the teacher enquired, 'Why is there all this talk? You're not at the junior school now.' He then claimed that, 'If your behaviour becomes more juvenile, you should return to the juvenile school . . . you're not in the junior school now, where you sit at little desks.' Discipline was therefore enforced by the use of stereotypical images of body size and age, not only in terms of bodily self-control but also in attendant academic ability and identity.

Children at school, then, are seen to be enmeshed in intricate webs of power, which utilize their bodies and a concern for their welfare to exercise discipline. However, this is not to say that children are passive victims of the process. On the contrary, children in the study demonstrated daily in the classroom their ability to resist actively the restrictions placed upon them. Because such restrictions often took the form of rules concerning embodiment, space and temporality, many forms of resistance also revolved around children's bodies and their capacity to manipulate space and time.

FORMS OF RESISTANCE TO DISCIPLINE BY PUPILS

Following Gordon (1996), it became evident that because discipline was enforced through correct embodiment, the fragility, sickness or 'wild nature' of children's bodies was often invoked, either formally or informally, to circumvent school rules. In a more formal capacity, pupils were only allowed to contravene the normal 'time–space path' if they were able to show, with corroboration from their parents, that they were subject to certain illnesses or bodily conditions. For example, they could visit the lavatory during lessons only if they could present a note in their school diary stating that they had a bladder 'problem', and similarly, those girls who were menstruating could avoid showers at the end of a physical education lesson only if they possessed such a note. One boy who had recently undergone chemotherapy for leukaemia and had experienced hair loss was allowed to wear a cap, thus contravening the usual dress code. Children whose parents claimed that they were allergic to chemicals in the swimming baths were able to forgo swimming lessons (although there was some doubt cast on the validity of this claim), and participation in games, physical education and drama lessons could be avoided only by the presence of illness or medical problems. However, teachers usually worked on the basis that if children were well enough to be at school, they were well enough to participate in these lessons, and one teacher remarked: 'It is no good saying that you can't do PE because you've got a blister or a boil on your bottom. If you want to be excused, I expect to at least see a piece of pot [i.e. plaster of Paris] or something serious.' Minor conditions such as rashes or verrucas were not considered serious enough to facilitate a pupil missing lessons, and children's access to the sick role (Parsons, 1951) was sometimes in question (Prout, 1986).

However, by far the greatest form of resistance to authority by pupils manifested itself in an informal manner, by way of relatively small acts of defiance which involved the use of their bodies, bodily functions or waste products. Hebdige has commented that 'the challenge to hegemony which subcultures represent is not issued directly by them. Rather it is expressed obliquely, in style' (1979: 17). Boys and girls habitually flouted the dress code by wearing plastic 'friendship bands' on their wrists, sometimes up to a dozen on each arm, and these were a source of real contention amongst the staff. However, resistance to authority was not simply played out through the medium of children's actual bodies, but also through the use of bodily functions and effluence. Csordas discusses the cultural specificity of the manner in which particular societies deal with body products such as 'blood, semen, sweat, tears, faeces, urine, and saliva' (1994: 5), and Mary Douglas (1966 [1992]) explains the important societal symbolism of the human body and the rituals concerning bodily substances which become dangerous when 'out of place'. Children take great pleasure in using their bodies as a medium of expression (Benthall and Polhemus, 1975) and revel in aspects of the body which adults have usually come to find distasteful and 'taboo', such as blood, excrement and saliva. They are also still fascinated by their ability to use different facets of sexuality both to shock and as a source of power over their peers (James, 1986). This was demonstrated by children's insistence on relating to me the unexpurgated, gory details of accidents they had suffered, and also their tendency to recount 'rude' jokes to other children, whilst ensuring I was within earshot.

GENDERED TRANSITIONS

It was evident during the actual transition that the use of the body as a source of power and resistance was gendered. Whereas girls generally resorted to more covert forms of resistance such as bodily adornment which contravened school rules on dress, boys were more likely to use their bodies as an instrumental source of rebellion, especially those boys designated by others as the 'Hard Boys'. These pupils lost no opportunity in disrupting proceedings by belching, breaking wind, spitting, pulling faces, yawning, snoring, coughing in an exaggerated fashion, pretending to sneeze loudly, making noises with their mouths or hands, drumming their fingers on the table, and shuffling their bodies on chairs causing them to squeak. Occasionally, pupils in the 'Hard Girls' faction would also use some of these tactics, but to a much lesser extent. A fieldnote demonstrates pupils' ability to interrupt the teacher's flow and disrupt a science lesson:

> As we enter the laboratory, Mrs. Carter says that some of the group will have to be moved around to different parts of the classroom, ostensibly so that they are better able to see the board, but I think it is probably an attempt to split up the more troublesome element. She says that Simon will have to move, so Simon says, 'All right, I'll move', and moves his stool two inches to the right. George is sprawled out on the workbench, and Mrs Carter tells him not to lie on the bench but to sit up. He does so, but starts rocking on his stool to make it squeak. Freddy makes a big thing out of breaking wind, so George holds his nose and makes a performance out of moving away from the smell. Simon is told to sit up and take his face out of his hands.

After previously identifying the disruptive element in the group, Mrs Carter had planned a strategy to separate them which gave her a legitimate reason to move them around and also to stamp her authority on the lesson. However, by their use of space and embodiment, the boys sabotaged her efforts to control them, and a large section of the lesson was lost as she attempted to bring the class back to order.

Boys were also adept at manipulating space by utilizing their bodies or bodily functions to remove themselves either from lessons or from the space they had been allotted, even occasionally injuring their bodies. At the primary school, during a music lesson, which he disliked, Billy deliberately stabbed himself with a pencil, drawing blood, and was forced to leave the lesson and visit the nurse. Also at the primary school, the children were sitting on the carpet for a lesson, and Patrick asked if he could stand up as he was suffering from cramp. The teacher agreed, providing he did it 'sensibly', but after receiving permission to stand, Patrick stood behind the bookcase, squatting down and occasionally peeping over the top. The other children, aware that they would not be personally punished, revelled in the spectacle, thereby indulging in bad behaviour 'by proxy'.

Once at the secondary school, boys continued to achieve their objectives through blatant manipulation of their bodies. They would insist that they needed to visit the lavatory, despite the usual school rule (see above). On one occasion, one boy repeatedly showed the teacher a small scratch on his finger, which he claimed was stinging, and asked to visit the nurse, until the teacher relented and allowed him to go, thus enabling him to miss a large part of a lesson he disliked. Boys who repeatedly misbehaved were eventually sent out of the classroom, but this strategy tended to backfire on staff members and demonstrate pupils' ability to utilize surveillance strategies for their own ends. Miscreants sent outside merely took the opportunity to pull faces at their classmates through the glass panel in the door, one boy going a step further and sticking a pencil in each ear. Once outside the classroom, pupils would often put their heads back inside the door and claim that they needed the lavatory. The teacher invariably refused, but boys would protest that 'I'm going to pee myself if I don't go, sir' and, in the last instance, teachers would be forced to acquiesce as they could not risk an 'accident' or a complaint from parents, and pupils were well aware of this.

One unusual aspect of some boys' behaviour was their tendency either to burst into tears or sulk, features usually associated with girls' behaviour (Askew and Ross, 1988). It was noticeable from the beginning of the fieldwork that some boys, if reprimanded by a teacher, would fly into a rage, put their heads down onto their desks and cry, especially if they felt they had been dealt with unfairly. Harry and Neil were reprimanded for 'messing about' (thereby disrupting the order of the classroom) and threatened with lines, whereupon Neil protested that he hadn't done anything wrong, put his head onto his hands and began to cry angrily. Later, in the line waiting to enter the hall for assembly, Neil continued to mutter angrily, with tears streaming down his face. This kind of behaviour occurred on numerous occasions, but apart from one was always related to boys. They became very angry if they felt they had been wrongly accused, and this threat to their identity as 'good pupils' appeared to be more important to them than allowing the rest of the class to witness them crying. Boys also showed a tendency to sulk if they were reprimanded or felt they had been wrongly handled by a teacher, and the Year Co-ordinator at the secondary school remarked to me that during 27 years of experience in the teaching profession, she had never previously encountered this kind of behaviour from boys. Patrick claimed on several occasions that his teacher treated him unfavourably. After a physical education lesson he claimed that two of the girls had swung a mat into his legs, but when he reported this to the teacher, she had appeared to dismiss the incident as trivial. Patrick felt that she should have at least confronted the girls, and claimed that she 'didn't do anything 'cos she never believes me, she doesn't like me. I'll get done for breathing next!' He related his perceived unfair treatment to the most fundamental and vital of bodily functions, and utilized his body (sulking, crying and throwing a tantrum) to protest.

Another way in which some of the boys expressed a challenge to authority was by utilizing their hair, again a method more generally used by girls. This strategy was adopted solely by members of the 'Hard Boys' group. Soon after the transition, it was noticeable that, one by one, they arrived at school with their hair bleached blonde. The staff appeared to adopt the line of least resistance (the Year Co-ordinator remarking that the less the school made of this tactic, the sooner it would burn itself out) so the boys went a little further, with the hair colour gradually progressing from blonde to bright pink or orange. As the staff had predicted, this behaviour gradually seemed to lose its attraction as the term progressed and, during follow-up fieldwork, it was evident that these boys had returned to their 'normal' hair colour. However, boys from the 'Hard Boys' group would often be chastised for combing their hair during lessons, and during the visit by the school photographer, it was noticeable that it was the boys, rather than the girls, who were more concerned about the appearance of their hair.

If this was the manner in which boys mounted a challenge to authority, not only in ways usually identified with boys in the school setting (Spender, 1989), but also by using strategies generally associated with girls, then what of the girls themselves? Hebdige's work (1979) has received criticism in that it fails to include the experiences of girls (Blackman, 1995). McRobbie and Garber (1976) pose the question of whether this is simply because girls interact amongst themselves to form a distinctive culture of their own and offer a different type of resistance, which is more in keeping with non-subcultural male groupings. Girls observed during the study usually used their bodies in different ways from the boys to resist control. Although they were obliged to wear school uniform, they tended to rebel in relatively small ways by altering or adding to the proscribed dress code, although this varied slightly as to whether they belonged to the 'Boffin Girls' or 'Hard Girls' factions. Girls in both groups used their hairstyles to stamp their identity on their appearance by wearing brightly coloured 'Scrunchies' (fabric ___ ered elastic bands which held their hair in ponytails), slides or headbands, some of which displayed their names in different colours. They also wore brightly coloured socks which often bore motifs such as Disney characters or similar icons of teenage culture, although these were invariably hidden by their long trousers. Also, during lessons which they found to be boring, girls would engage in a kind of game which required them to change shoes under the table with their female neighbours, until they were all wearing odd shoes. Because staff were unaware of this practice, and because the boys were excluded, it represented to the girls a source of secret power expressed through the body. Those girls belonging to the 'Hard Girls' faction, however, were more outwardly confrontational. They would wear brightly coloured nail varnish, either sparkling green or bright blue, or wear earrings other than the regulation small studs. These girls would also regularly contravene the rule which disallowed chewing, although they would often protest that they were not actually chewing gum, but small pieces of plastic or other items, thus attempting to 'sidestep' rather than actually break the rules.

However, I only witnessed two incidents involving girls which may be construed as the use of possible illness to avoid lessons. In the first instance, Alice confided to me that she was worried because she had forgotten to bring her trainers for a physical education lesson. When it came to the actual lesson and the register was being taken, her friend reported that Alice was with the nurse, as she felt sick. This may have been coincidence, but it did appear rather convenient that the sickness had arrived in time to cause Alice to miss the lesson about which she was so concerned, although the phrase 'worried sick' springs to mind. The second incident occurred in similar circumstances. During a maths lesson, the teacher asked Rhiannon, who was fairly timid and rather weak academically, to come to the front of the class and write a sum on the board. She refused, and when pressed, became very agitated and began to cry. The teacher asked me to take her to the lavatory, where she remarked: 'My mum said that when I'm dizzy I have to go home.' She claimed to feel dizzy and unable to see properly. I took her to the nurse, who eventually sent her home. Once again, the illness seemed to appear suddenly and without prior warning, begging the question of whether these two girls had realized, in common with some of the boys, that claims of physical illness could be manipulated to remove them from potentially hazardous situations, and that the body could be used as a vehicle for removal from a particular space.

CONCLUSION

From an analytical point of view, the classroom can be seen as a battleground, with both sides striving to capture the high ground. Teachers have been forced to relinquish their right to chastise pupils by the use of physical force, and so must find an alternative source of power. With the increase in class sizes, gradual erosion of resources allocated to education, and the exigencies of mounting paperwork, this is proving ever more difficult. Nevertheless, the main site of power used by staff during the current study was that of attempting to control children's bodies. From the moment they entered the school, pupils were introduced to a strict regime of constraint, which not only determined where and when they should be throughout the day, but also how they should comport themselves. The need for this was often explained through the medium of a concern with pupil safety, which is understandable. One staff member, when faced with the idea of teachers enforcing discipline by constraining children's bodies, enquired how else they might keep control. Unfortunately, the main drawback to the strategy of advocating safety as a medium of control is that children often display a rather cavalier attitude towards their own bodies, as has been demonstrated by similar approaches to health (e.g. anti-smoking, drugs and alcohol) education. Consequently, pupils continued to contravene the rules designed to ensure their safety. They dropped heavy bags down stairwells, hung precariously over banisters on the top floor, and either jumped, or pushed each other, down whole flights of stairs.

Because staff attempted to instil discipline by controlling pupils' bodies, it was by utilizing their bodies that pupils rebelled. This power struggle was gendered, with boys and girls at least in the initial stages of the transition using their bodies in different ways – the boys exploiting parts of their bodies and/or bodily functions to disrupt the lessons, and the girls pushing at the boundaries of the school dress code. However, the boys did utilize some ploys which could have been perceived as arguably more feminine, such as dyeing their hair pink, and resorting to tears and sulking if they felt themselves to have been unjustifiably reprimanded. None the less, whatever the particular nuances of gendered embodiment, there is no doubt that children will continue to use their bodies as an effectual source of power.

NOTES

1. A child has Special Educational Needs if s/he has a learning difficulty which requires special educational provision. A child has a learning difficulty if s/he has a significantly greater difficulty in learning than the majority of children of the same age, or if s/he has a disability which means that that s/he is unable to use the normal educational facilities provided for children of the same age in the area.
2. Corporal punishment was formally abolished in state schools in England and Wales in 1986.

5 Parents, Children and the Construction of the Healthy Body in Middle-class Families

Kathryn Backett-Milburn

INTRODUCTION

Although health and healthy lifestyles have emerged as central motifs of the late twentieth century there has been little empirical study of the part played by the body in their construction. This is particularly interesting in view of the emphasis on body monitoring and maintenance which characterizes much of this discourse. Thus, not only have health-relevant behaviours often been studied in detachment from the social contexts in which they are embedded and given meaning, but also they have been detached from the vehicle through which they are enacted and experienced: the body. If this is the case for adults, it is even more so for children whose views on health and illness have only recently begun to be researched (Prout, 1986; Backett and Alexander, 1991; Oakley et al., 1995; Mayall, 1996).

Lay accounts of health and illness from both children and adults regularly demonstrate a tension between what are understood as the currently approved tenets of healthy lifestyles and body maintenance, and their practical enactment in everyday life. It has been suggested that this tension between knowing and doing may be partly explained by an appreciation of the socio-cultural context which, it is argued, transforms what is thought to be scientifically 'rational' behaviour into what is viewed by lay people as culturally appropriate 'reasonable' behaviour (Backett and Davison, 1995). Further understanding, however, may be gained by considering the part played by the body or, more precisely, the lived experience of the body, since this is crucial for the practical accomplishment of social behaviour. Indeed, the body itself has become a site for resistance to prevailing conceptions of appropriate health-relevant behaviours (Crawford, 1984).

This chapter reports research which accessed the lived body implicitly rather than as an explicit empirical project. The study, carried out in Edinburgh in the late 1980s, explored health-relevant beliefs, behaviours and experiences in middle-class families within the context of their daily lives (Backett, 1990). The two-year qualitative study was carried out with 28 couples each with two children initially aged between 3 and 10 years. Three rounds of interviews were carried out with the adults, involving separate and joint interviews with partners; 52 of the children were also interviewed. These home-based semi-structured interviews employed innovative methods which encouraged children to talk about health in their own terms and in the context of their own daily lives (Backett and Alexander, 1991).

The study provided rich data which have been re-analysed here to get at the lived body that may be embedded within everyday accounts (Watson, 1995: 15). The chapter argues that for these families there were a number of uncertainties which made problematic their construction of health and the healthy body. Such uncertainties, combined with conceptualizations of difference and change in bodies within families, meant that making sense of the healthy body was a dynamic and life-long project which was never truly 'finished'. The chapter discusses these areas of similarity and difference in the meanings attached to health and the healthy body, and their practical enactment. It concludes with an analysis of contested areas of bodily practices which highlights the importance of seeing children as social actors in their own right who not only have to negotiate their way through the adult world but also have to engage with other children in the construction of their own social worlds.

THE PROBLEMATIC NATURE OF THE CONSTRUCTION OF HEALTH AND THE HEALTHY BODY

On first asking, and at the outset of the fieldwork, it appeared that these middle-class adults and their children were reasonably sure about the ingredients of good health and body maintenance. Early fieldwork accounts were dominated by a reiteration of the currently approved broad guidelines for so-called healthy behaviours, and there was a general acceptance of an ethos of personal responsibility for health. The adults talked about a healthy diet, taking exercise, not smoking, drinking alcohol in moderation, reducing stress, and having a happy and healthy environment. In their interviews the children drew lots of fruit and vegetables, and pictures of bodies swimming and generally doing physical activity. The older the child the better able s/he became at identifying what was currently thought to be good or bad for health.

It appeared, therefore, that the characteristics of a so-called healthy lifestyle were familiar to all family members and apparently shared. On further questioning, and with greater familiarity with the researcher, it was evident that not only were these ideas about healthy lifestyles and healthy bodies far less clear to respondents than their first accounts suggested, but also that their translation into actual behaviour was problematic, both on an individual and family basis. Respondents were uncertain about the precise implementation of health guidelines: How much? How little? How often? How regular? These were frequent topics as they ruminated over healthy behaviours. They were uncertain whether they actually believed in the efficacy or outcome of suggested healthy behaviours; i.e. would it really result in healthier bodies? They were uncertain about the fit of various behavioural guidelines with their own daily lives; i.e. was it practically possible to manage the body in these suggested ways?

Although these observations apply particularly to the adults' accounts, uncertainty and partial knowledge also characterized the children's interviews as they unfolded. For example, the children who were 8+ were asked to reflect on why healthy food is good for you and unhealthy food is bad. If they were able to reply at all, many of their responses suggested, at best, partial knowledge about effects on the body but effects which, in the main, would be highly visible both physically and socially. For instance, a boy said that good food was 'number one' for keeping healthy because, otherwise:

> You'll get sick or your teeth will drop out, or you'll get fat. Because if you haven't [had good food] you'll just fall over.

A girl, who had seemed well informed about the relationship between calories and weight gain, said later when considering what might happen if you did not take much exercise:

> All these calories will be clogged up inside you and you'll just, I think you might want to go to the toilet a lot. And I think you wouldn't be feeling that well.

This background of uncertainty about how health is to be understood, achieved and maintained in families (Backett, 1992b) meant that making sense of the healthy body was a complex and ongoing social accomplishment. The unfinished nature of this negotiated task was imbued with even greater sensitivity with regard to parents' care of their children's health and bodies. Keeping children's bodies healthy and well maintained was a major objective for these middle-class parents, but how this was accomplished in practice was often unclear and, therefore, contested both between parents themselves and between parents and children. For example, for these parents it was almost axiomatic that parents should take greater care of their children's health than of their own and the majority described how they carefully monitored and observed their children's physical health and bodily well-being. In this respect it appeared that children's bodies were seen as potentially more vulnerable and necessitating a greater and more immediate attention than those of adults. In reply to my question 'Do you look after your children's health in the same way that you look after your own health, or do you see them as having special concerns?' R9(F) said:

> I think, broadly speaking, it's the same. [KM: Yes]. Just make sure that they have plenty of exercise and that they are using their arms and legs, keeping everything working and trim, and eating the right things and going regularly to the toilet and that sort of thing. Just keep an eye on them.

However, at the same time it was often claimed that becoming a parent had resulted in their putting their own health and care of their bodies second to that of their children. Thus, most respondents also emphasized that they would seek help for their children much more readily than they would for themselves. For example, R24(F) contrasted how she would deal with her own health compared with the children's as follows:

> Children are so obviously well, you know when they are well, that when they are ill it's a sort of immediate situation that has to be dealt with straightaway, em, because it deteriorates. Em, with my own health, or with adults you tend to, if you're feeling tired or if you're sort of under stress, you just wonder whether it's a problem that's really needing dealt with, so that you tend to leave it a bit longer.

Thus, *not* having to seek outside medical help to look after the child's body was a marker of healthiness but knowing when and how quickly to seek such help for children's physical ailments, because of their greater potential vulnerability, was seen as a social sign of good parenting. Evidence of a lack of unnecessary attention to the body was, therefore, paired uneasily with a social obligation to pay close attention to the bodies of the younger family members.

An Example: Cuts, Bumps and Bruises

In some ways these contradictions coalesced around the issue of children's everyday minor injuries to their bodies: cuts, bumps and bruises. Two main themes emerged. First, everyday accidental damage to the child's body was so mundane and commonplace that it was not worthy of mention. As the R1's discussed in their joint interview:

> R1(M): Well I notice that, you know, bathing them, now they have a great variety of bruises, (R1(F): Well, because they are in their shorts or without tights and their legs are all battered.) they both have grazed knees. (R1(F): Grazed knees, but they're not really accident-prone.) No. (R1(F): They're not bad, K. did, she banged into a girl with her bike. If there is an accident it's usually K.) Yes, cycles into the wall and things, she cycles into walls, she gets her fingers caught in doors, black eye.

Such events were seen as part of childhood and, while they might prove a topic of family conversation, say at bathtime, they did not merit close attention or concern. Children's bodies were seen as quickly healing, resilient, and minor pain or discomfort would soon pass. Also, children were not expected to complain too much about these minor injuries, but rather to take them in their stride. If children *did* request too much adult attention or sympathy, parents reported that this was either given in a superficial way or that they were told to put up with their bodily discomfort. Thus, children's bodily problems appeared to be distinguished into two main categories of 'minor/expected/minimal attention' or 'major/unexpected/considerable attention'; and parents not only had to make these decisions about the latter accurately, but also to socialize the children into appropriate social reactions to the former.

A second main theme was that drawing too great attention to damage to children's bodies, by, for example, seeking help at an

Accident and Emergency Department could easily result in some construction of social suspicion about inadequate parental caring or even of parental abuse. The accounts of these middle-class parents showed an awareness that authorities outwith the family took it upon themselves to monitor what was happening to children's bodies. Many of them expressed a fear that asking for medical help for minor accidental injuries to children's bodies or for ailments to certain parts of the body, notably the genital area, might draw inappropriate attention to their parenting or personal behaviour towards their children. Some actually described the cross-questioning they had experienced from a health professional. It was, therefore, socially important to normalize bodily injury or even to keep some physical ailments within the sphere of domestic medical care. In this respect this analysis of lay conceptualization of damage to children's bodies highlights the intersection between culture, individual action and social control.

Bodies in Families: Conceptualizations of Difference and Change

It was apparent from both parent and child accounts of health and illness that difference and change in bodies was a dominant theme. This added a further dynamic element to the uncertainties about the ingredients of health and body maintenance discussed in the previous section. For example, making sense of the body and health was compounded by perceptions of temporal fluctuations related to seasonality, lifecourse or cohort historical experience.

In the parents' accounts both adult and child bodies were described as different, for instance, in response to different seasons, times of the year or weather. Most adults said that they felt that they were less physically active and less energetic in winter-time. R26(F) said, for example, of her husband:

> He can get run down a bit, I think, em, and he can go very pale, waxy look, ghostly look about him. (KM: Oh yes) But, em, he seems to be, a bit sunshine and he's picking up again. But he seems to get down a bit over the winter months and then during the summer months he boosts up.

Some described how their children might be playing happily outside on light summer nights but were harder to motivate physically in winter. For instance, the R15's described, as follows, how their children were more lethargic in winter:

R15(M): In that they will sort of lie about (R15(F): They are more happy to sort of lie around, watch the telly, or if you are going out in the afternoon 'Where are we going? Oh must we?' and so forth.) Whereas in the summer if they don't want to go somewhere it's more because they are out and they are playing with people.

Also, bodies were seen to change over the life course and to require more self-conscious maintenance as they aged. Younger bodies and children's bodies were described by respondents as able to withstand many things such as poor eating, inadequate sleep or being pushed to physical extremes with little or no apparent damage or ill-effects (Backett and Davison, 1995). As R5(M) said of his health-relevant behaviour, 'When I was younger I probably reckoned that I could do everything I wanted to do without it creating any problems for me.'

Equally, though, respondents perceived that there had been changes over time in socio-cultural evaluations of what may or may not affect the health of the body. Many spoke of how what was re-garded as appropriate physical care by one generation might be regarded differently by the next. In their accounts, many respon-dents gave examples of how their bodies had been looked after differently in their own childhoods, and how their own parents still had different attitudes from their own towards physical care, particu-larly with regard to food and eating. The fact that some of these differences were still present in grandparents' behaviours towards their own children was often described as a source of tension be-tween themselves and the grandparents.

These perceived changes in ideas about physical care were not, however, unproblematic for respondents. Indeed, the majority of respondents also expressed scepticism about these very changes. Nevertheless, alongside this they voiced concern that if they did not *try* to carry out these current ideas, at least in respect of care of their *children's* bodies, they might risk jeopardizing their future health and thus be judged as less than adequate parents. In this regard, therefore, knowing the 'right' way to look after children's bodies was, for these respondents, a greater source of concern than was looking after their own.

Furthermore, the conceptualization of the current resilience of the child's body was muted by the worry that this might be decep-tive in the longer term and that in fact their bodies might simply store up trouble for the future. For example, R15(M) articulated this kind of view when he reflected as follows on his eight-year-old son's poor eating habits:

> Em, one slightly worrying thing is, I remember seeing a documentary on the telly which said a lot of damage is done to children in their early teens by eating the wrong sort of foods you know, if you tend in your later teens to suddenly wisen up to the whole thing, but, er, the build-up of cholesterol and so forth in the blood and this type of thing, a lot of damage is done by then.

DIFFERENCES WITHIN FAMILIES

Alongside these general constructions of differences in bodies and how they were to be looked after, respondents theorized a range of particular differences between adult and child bodies within their own families. One major difference was that whilst children's bodies were described as still developing and having potential for positive change, adults' bodies were described as at best static or, more frequently, as deteriorating. Thus, current malfunctionings in children's bodies were seen as remediable or self-rectifying. For example, the parents of several children with asthma and the mother of a boy with enuresis, expressed the hope that they would 'grow out of it'. In comparison, adult bodies were viewed as potentially now subject to damage or illness which might have permanent effects and, indeed, several respondents described how they currently lived with assorted bodily malfunctionings. For example, several men said that they were more careful with their sporting activities in case they did themselves irretrievable damage. Similarly, R1(F) worried about physical effects on her husband because 'he pushes himself all the time' and 'I feel it will catch up with him one day'. She explained:

> He just seems to thrive on being very busy. He's only 31 so I feel while he's this age he can cope with it. In fact, this morning I got a letter from friends in Hong Kong and P has ulcer trouble due to stress, he pushes himself as well and that made me think about J [husband], can his body cope with this? (KM: Yes), But I think at his age he probably can, I feel he should relax more.

The effects of ageing on the adult or child body were also perceived differently. Children's bodies were seen as ageing positively, for example they would get bigger, stronger and get over childhood illnesses. R24(M)'s description was typical, he said:

> The kids, well they get colds and chickenpox and all the usual stuff. We seem to be sniffing all the time because they're sniffing all the time. (KM: Yes, I see). Well, they're getting past that, I think.

In contrast, the adult body was generally seen as ageing negatively, as potentially subject to serious illness and as declining in capability. This was particularly evidenced by respondents' references to men having either to give up vigorous sports or perhaps to settle for activities which were less demanding on the body. As R5(M) eloquently expressed the issue: 'Body's starting to rebel a bit, takes me longer to get over the wee knocks and strains.' Other men spoke of now 'shuffling round the rugby pitch' or settling for 5-a-side football, curling or even bowls. Some women spoke of similar curtailments of physical activities, but also of having to watch their figures more or of being aware of potential deterioration of the body. As R10(F) explained:

> As you get older, if you don't keep fit then your joints and your heart and things tend to get used to you not keeping fit, then if you do make an effort, if you do, then your problems are that much harder to get back.

In this way, adults were described as having self-consciously to maintain their bodies whereas children's bodies generally maintained themselves unselfconsciously, or as a natural consequence of their ways of living. For instance, R9(F) said of her body: 'I don't want to be superfit but I do want to keep everything in good working order.' In contrast, children were perceived as unselfconsciously keeping their bodies in good working order, and parents regularly made statements about children keeping their bodies fit naturally through games and play.

This ideal of the child's naturally active body stood in contrast to many accounts of the sedentary or inactive adult body when adults described their typical days. R15(M) reflected the accounts of many of the men when he said: 'My job tends to be sitting on my backside most days.' The majority of women also bemoaned the lack of naturally occurring physical activity in their daily lives.

However, their accounts tended to highlight the issue of having to use cars rather than walking so that they could fit in their work and domestic tasks with the exigencies of childcare. Overall, physical exercise of the adult body tended to be described as a self-conscious activity separate from the sedentariness of the daily work routine.

PARENT AND CHILD CONSTRUCTIONS OF THE 'HEALTHY' BODY

Looking after the Health of the Body

In general terms, both parents and children talked about the healthy body in terms of how it appeared and functioned from the outside and how it appeared to function from the inside. For both the adult and child body, its health was also described in terms of what was done to it, what was put into it, and how it was affected by social contexts and physical environments. Most respondents described processes of monitoring the health of their own and their children's bodies, often encapsulated in the term 'keeping an eye on things'.

Throughout, it was also either explicitly stated or implicitly assumed by adults that children needed guidance and supervision in bodily care; and children showed in their accounts that, even if they chose to disobey, they took it for granted that their parents would set some rules about how they as children cared for their bodies. For some parents this meant enforcing corporeal routines on their children which they did not always adhere to themselves. R1(M) commented:

> I'm a lot more careful with their things than I am with myself. It's a bit like 'don't do as I do, do as I say', sort of thing. (KM: Yes). We don't ever send them to bed without washing their face or brushing their teeth, although I quite often do it myself.

The effects of body maintenance, the efficacy of health-relevant behaviours, and the conceptualization of the healthy body were, however, described and understood by both children and their parents in terms of *immediately* identifiable and/or visible *short-term* signs and signals. Adults were often well able to describe *potential* long-term health outcomes of ways of living, social or environmental circumstances, or health-relevant behaviours; and some of the older children were beginning to make statements connecting, for example, certain behaviours with heart disease or future ill-health. However, both parents and children spoke about health and healthy bodies predominantly in terms of, for instance, *immediately* observable or experienced physical and psychological signs, energy levels, social functioning, physical and mental activity and performance, and feelings of wellness and fitness. If the fruit and vegetables, the additive or sugar-free food, the exercise bike, the decaffeinated coffee or the sunny holiday abroad, did not have immediately identifiable corporeal benefit, then their longer-term value to health might be rendered more mysterious or even questioned.

The Social and Cultural Location of 'the Healthy Body'

It was evident from parent and child accounts that the concept-ualization of the 'healthy' body involved drawing on social, cultural and moral spheres of knowledge as part of making sense of perceived corporeal realities. However, children's conceptualizations of health and bodily practices were shaped only in part by their parents and family context. Children also drew on their own social worlds and experiences which were partially hidden from adults and constructed by children themselves. For example, it was regularly claimed by both adults and children that outward appearances of physical healthiness could belie inner states of unhealthiness, but children emphasized different physical markers. Similarly, a major theme of the adult interviews was that physically healthy bodies could be achieved either despite a lack of attention or through a narcissistic *over*-attention, both of which were open to social or moral criticism. (Backett, 1992a). Such self-conscious awareness of body maintenance was less evident in the children's accounts.

For both adults and children, however, conceptualizations of the healthy body were complexly interwoven with its location in wider socio-cultural contexts. Interestingly, however, this was best illus-trated by respondents' difficulties in empirically accessing healthiness, healthy people or healthy bodies. Both adults and children could point out health-promoting ideals or practices, or features of healthy bodies in the abstract. However, on the basis of daily personal ex-perience and observation, they were much better able to identify what they considered to be 'unhealthy' behaviours, people or bodies, rather than those which were 'healthy'. Adults described individuals they knew who were overweight, ate the wrong foods, drank and smoked to excess, worked too hard, were stressed and who were inactive physically or socially. Similarly, children talked about unhealthy peers who were fat, physically lazy or unfit, and ate too many sweets or had rotten teeth.

By contrast, it appeared to be much harder to feel confident in identifying '*healthy*' people; and knowing whether or not people whom they knew personally *were* actually carrying out behaviours which might impact positively on their physical health, was even more mysterious and uncertain. As several respondents pointed out, there were healthy people and people who led healthy lives and took good care of their bodies, but the two were not necessarily the same. Both adults and children said that it was hard *really* to know what other people might be doing which was good for health. Some children in particular said that they could not tell if, for example, others in their class were healthy or not because they did not see what they were eating all the time at home or what they did out of school. A common response from the children was: 'I haven't been to their house, so I don't know.'

However, even if respondents *did* have direct access to more extensive knowledge about others' bodies or body maintenance, as is the case with family members, conceptualizations of healthiness or healthy bodies were again filtered through a cultural and moral lens. For example, one area in which children found it very hard to talk about unhealthy behaviours or physical signs was when they were asked to talk about anything their *parents* did or ate that was unhealthy. Several children reacted by saying 'we're all the same' or 'we don't do anything unhealthy'. One child said that his mother just would not ever give him anything unhealthy to eat. However, almost all of the children who had a parent who smoked did not divulge this to the interviewer and, although mention of parents' being on diets was made by a few children, overall, they did not comment on parents' fatness or laziness (which they did readily with peers!).

There are several possible understandings of these blinkers to or lack of disclosure about parental behaviours relevant to health. They could indicate that, literally, the closer to home one got, the more difficult it became to see or acknowledge unhealthy behaviours or bodies and the stronger the social and moral pressures were experienced. They might also indicate that children in fact had different markers of unhealthiness, for example, rotten teeth, physical laziness and fatness were prominent in their accounts of peers; and these might also be assessed differently when observing adults. Also, however, they might reflect the child's partial knowledge of adults' physical health and the lack of visibility of the full range of their parents' behaviours to them. For example, one girl said she was *sure* her mother ate sweets and chocolates later in the evening when she could not see this; and one boy's speculation on his parents' possible unhealthy behaviours set him wondering, 'Maybe there's something they do when I'm asleep in bed.'

It seems, therefore, that when children conceptualized health and the healthy body, they attempted to draw on similar socio-cultural and moral frames of reference to those of the adult respondents. However, because they had only partial access to adult knowledge and experience, and also drew upon their own social worlds, their assessments and priorities revealed some differences from those of their parents.

The Healthy Body is an Active Body

The most dominant and recurrent theme in these middle-class parents' and children's conceptualizations of the healthy body was its equation with activity. For these families, the healthy body was the active body. This provides an extension to earlier work on lay concepts of health as the ability to function in the world (Herzlich and Pierret, 1986). From these accounts in middle-class families, the active body was not only essential for everyday social functioning, but it was also seen as both instrumental to and symbolic of effective and successful social functioning. The active body was imbued with social capital.

Conversely, inactivity, or the inactive body, was seldom celebrated and, for example, it was only a small minority of adults or children who said that sleep was one of the ingredients of good health. Those who did so often felt the need to justify their position. For instance, R20(F) was apologetically assertive about her belief that retiring to bed was *her* way of coping with bodily sickness or discomfort. Also, R9(M)'s need to rest and sleep a lot, particularly at weekends, was presented as a sort of necessary indulgence in order to cope with a demanding job.

Many adults' descriptions of their busy working lives illustrated how they felt that it was almost impossible to find an adequate place in their lives for the resting, sleeping or inactive body. Furthermore, when adults were asked to reflect on days when they felt unhealthy, the theme of the lethargic, sluggish or inactive body predominated. Respondents spoke of not being able to be bothered to do anything or of giving in to laziness. As R10(F) explained:

> The fitter days, em, I'm full of energy (KM: Yes) and I can sort of take anything on and make decisions, and on other days I can't think straight.

For the majority of the women in the sample, such days often occurred prior to their menstrual period and many gave vivid accounts of PMS and how it affected themselves and their family lives. As R9(F) explained:

> There are days when I feel a bit heavy and a bit can't be-botherish, and then other days when I have the energy to do a million things. There are days before my period in particular (KM: Oh, really) when I am sort of on a short fuse and also feeling a bit yuck, but then, that passes and I feel fine again.

The theme of the active body also dominated parents' accounts of their children's health and everyday lives. It was the rare respondent who felt that his/her child was inactive either physically or socially. Descriptions were given of a wide-range of organized activities and club membership in which their children participated and this was paralleled by an outlining of complex parental arrangements to transport or accompany children to these events. This could be so time-consuming for parents that it dominated their own free time.

Respondents also portrayed a 'healthy family' as, ideally, involving its members being active together. However, conceptualizations of differences between bodies were put forward to explain why this was difficult to achieve in practice. For example, it was evident that even if adults took some exercise it was often impossible to include children in it. One keen footballer recounted, for instance, the fact that as his daughter became older it became inappropriate to take her along each Saturday because of having to supervise her near to the men's changing rooms. Equally, constructions of the consequences of physical ageing meant that parents stopped aspiring to the *same* activities as their children. It was expected that, as adults, they became spectators or coaches or organizers or pleasure players rather than active regular participants in previously enjoyed sports. It was the *unusual* family who could sustain in practice the construction of being a physically active *group*. Even the two generalized claims initially made by some of the families that 'we go for walks at the weekend' or 'we all go swimming regularly' were shown to be contradicted by the subsequent fieldwork accounts over time or when one weekend was examined in great detail.

The high value accorded by parents to the active body was also very much reflected in the children's interviews. Although one aim of these interviews had been to access views about activity and health in its broadest sense, the children talked overwhelmingly about forms of exercising the body as being healthy things to do. For example, in their drawings, general types of physical exercise were depicted by 50 out of the 52 children. When this was explored by the researcher, the main reasons given for these being healthy were related to exercising bits of the body, 'making you fit and strong', or being 'good' for muscles.

Similarly, when assessing photographs of children doing a wide range of things such as sleeping, riding a bike, playing a computer, or hugging a puppy, the majority of children continued to define 'healthy things to do' in terms of exercising parts of the body. At times this conceptualization was clearly hard to sustain as, for instance, when the occasional child explained that computer games involved exercising the fingers or that watching television exercised the eyes! Although some of the younger children reacted to the photographs of more sedentary pursuits in terms of what they personally liked or enjoyed, any interpretation of 'healthiness' as involving simply pleasure or feeling good was seldom expressed in the responses of the majority of the sample. Thus, many of the older children actually interpreted some of the photographs depicting less active bodies at play or rest as *'just* playing' and, therefore, as not healthy. Mental activity or creativity were also infrequently cited as 'healthy things to do' and photographs showing such pursuits were often deemed 'not healthy' *because* they were physically inactive.

In other parts of the interview children also made reference to their active social lives and it was evident that, overall, this sample of children were activity conscious and activity approving. However, the process of accommodating inactive bodies into a conceptualization of health as entailing active bodies, physically and socially, appeared to be as problematical for the children as it was for their parents and some contradictions began to emerge from their more grounded accounts of their usual/most recent out of school activities. Here, choice and enjoyment of sedentary activities was shown by almost all children as they claimed to watch television daily or often after school and on weekend mornings. In fact, the majority of children all cited an indoor, sedentary activity (TV, computers, reading, games and drawing) as their first response when describing their most recent after school activity.

Similarly, the children's interviews gave little indication of regular shared physical activity with one or both parents. Moreover, children's perceptions of healthy activity as including, for example, running about and lots of movement, perhaps meant that several of them in their interviews saw *parents'* activities such as golf, curling or bowls as 'not exercise' and, therefore, as not worthy of mention since, in the child's terms, they had little relationship to health or body maintenance.

Disruptive Bodies

An extension of the concept that healthy bodies are active bodies was the great emphasis laid by respondents on not allowing the body's sickness or malfunctioning to disrupt everyday social functioning. A marker of healthiness, particularly for the male, was that he seldom or never took time off work; and many respondents even emphasized this by detailing *actual* numbers of days off during the past few years. Women also claimed that they kept going during sickness; few described being able to take some bed rest if they were working mainly in the domestic base; and those who were in paid employment said they tried even harder not to go off sick in case they had to take any time off work to care for sick children. In this respect, children's sick bodies were seen to take precedence over social obligations in less questioned or more legitimate ways than were those of adults. The self-conscious resistance of symptoms of physical sickness, so that it did not disrupt social activity or obligations or impede these for any length of time, was well described by R8(F). She spoke of a recent cold, which had stopped her from sleeping well for a couple of nights, and explained:

> I felt really jaded so when they went to school that day I thought, oh, J [husband] was away on a course and I decided to go back to bed till 11 o'clock and I slept, and I got up. But I only did

that because there was no one around and I wasn't, you know, there was nothing to do and nothing to hurry for at the end of the day.

Age was another dimension of difference within families with regard to responses to the sick body. As has been discussed earlier, children's illness was described as requiring a greater and more speedy attention than that of adults. Similarly, although this did vary between families in the sample, children were, by and large, more likely than adults to be allowed time off from social obligations, such as school. In addition to previously mentioned difficulties in accurately deciphering children's symptoms, the illness trajectory was itself viewed as potentially more risky and unpredictable. In this respect, parents described how they took no chances with children's illnesses and the children themselves described the processes of taking their sickness symptoms to, primarily, their mothers and of being encouraged to stay in bed, at least for a while. Even these decisions about care of children's sick bodies were, however, also made by locating them in the context of the wider family circumstances and social obligations.

This relegation of the sick body to a minor and transient concern which did not reflect overall healthiness was again reflected in the strong ideology of keeping going and giving social obligations a supremacy over symptoms. Being healthy meant claiming to ignore potentially disruptive sick bodies. The empirical proof of all this could have been that not one interview was ever cancelled owing to illness. The researcher also at that stage unwittingly colluded in this by conducting interviews whilst suffering from a bad chest infection which resulted in paroxysms of coughing during a few interviews.

Here again, however, this social construction of healthiness was found to be contradicted by empirical accounts of the lived body. Interestingly, respondents' accounts during the fieldwork revealed quite clearly that illness resulting in time off work or stopping everyday functioning was a regular occurrence in most of these families. Several of the men did, in fact, report time off work for illness during the study but still claimed that this was highly unusual for them.

In their interviews, the children scarcely mentioned illness when considering health. Neither did illness enter into their assessments of friends' or peers' healthiness. For the children it appeared to be unimportant when considering their own health; and even when invited to talk about what happened when they were ill, those who had illnesses such as asthma, eczema or epilepsy made little reference to them. Perhaps R17(M) was right, when he commented about his daughters:

> The business of living is too important for them. They want to be at their games or whatever. So it's a sore ear when it is *really* a sore ear.

CONTESTED AREAS

The uncertainties surrounding the construction of the healthy body and the differences within family groups, all contributed to many contradictions between and within parent and child accounts, and with the lived daily experience of the body. Many contested areas between parents and children in health and bodily maintenance were reported. The child's agency often shone through the parents' accounts, albeit experienced and described as challenges to adult authority. It was also clear that, even in this context of parental management and surveillance of their physical health, children sought to carve out areas of corporeal independence, whether through active effort or passive resistance. Children's practical accomplishments of health and body management were expressed by them in a less abstract and more concrete way in terms of likes and dislikes, constraints and opportunities, and very immediate situations and decisions to be interpreted and managed.

Two main contested areas were regularly described by both parents and children. These were imposed physical activity, and food and eating behaviour. Here parents explained these contested areas in terms of children exercising willpower or acquiring tastes about what went into their bodies or how they chose to use them. Children expressed their resistance in their interviews in terms of stating their likes and dislikes and by describing experiences of challenging or subverting parental authority.

Physical Activity

Many parents described how their children resisted walking either for pleasure or as a means of transport if the parental car was available. R5(M), for example, felt that his children needed positive encouragement in this respect and was also critical of his wife's regular car use for short journeys. He said:

> Em as far as the kids are concerned, as long as they're getting outside and getting fresh air, and I certainly encourage them, even if it means taking them for walks and that kind of thing to, to get them out, if they're not all that keen and generally try and ensure that their growing up is not em, impaired by a lack of anything in particular, such as exercise or basic good quality foods, despite the fact that they might eat a lot of rubbish as well.

However, several women explained that one or both of their children much preferred travelling by car and that it was consequently very difficult to make everyone walk. R15(F)'s account was typical, she said:

> I have to take the car simply because of the time factor, and I feel it's made S lazy because he's the one that gets dumped in the car whereas R walked more when he was younger. S's very lazy, he doesn't like walking and I think that's why.

Clearly, however, walking or taking certain kinds of exercise as opposed to others were construed and evaluated differently by many of the children. For them, exercise had strong immediate purposes of social inclusion, pleasure, personal credibility and peer acceptance, and these were not relevant either to the more self conscious exercising of the body by their parents or the use of the body as a more time-consuming mode of transport. When asked what would happen if you did not take lots of exercise, one boy said:

> You'd get laughed at. You wouldn't be fit, you couldn't run, chase someone who took something off you and get it back.

A girl explained:

> When you're not that healthy you don't run as fast or they'd say, 'No you can't play because you would just get us all caught.'

Food and Eating

In these families a considerable amount of catering for individual food tastes took place, and children also exercised considerable volition over a particularly visible arena of food choice, their packed lunch boxes (Milburn, 1995). Parents, however, had an ambivalent attitude towards the food choices they were in a position to offer to their children, since making choices also involves making rejections. Consequently, the child's exercising agency over the food s/he chose to put into his/her body was often portrayed as a contested area, especially when the child chose foods which were defined by parents as potentially harmful to the body. Sections of the interviews were dominated by parents' accounts of their tactics to encourage children to eat certain foods; and this area was often contested between the parents themselves. For example, R5(M) said to his wife about their son:

> You don't do enough to make him any better. I mean he is still, he gets away with dictating what he is going to eat and I think he's getting old enough for us to be telling him.

There were various ways in which parents accounted for their child's exercise of agency over foods which s/he chose to eat. First, parents conceptualized such contested choices as children 'developing their own tastes'. In this respect, it seemed that physical desire for certain 'tastes' was at best avoided or at worst to be regulated. Sweets were the most frequent example. R2(F)'s views were typical, she felt that:

> I don't think it's valid to sort of deprive children completely. I know people who have done this and it usually backfires the first time a child gets a taste of sugar and gets sort of hooked on it.

Second, external influences, particularly when a parent was not present and the child, therefore, had greater agency over his/her body, were seen as affecting choice. Here the child's tastes were seen as affected particularly by peers, choices at school lunches, and grandparents. Third, children's competence to make so-called healthy choices in foods was challenged by parents' conceptualization of their not having an active or pressing concern for health or their bodies. Because children took their bodies for granted, this concern for health was perceived as something which children had to learn, but which they were also seen regularly to ignore or to challenge. For instance, R25(F) explained that her elder son knew that sweets were bad for them but still had them, 'but he thinks about it before he takes it', whereas her younger son 'eats as many sweets as anyone – anything he can get his hands on'.

Thus, parents' accounts showed many contested areas of body management with regard to children. In turn, the children made their own decisions about body management partly through negotiations with parents and significant others, but partly also on the basis of their own conceptualizations of health and their lived experience of their own social worlds. Like adults, many of their decisions about body management were also made pragmatically and for non-health-related reasons. Thus, for example, almost all identified fruit and vegetables as good for health and the body, but only a few claimed either to like vegetables or to eat them regularly. Similarly, as has been described, exercise of the body was seen to have as much of a social as a health payoff, and decisions about eating the contents of a school packed lunch were affected by time availability, the lure of playtime and the approval of certain foods by friends.

CONCLUSION

This chapter has shown how, for these middle-class parents and children, the lived experience of the body, corporeal and social, often sat uneasily alongside currently approved tents of healthy lifestyles and body maintenance. Thus, the study revealed many tensions and contradictions between respondents' expressed ideals of health and body maintenance and their practical accomplishment. In this respect children's accounts reflected those of the adult world where knowing and doing were often unrelated. This was clearly shown, for example, in difficulties in sustaining in practice the image of the healthy body as the active body, and the associated problematic of legitimating and accommodating the inactive, resting or sick body.

However, the study also revealed many differences between parents and children in their lived experiences of the body (see also Christensen, this volume). Such findings underline the importance of questioning the assumption of similarities of health relevant beliefs and behaviours and body maintenance within family groups. Given

6 'To Become Dizzy in Our Turning': Girls, Body-Maps and Gender as Childhood Ends

Shirley Prendergast

The world about me presents me with an invitation – I respond. That invitation itself is only explicable in the light of the original question my body has put to the world. We may turn back and forth and become dizzy in our turning, but we will not discover an absolute priority in either body or world. I am free to act in the face of my world: my freedom is in its turn shaped by that world. There is neither absolute freedom nor an absolute and passive determinism. There is only the reality and life of a 'situated freedom'. (Merleau-Ponty, 1962: 102)

INTRODUCTION

In Toni Morrison's novel *The Bluest Eye* (1990) the nine-year-old Peccola, uninformed and unprepared, starts to bleed with her first period as she plays with her friends on the front porch. Finding them attempting to deal with this frightening predicament, Peccola's mother is at first angry and then, strangely, inexplicably, her manner softens, becomes tinged with a knowing sympathy and curious regret. In like fashion Janet Frame (1984) describes in her autobiography running to her mother in terror of bleeding to death. Her mother, hugging her, strings a cumbersome and scratchy wash towel between her legs with a mumbled warning that now she is grown up, 'she must be careful'. For Peccola and Janet the onset of menstruation was etched on their imaginations, in all its vividness and detail as the day that something significant changed. However, marked by a powerful and novel response from adults, what *exactly* had changed, and why, was unclear, implied in looks and tone of voice, guarded warnings, hinted at in overheard conversations. Now, they seemed to say, life will never be quite the same again. These aspects of what Bourdieu (1976) has called 'embodied memory' are very powerful. Looking at old primary school photographs brings back similar half-understood premonitions about my embodied self before puberty. As with other girls my hair is plaited, painfully scraped and clipped back 'off my face' in the way that my mother thought proper at the time. There are the sexless, skinny, active bodies of children born during the war. Our playground was also the village cricket field where, directed by our head teacher, we often played cricket in games lessons. He made no concessions to size or age: we used the same wicket and the same hard, red leather ball with stitched seams used at proper matches. I was good at batting and I loved catching the ball when it was thrown high or hard. On the other hand, I was absolutely hopeless at throwing: I just couldn't flick the ball with my wrist; I was awkward, ungainly; my arm almost jumped out of its socket; I threw myself with the ball and it went wildly in unexpected directions. Exasperated, he would say: 'Shirley: you throw like a girl!'

Once I reached my teens I began to hate cricket and most sport. It brought back (and still does) a volatile mixture of feelings: an overwhelming sense of boredom and inevitable failure: a shameful sense that my body was in some way wrong, 'disloyal' to be skilled in one respect and so incompetent in another; a disbelief that only boys were good at sport; a stubborn determination and pride in proving adults wrong; resentment that the road to the teacher's regard was to overcome the things that 'naturally' belonged to me as a girl. Perhaps above all, a sense of injustice: was it fair that this regard was denied me because the bodies of girls were, in some utterly incomprehensible way, different from the bodies of boys?

Of course, these three accounts of childhood embodiment range across place and culture: Peccola a poor black child of the American South, Janet a poor white child from New Zealand, myself a white child from middle-class England. Moreover, all three describe children many years ago. What possible relevance could they have for today? And yet we find numerous echoes of Peccola's and Janet's experiences of early adolescence not just in the literature more widely but also in younger women's memories and stories, and most particularly in my study of English schoolgirls, completed in 1992. As we talked, and as I listened to the girls in the study talking with each other, there was a powerful sense of fragmented, unacknowledged embodied experience being spoken. As events, feelings, memories were described, named, compared, fitted together, a map of a hitherto secret knowledge came into being. I often experience this again when I speak about my research to adult women, a tangible sense of shock, a pained recognition of the unspeakable: 'This happened to me ... I felt so ashamed ... I never talked to anyone ... I'd forgotten until now ... surely it's not still the same ...'

As Turner (1992), Keat (1986), Freund (1988; 1990) and others suggest, these powerful feelings, memories and perceptions about the habitual actions of embodied existence, and how they come about, touch on some of the most interesting and complex issues in philosophy and the social sciences: are they learned or natural? What, if any, is our conscious understanding of them and how do they come about? When and why do they change? What is the significance of collective interpretations of embodiment within social contexts of power and value? To what degree do we have individual agency within these frameworks? Above all, how do we come to carry at one and the same time the characteristics of our culture (the Gallic shrug, an English reserve) those of gender (throwing like a girl, acting like a man) and our age and class (a bent old lady, a stiff upper lip) and yet remain identifiably, uniquely embodied as ourselves? These are fascinating and complex questions. They are also questions that, despite a burgeoning literature, remain persistently abstract: one either does empirical research on the body *or* discusses theory. In this chapter, difficult though the process may be, I hope to bring the empirical and the theoretical a little closer together. I argue that menarche carries weighty presentiments for girls, marking an abrupt ending of childhood characterized by and necessitating radical new mappings and remappings of bodily experience, meaning and value. These herald a more intense phase in the taking on of gender, an embodied transition, a new being-in-the-world dominated by the need for excessive 'mindfulness' and 'closure' in comparison both with girls own earlier childhood experiences and with those of boys in their peer group. This is magnified by the fact that such mappings are often done by each girl on her own, in isolation from both her peers and from adult women.

It is proposed that mindfulness and closure are not natural corollaries of girls' bodily changes, but are wrought within and by the embodied practices and material realities of social contexts, particularly school, which shape lived experience and give it value.

In particular these are about the ways in which gender is collectively, *socially* held, carried and mediated in the everyday, such that each *individual* comes to embody gender, to act, feel and be authentically gendered in their own lives.

LEARNING EMBODIED/GENDERED RULES

Using the example of early menstrual experience and describing events and memories from the middle years of childhood, this chapter explores some issues concerning girls' bodies at a critical time of transition into adolescence. This is not to privilege the body or processes of embodiment in terms of a biological reductionism, rather, by seeing the body 'as the very fabric of self', as Diprose (1994: 108) puts it, to expand our understanding of how social interpretations, material practices and bodily experience are essentially intertwined. Its project is to use a phenomenological perspective, as described for example by Olesen (1992), Freund (1988; 1990) and Buytendjik (1974) to think about the ways in which gendered identities are shaped at this time. Such an approach moves beyond the usual call for the reconnecting of body with mind, towards some synthesis of being embodied as human in a social and material context, in a place, in a world which is itself the product of our labour: of what has been described as our 'being-in-the-world' (Moss, 1989; Csordas, 1994).

Csordas, in speaking of the body as 'the primordial ground of culture', emphasizes the primacy of embodiment as that which we all know, we all share. Being-in-the-world constantly involves mediations between material, biological, symbolic, individual and social processes, between body, mind and context (see also Prout, this volume). It is only through collective, shared experience of these mediations that we can know the world. Further, it can be argued that these held-in-common experiences and transformations are an integral and essential aspect of what it means to be human: cultural bodies transform the world but are also, in the process, themselves culturally made and transformed. In the language of embodiment, in forms of embodied experience and value then we might expect to find the variety, complexity, processes of metaphor, paradox and symbolism that are the very stuff of cultural meaning.

For example, the lived experience of the body, the ways in which we express and give value to it, and informal and institutional frameworks of rules that determine how these can be privately and publicly demonstrated, are little discussed within our own culture. At the same time, the issue of embodiment as a cultural process surfaces most poignantly at key points in the life course. Hockey and James (1993) have pointed out how, in Western systems of thought, metaphors of growth and value are closely allied: most valued is that period of adult maturity, to which childhood and youth aspires to *grow up* towards. Perhaps least valued is the so called *decline* of age, when the cycle loops back and an old person progressively enters a 'second childhood'. This time we are not being brought up towards adulthood, but diminishing, downwards in the 'wrong' direction. The trajectory of the body through time carries symbolic and moral value: bodily forms are paradigmatic of social transition: birth, hope; reproduction, maturity; age, decay. Each requires that we adjust to and attend to our body, or that of others in an appropriate and special way, as carers or as cared for, as male or female or as independent or dependent beings. These configurations of size, maturity, dependency, power and value may take very different forms in relation to gender and age (Prendergast and Forrest, 1997a) and other cultural contexts (La Fontaine, 1985).

Clearly we might identify a number of positionings, periods and moments when embodied processes are critical to social interpretation and regulation of transition within the Western life course. For example, the early years are driven by the operationalizing of (somewhat arbitrary) embodied distinctions between and transformations of, newborn to infant to toddler to child regulated by a conceptual framework of developmental 'stages' (Burman, 1994; Morss, 1996). Puberty signals the socially embodied shift from childhood to adolescence (even though, in reality, some aspects of physical puberty may be as early as 9 or as late as 19 years of age) and another comes, as Diprose (1994) notes, when a woman's body is irrevocably physically, emotionally and socially changed by pregnancy and birth.

From the moment it is born the child is embodied both as small in relation to adults and as a sexed and gendered being. The child body as smaller than, as a body becoming adult, poses particular and interesting questions regarding the nature of adult/child relations. Within the structures of dependency inherent in such relations in Western society to be a 'child' to be 'childish' or 'childlike' always therefore implies actual or metaphoric powerlessness. At the same time we are not brought up to be a *child* (because it is part of the social definition of childhood to be 'brought up', which children themselves may well resist) but as a *girl-child* or a *boy-child*. This combination of size in relation to and gender (what Bob Connell, 1987, has famously called the 'discourse of the pinks and blues') carries and shapes the whole process of socialization. We can see this if we look at how being embodied as 'small' has different gendered significance even in childhood. For a girl to be small and thin connotates fragility, gracefulness, an image of femininity we find everywhere reflected in the birdlike, anorexic teenage supermodels in fashion magazines. Revealingly, we often call girls who take other embodied routes, who perhaps might be said to 'act large', tomboys. For boys, dominant images are of toughness and strength drawn from heroes on the football field, in which to be tall and big is to hold your own in a company of peers, and where to be small is a powerful risk factor. This is borne out by psychological findings from the USA, which (crudely) conclude that in general the timing of embodied transition into adolescence that is *best for boys* – to be taller, bigger, earlier maturing than ones peers – is the *worst outcome for girls* (Simmons and Blythe, 1988). It seems that we cannot address embodiment unless we also address gender: the study of childhood requires that we look at both together.

THE MENSTRUAL BODY

Certainly it is my experience (Prendergast, 1994; 1995) that for all our theorizing about the body and sexuality, menstruation is still something that it is not quite right to talk about. As Emily Martin (1989) has written, how strange that a key and continuing event in most women's lives, the onset of menarche and the experience of menstruation, which can have huge implications for women's general health and well-being throughout the life course, has been so generally ignored in research. One might imagine that the onset of menarche for girls marks a key moment in embodied transition from the world of childhood into that of adulthood. More so perhaps in that it does not happen gradually, creeping up and passing unawares: as Peccola and Janet and the girls in my study themselves say, suddenly, one day, something is very, very different. There is little sense of celebration, of peer, public or even family recognition of this shift but as something within the confines of the most private, personal, individual realm of being, possibly shared with a best friend or your mother. At this time girls frequently describe feeling lonely, talk as much or more about loss and ambiguity as about pleasure at a new status.

The following section draws on young women's accounts drawn from a major study[1] of girls and menstruation in English secondary schools as they observe, experience and recall this time in their lives. It describes information from observation, interviews and questionnaires with a large sample of girls between the ages of 13 and 14 years (in the third year of secondary school) and 15 and 16 years (in the fifth year). It starts by looking at girls' earliest intimations of knowledge and the significance of when and how they were informed about menstruation by parents and in school, and follows through the realities of menstrual experience as it is lived out in the context of primary and secondary school. The chapter concludes by exploring the implications, consequences and effects of these processes for girls' sense of being-in-the-world as they look backwards to childhood, forwards to 'growing up' and sideways to the behaviours and experiences of the boys in their peer group.

SOMETHING HAPPENS TO GIRLS . . .

It was my best friend in primary school. She sort of came in one day and she was totally different, a different person. She didn't want to play or run around the playground, she just wanted to sit down. She told me what had happened, and I thought, God, you know, if that happens to me I don't want to start. (Sally, aged 15)

We were nine, on the school holiday, and she woke everybody in the middle of the night, and said, like, 'I'm bleeding, it's happened' . . . and my friend said that she would go and get a plaster, but the girl knew . . . And sort of bleeding from *there*, we had never heard of it. (Jen, aged 16)

While it is difficult enough for many adult women to discuss menstruation openly, I discovered that for young women the difficulties could be multiplied a hundred times. Even now, in the late twentieth century, more than one in ten girls in the study still had not known about menstruation in advance of it happening, and many could not and did not talk about it to their mothers. Although about 10 per cent of girls started their periods in primary school, some

as young as nine years of age, the majority had little or no adequate information about them from that source.

A powerful theme in girls' narratives about the time before
menarche could be summed up as 'knowing that *something* (strange
and rather frightening) happens to girls that does not happen to
boys'. Clearly there are different kinds and degrees of knowing about
bodily events. Girls recalled how there was some indeterminate time
when they knew 'something', and gradually, spread over some years,
they were given formal information, including perhaps the biological facts of the menstrual cycle. Usually after this, but sometimes
before, a girl 'knows' in a different way because she experiences
irrefutable changes to her body. Because the cycle is often erratic
and irregular in the early years it may be very much later on that
she assimilates yet another kind of knowing, the rhythms and vari-
ations, the realization and consequences of her personal version of
what it means to have a period. Interwoven through all of this,
girls also acquire informal social knowledge about menstruation:
how it is viewed and dealt with in the world, to whom and how she
might speak about it, and the practical arrangements that must be
made so that rules and etiquette as to its visibility and management are not contravened (Laws, 1991).

While many girls could remember and discuss how they had been
formally told about menstruation, at home or at school, they also
began to recall other kinds of knowing, knowing 'something' which
didn't count as proper knowledge, at a much earlier age. For many
girls this half-knowing had been in place by the time they were six
or seven years old, and had come about as a result of seeing, over-
hearing or being told odd and inexplicable things: about 'blood';
about what girls could or could not do when they were bigger;
about being careful; about secrets that they should not tell. In her
interview, one girl suddenly recalled being told that sanitary towels
were 'linings for slippers that only ladies wore'. The embarrassed
amazement of her mother and the shop assistant when she asked
her mother to buy her some had been deeply perplexing. Many
girls remembered hazy events in primary school, where girls had
cried and had been hustled away by teachers, or their confusion
when a friend wanted to sit quietly in the classroom, a changed
being, who would no longer join in their games.

Such incidents set an emotional tone which framed expectations
of later experience; not understood at the time they nevertheless
made a vivid impression and were stored for future interpretation.

The effects of these incidents were not easily redressed by the later giving out of correct factual information, even if it were forthcoming in the primary school context. Not only did they pre-date and influence later formal teaching, but they continued to colour responses and feelings for some of the oldest girls in the study. Indeed in many instances these early observations and experiences remained intact, alongside and untouched by more formal learning, frozen as worst-case examples, continuing to convey messages of collective and individual embarrassment and shame for many years to come.

IF I'M LUCKY IT WON'T HAPPEN TO ME . . . FIRST HEARING ABOUT MENSTRUATION

> When I first found out I thought that I was one of the lucky ones who wouldn't have it. I thought that you didn't need to have it. (Birgit, aged 13)

> I kept saying to myself I hope that I start at 17 or 18. I don't want to wear sanitary towels, I hope that I start as late as possible. (Cathy, aged 15)

> Like this girl in primary school, she said her sister had started and that there was blood everywhere, and all the boys were taking the mick. And we used to dread it. I thought that it would be permanent and that you bled all the time. (Prettie, aged 14)

In contrast to early informal knowing, the sequence and timing of formally given information, from home or from school, was characterized as late in three significant respects. First, formal information from primary school about menarche and menstruation was given later than information about sexual development, if it was given at all. This is similar to findings by Thornburg (1981) and Goldman and Goldman (1982). Farrell (1978) also describes a similar sequencing of information giving between mothers and daughters ('where babies come from', 'menstruation' and finally 'sexuality'). Second, formal giving of information from adults was also late compared to the informal and accidental ways of knowing described above. Third, formal information was also given chronologically late in that some girls were very close to the event, or had actually started their periods before being formally told, particularly if onset was early.

Perhaps it is not surprising that by the time girls were formally told about menstruation, their reactions were often rather negative. Many described feelings of disbelief, followed by a variety of distancing and qualifying thoughts that pushed the whole event as far away as possible from their own experience. For example, girls reported thinking that the information they were given might be wrong, that such things didn't happen to most girls. Even if the information was correct, they personally might be able to escape the experience, to stop periods happening, or that they personally would be 'lucky' and start very late. These distancing measures were even more creative when girls tried to make sense of information gained as a result of accidentally acquired knowledge. One girl described how a primary school friend had unexpectedly started her period and been discovered crying, locked in the school toilet. The teacher explained that it was just a normal process, she was only 'growing into a big girl'. Discussing this, the other girls had thought they might avoid the same fate if they ate less at school dinners. Another thought that you might be able to avoid periods altogether because she had heard that you could wear tampons in the swimming pool 'to stop the bleeding'.

We can see that these are not the bizarre, irrational beliefs so targeted for eradication by health education experts keen to set children right about the facts. Such responses are shaped by children struggling to make intelligible the very processes that deny them knowledge in the first place. Common interpretations included misunderstandings about the timing, duration and amount of bleeding, the cause of bleeding and menstrual pain, ideas about menstruation and sexual intercourse and pregnancy, not knowing that periods were related to being fertile and assumptions that boys had periods too. In some cases these ideas had persisted for many years before becoming clarified by discussion, teaching or actual experience.

PRIMARY SCHOOL LESSONS

We had a lesson, but not about periods. Just about how the body works generally, the circulation. They did one on frogs and rabbits, and we saw a baby rabbit born. (Jacqui, aged 14)

They told us about sexual education first with the boys, but then the girls were taken into the video room on their own. It was good they told us a lot of things, I don't know what the boys knew. (Natalie, aged 15)

Formal sex education about menstruation in primary school, as it was recalled by the young women in the study, was mostly conspicuous by its absence. Over half of the sample said that they had nothing in primary school on this topic. Even so this is a better state of affairs than the situation reported by Allen in 1987, where just over one third of girls reported having some teaching on 'changes in a girl's body' in primary school. Many remembered seeing a television programme about rabbits or frogs, and how babies are made, with perhaps some fragmented and often incomprehensible mention of what was to come. This reinforced the feeling described above, that something had been held back particularly, to be announced at a later date. This something which is revealed later is of course bleeding, which will happen only to girls.

Such teaching was often given just to girls, and might take place as an emergency session, for example just before a school visit or holiday, so they could be prepared. Boys appeared to know little and to have little interest in the topic. Knowledge and experience of menstruation were likely to be seen by younger girls as something intrinsically embarrassing and difficult, to be hidden *per se*, in contrast to the problems girls had later, maintaining secrecy against the more heightened sexual teasing of boys by the second year of secondary school. This reflects perhaps the 'developmental gap' between girls and boys, in which girls are approximately one to two years ahead of boys at puberty (Simmons and Blyth, 1987). Even where it takes place in primary school such teaching is often in stark opposition to the reality of the facilities available to such young girls. Although about one in ten girls actually begins to menstruate in primary school, as we shall see below, practical provision was often non-existent or such as to single out early starters and make them even more visible to their peers. The gap between teaching and provision, rhetoric and reality, prescription and practical possibility was a theme that also continued into girls' experiences in secondary school.

TALKING TO MY MUM

When I was in the first year of this school, suddenly this thing happened to me, and I thought that I had better tell my Mum, you know. I was embarrassed to ask her. I didn't tell her anything usually. Friends had told me it all, not her. (Emma, aged 13)

And I hid it from my Mum for three days I think, and I just couldn't bear it any more, so I ran downstairs and said, you know, 'I'm bleeding'. She sat me down and said, 'Calm down, remember all those things I told you'. And it was sort of like rushing through my mind, because you know its a big change. I wanted to know everything at once. But I wouldn't say that my Mum told me everything. She sort of explained what to do, what to use, but she never explained what a period was. I think that I learned that more from school and friends. (Nicky, aged 16)

I told my Mum about our lesson then I heard all about it, all my Aunts, and that they had heavy bleeding, my Mum and even my Gran. So she thought that I would have that too, and I did! (Jane, aged 15)

Mothers had been one source of early information about menstruation for the majority of the sample. However, about one girl in ten had not been told about menstruation by anybody in advance of it happening, and of those who had been told in advance, only three-fifths had been first told by their mother. Even the girls who had been told in advance by their mothers described how the information still came late, and about a quarter of girls found early discussion with their mothers embarrassing or unsatisfactory. For those girls who had positive experiences of it, mothers were an ideal sources. They were seen as good informants not because they had biological information, but because they could be understanding of, and sympathetic to, the implications of menstruation for girls' everyday lives. Practical advice and personal information about pain and discomfort was most valued, indeed some girls learned the menstrual history of not only their mothers, but of friends, aunts, sisters and even grandmothers in this fashion. Mothers could smooth the transition and mediate if and how male members of the family became aware of what had happened and how they responded. In addition, mothers could ensure that girls did not have to deal immediately with remembering dates and buying their own supplies unless they so wished.

The ways in which mothers came to give information to daughters was often complicated. While some mothers seemed to decide unilaterally that their daughter needed to be told about puberty, many waited until prompted to talk by external events. This could be at a relatively late age, and often close to the time at which girls might actually be starting their periods. Most prompts came when daughters began to physically mature or when they asked specific questions about accidental events, things that other girls said or lessons in school. Indeed school lessons were an important prompt and appeared to legitimize both asking questions on the part of the girl, and the giving of information on the part of the mother.

With the onset of menarche not only can girls receive strong messages about the need for hygiene and secrecy, but it also acts as a harbinger of what Thomson and Scott (1991) have called the 'protective discourse' that characterizes communication about sexual matters between mothers and daughters. Warnings about 'being careful' of boys were particularly mysterious and distressing. For many girls menstruation is not associated with positive feelings of growing up or of a positive developing sexuality, and tentative explorations of sexual feeling may also became tinged with a sense of shame.

LOOKING AHEAD: 'I THOUGHT, OH NO, IT'LL ALWAYS BE ON MY MIND NOW . . .'

Afterwards I didn't know how to do things, like I felt I didn't even know how to *sit* normally anymore. I thought, oh no it'll always be on my mind now, how on earth will I manage? (Siri, aged 15)

Clearly menarche poses some kind of Rubicon to be crossed. Although it demarcates for girls a physical end to childhood, what it heralds, what girls enter into, is not quite so clear-cut. This new place seemed not so much 'becoming a woman', as it is often euphemistically described, but more a lobby, a waiting place from which this more distant prospect is observed and judged. From the age of 10 or 11 girls talked of looking ahead, balancing possibilities: would it be late or early, what would it be like, would it change your life, would you manage, would you actually feel and be treated as more grown up? Three issues were key: first, the immediate intimate, personal effects of the menstrual cycle as they changed girls sense of themselves. Second, the use made of this new embodied status in peer group relations, particularly with boys. Third, the facilities and provisions made by school which enabled or disabled girls coping strategies. First, we can see girls looking ahead to the immediate, intimate, personal effects of the menstrual cycle as Amrit describes:

> It depends on what yours are like. If you are really ill then you are at a disadvantage, if not then, no . . . lots of girls do get pain though, and boys don't. If you are in a class and can't concentrate, and the boys are perfectly happy, not having to care about stomach aches and that, then you are disadvantaged because you are not learning so much. (Amrit, aged 13)

Girls of all ages discussed a wide range of physical and mental effects, often as frequent and as severe as those reported by adult women in other studies. While these are personal and private, the conditions and demands of school are such that private experiences often became public knowledge. While at primary school and in the first year of secondary school less mature and younger girls might hear about 'uncontrollable' bleeding and severe menstrual cramps, headaches, about feeling depressed, irritable and fed up, about missing school and feeling unwell in exams, or see girls crying or going to sleep in a lesson, staining their clothes, having accidents in mixed PE classes, missing games and being forced to take showers. Many of these things actually happened to a high proportion of the girls in the study. Moreover such events entered into school mythology as worst-case scenarios (as described for Mary below). Alongside such knowledge was a fatalistic sense that personally there was little that could be done to mitigate such effects. If you were lucky they wouldn't happen, if you were unlucky the only thing was to go to bed or 'take a tablet'. There was evidence of very widespread use of painkillers for period problems by girls in the study. It was even more disturbing that the majority of the painkillers they named were likely to be ineffective for the reasons for which they were taken.

At the same time girls also looked ahead to a new embodied status in peer group relations, particularly with the boys. While for some girls menarche was a prelude to closer emotional and physical relations with boys, for many, like Fiona, their newfound maturity was a nuisance and source of embarrassment in this respect:

> At my last school there was a girl, and the boys found things and tampax in her bag, and they were chucking it around the

classroom and kicking it down the corridor. And she was just crying, and really they didn't care, they don't really feel or anything. (Fiona, aged 13)

Girls' bodily status provided rich material in terms of conflicted gender relations, particularly during the second and third years (aged 12 to 14) when girls are becoming more physically mature. Boys usually acted in groups, with a strong element of bravado and daring, manifested in provocative behaviour that suggested collective breaking of taboos. Most commonly, boys would rifle through with girls' bags in an attempt to find their spare supplies of towels, tampons and other material necessities. Behaviour of this kind was exacerbated by a number of other factors. The lack of adequate facilities in school generally meant that girls had to bring and keep in their bags everything they needed for the day. Bags and coats had to taken everywhere, few schools provided lockers for this purpose. In addition, many girls had irregular periods and carried supplies all the time in order to be ready for any emergency. In every school girls spoke about boys raiding their school bags, publicly displaying their 'stuff' to the rest of the class, and throwing or kicking tampons around. Even if this had not happened personally, all girls knew of a recent incident in their school.

Boys would also keep a watchful eye on girls' behaviour. For example a girl suddenly leaving the classroom and taking her bag with her, being touchy about letting someone look in her bag for a pencil, having an argument, getting upset or angry, feeling unwell or having stomach ache, being concerned about clothes or missing games, had all been used by boys as evidence that a girl was menstruating! In addition boys had many imaginatively unpleasant words for menstrual events that graphically conjured up the physical nature of the experience. This is a shaming language because it both draws attention to a personal part of the body and visualizes it as dirty and polluting. Sometimes boys might pick upon a particular incident for such attention. For example, Mary, aged 15, described how she had been called Bloody Mary for almost two years after a humiliating incident when the teacher would not let her leave the classroom to go to the toilet, and she had stained with blood both her skirt and the chair she was sitting upon.

In this respect girls also looked ahead, not in the abstract, but in the social and material context of school, where they had to be, day by day, year by year, and over which they had little control.

The toilets in primary school, well there was *nothing at all* for girls like me. I had to be taken up to the teachers' (toilet) and have it unlocked each time Then in secondary school it was worse in a different way . . . they were locked in lessons and at break they were broken, flooded, no loo paper. We couldn't even wash our hands properly. (Donna, who had begun her periods in primary school, aged 13)

I came on suddenly and blood was running down my leg . . . there was nothing in the toilet and the secretaries' office was miles away. I tried to get a girl to tell my friend, but she didn't come. In the end I had to go myself and explain while everybody heard, and I got into trouble for being late back to lessons. (Seyla, aged 15)

It is not just a question of giving information, of changing knowledge and beliefs, attitudes and behaviours towards menstruation, as much of the literature would lead us to believe. As for Mary, and for Donna and Seyla, schools in the study generally failed to provide conditions where menstrual experience could be adequately let alone positively experienced. It is above all an embodied experience, shaped by and lived out in social contexts and processes, within frameworks of needs and expectations, requiring practical facilities and careful organization in order to manage it in a socially approved fashion – to render it invisible to the outside world.

TO BE CONSTANTLY MINDFUL

One of the most disturbing findings of the study was the very inadequate provision for girls in school toilets. For example, the majority of girls reported that there was no reliable provision of soap, hand drying or toilet paper. When toilet paper was available it was often ineffective, hard, shiny 'tracing paper'. Door, locks, toilet seats and mirrors were often broken and disposal bins inadequate or missing. Toilets were frequently dirty, blocked and flooded. If girls needed emergency supplies of towels or tampons they had to queue at the secretaries' office; none were provided in the toilets themselves. Toilets were mostly locked in lesson time, and pupils were not allowed to go to the toilet in lesson time without a note from the teacher. Finally, most of the schools in the study did not have a sickroom, and painkillers could not be taken without a doctor's note.

Girls tried many strategies to mitigate the effects of inadequate provision, for example by avoiding using school toilets, waiting until they could go home or to a local shopping centre or pub. Not only was this inconvenient but it caused physical discomfort and affected concentration in lessons. There were many other examples of strategic preparation in an attempt to overcome bad conditions. Girls might try to go to the toilet in pairs, so that one person could hold the door shut, they carried 'stuff' around with them in their bags most of the time so as to be prepared and they often used two towels at a time, or super-absorbent tampons which would last longer without changing. Not only do such conditions have immediate consequences for girl's everyday health and well-being, and possibly for their achievement in school, but overall they burden girls with a weighty legacy of 'mindfulness'. This becomes clear if we ask the question: What is it that the average girl must do in order to successfully negotiate a day in school when she has a period?

Most basically she must know in advance that her period is likely to start that day, and be prepared with appropriate supplies. She must learn how to keep these in a safe place so that they are both readily accessible but not likely to be found, deliberately or accidentally. After that she must judge the appropriate time to change in order that no accidents happen, timing this with lesson breaks, and finding a toilet that has the facilities that she needs. If a girl has any kind of negative effects from menstruation (which, as we have seen, they commonly do) she must assess how she is likely to feel and be appropriately prepared (for pain, for example) in order to stay alert and complete school tasks successfully. She must have considered the day's lessons, and brought a note if she wishes to be excused from any of them.

This list suggests that the circumstances of school were such that all girls in the study, to lesser or greater degree, *lived* menstrual experience as a constraining, secret and negative event, whatever their attitudes or approaches. Above all they must manage all of these things unobtrusively, without calling attention to themselves. Most ironically, then, girls' last task is to forget and make invisible everything they have done in order to accomplish this successfully. This I would argue is what it means to be constantly and completely mindful.

A MOMENT OF RESISTANCE AT THE EDGE OF
ADOLESCENCE

> That girls' knowledge – of the body, of relationships, and of the
> world and its values – and girls' irreverence provide the grounds
> for resistance has been known since the time of Lysistrata.
> (Gilligan, 1990: 504)

Carol Gilligan speaks of 'a moment of resistance which occurs in
girls' lives at the edge of adolescence', a moment when they seem
to speak the truth about the world that they see. Later on, as they
enter it, they lose this ability. 'Why is it that girls who seem more
intelligent and livelier than boys at the same age; [who] go out
more to meet the external world and at the same time form stronger
connections with people seem to become less intelligent and lively
when they reach adolescence?' (1990: 530). Her answer is another
dilemma. At first, Gilligan says, on the threshold of adolescence
girls see and are angry that they must 'both enter and stay outside
of, be educated in and then change, what has been for centuries a
man's world'. Later, after adolescence, they silence this knowledge
and 'forget what they know'.

Gilligan addresses a key moment in a new taking-on of gender
from a predominantly psychoanalytical perspective. Although she
repeatedly mentions 'the body' and her text is full of quotes with
metaphoric implications of embodied change (at 11 years 'Tessie's
free-flowing world has suddenly stopped', 'she must be more careful
about her body, more attentive to the warning signals and the flags
of danger' (1990: 521–4). Gilligan never goes into any further detail.
In her overriding concern with 'voice', the girls she discusses seem
to live in a disembodied, almost contextless world of relationships,
feelings and ideas about growing up. Above all, she does not ask
about the body at such a crucial time for girls (in contrast with the
time of early childhood for boys): why is it that this critical awareness for girls surfaces and vanishes again in relation to adolescence?

This chapter proposes that the transition from childhood into
adulthood carries gendered meanings, which can only be fully understood by reference to the ways in which these are embodied. For
young women, the onset of menarche is a significant marker, a key
moment of embodied transition through which they begin to realize
the project of growing up, of becoming an adult woman, a new
being-in-the-world. At the same time, this moment carries a par-

ticular and powerful charge of secrecy and shame in Western culture, expressed in negative beliefs and attitudes and in associated behaviours. This chapter has argued that what girls encounter are not only negative attitudes and beliefs, but also the material shaping of gendered value within formal and informal aspects of institutional rules. Following Mauss (1973), these might be seen as embodied techniques of being a proper woman, literally incorporated into everyday, lived experience.

Looking ahead, girls observe and record both the social structures that shape this negativity, and the experiences, feelings and reactions of others who have encountered it already. As we have seen, even at a relatively young age girls are never entirely cut off from the experiences of older girls and women around them, and as they approach the early teens their awareness seems to grow more acute. One day nothing is the same again, her body has gone through irrevocable shifts, which necessitate a new sense of embodied self. Even the most commonplace everyday actions, to sit, to walk, to run, to behave normally, can become problematic. As Moss (1989: 79) notes, bodily changes, even minor ones, create a disjunction in our sense of being in the world. There is a lag, sometimes a considerable one, when one lives as-if things were still the same. We often describe this contradictory state as one of 'not-being-myself', or more dramatically, 'that inexplicable ugliness that comes from within and is referred to as "having a bad day"' (Rudberg, 1995: 36). Not only do girls experience an abrupt loss of the taken-for-granted embodiments of childhood, but their new embodiment itself heralds continuing fluctuation. The young girl is precipitated into sudden change, changes which are not just personal and private but which must also pay heed to, account for and monitor the actions and thoughts and behaviours of others, particularly boys, in a social world. In this sense at the very least, that which is desired, to grow up, must be weighed against this negativity, at worst it can be surrounded by an intensity of ambivalence, dread and loss regarding the ending of childhood.

MAPPING THE DIFFERENCE

Gender is an effect of the body's social morphology. What is mapped onto the body is not unaffected by the body onto which it is projected. (Grosz, 1990: 74)

The onset of menarche therefore necessitates a complex mapping and remapping of the gendered body to take account of these factors. Ask any adult woman about the ways in which she plans her life to account for menstrual experience and she will look surprised. Gradually, probing, a list emerges: in regard to choosing and buying towels and tampons, painkillers, their cost, where and how she keeps supplies safe and available, the importance of a comfortable bathroom or washroom with soap, hot water and the privacy and time to do what she needs. Further, she will probably account for her cycle in a diary, and think about these dates when she prepares for work, takes exercise, sleeps a little longer; plans holidays, interviews, exams, Christmas, has sex; explains being off-colour, feeling ill, depression, headaches, allergies, skin conditions, having rows; cuts down drinking, driving; in choosing what clothes to wear; monitoring her general health, stress, conception, contraception, the menopause . . .

Elizabeth Grosz writes about the body as text, as a surface for the inscription of what she calls 'body-maps' via both regimes of imposed control (regimes of the body in institutions) and through more voluntary, individual systems of cultural and personal value (like diet, makeup, clothing or body-building). 'There is nothing natural or a priori about these modes of corporeal inscriptions', she notes 'through them, bodies are marked so as to make them amenable to prevailing exigencies of power. They make the body into a particular kind of body . . .' (1990: 65) At the same time bodies are not purely blank surfaces capable of taking any inscription that we chose at will. They also present what she calls a biological bedrock, itself not fixed, but 'which interacts with and is overlaid by psychic, social and signifying relations'. She suggests that such universal or quasi-universal physiological features includes menstrual, anatomical or hormonal factors. What adult women learn are specific techniques of the body, as Mauss (1973) has described them. These can also be seen, to adapt Grosz's term, as three-dimensional corporeal inscriptions, complex, multifaceted maps which chart embodied manoeuvres through social time and space.

The body-maps that girls must make are both similar to and different from those charted by adult women. At the same time, practical and conceptual, private and social, some of the territory to be mapped is unknown, some is partially if vaguely apprehended, while some cannot be known until the experience actually happens. Above all young women must set about these tasks partly in a hostile public environment, in conditions quite unlike those available to older women. Three mapping tasks are described here. The first is how to map one's private, personal body through a process of radical change in which, quite literally, much of what happens is unknown, is 'off the map'. Each month girls can be drawn into a time of doubtful agency as, in the fluctuations of these changes the markers of normality vanish. Not only is your body very different from what is was before menarche, it changes again in a cyclical fashion, and even this may be unpredictable and unreliable. Suddenly your body has a new interiority to be understood: a new paradigm in which the appearance of blood (which usually marks the breaching of significant bodily boundaries) and possibly irritability, pain and headaches, are not now signs of illness but to be judged as 'normal'. In addition these changes may bring new feelings, experiences and sensations, new moods, which must also be attended to and incorporated into the everyday. Leaking, staining, flooding, feelings: what should be kept hidden might become exposed, inside–outside, private–public. All of these must be mapped.

A second task is learning how to live with and manage personal experience in a public setting which makes specific physical, practical, social and intellectual demands, in conditions that are negative if not downright hostile. In the face of teasing, harassment, unsympathetic school rules, grossly inadequate material provision and disgusting toilets, girls describe how they must keep a mental list or map of practical tasks, be constantly watchful and on their guard in order to keep menstruation hidden in school. This includes not only watchfulness of the body, constant monitoring to forestall accidents such as staining their clothes, but also watchfulness of their bags and possessions and of their own and boys actions. The combined effect of these kinds of watchfulnesses, both in producing and repressing the body, might be summarized more abstractly as housekeeping the body or 'regulating the self'(Martin, 1989).

A third task is making a conceptual map of social interpretations of the sexed body and their implications for gender; how to understand attitudes to bleeding and sanitary protection, to pain and emotional upset as negative, secret and shameful aspects of what essentially makes you a woman. At a young age, girls know that 'something' has been withheld from them. Adults were often embarrassed about raising the topic and spoke about it relatively late, even mothers, who waited until the questions came. This was in a context of earlier information/overheard stories/incidents which created a sense of shock, dread and shame which continued to shape girls feelings in later years. These feelings come both from a sense of withholding and from the content of what is withheld. Indeed these two aspects can be seen as interconnected in that the with-holding itself implies something difficult, embarrassing, secret or shameful about the nature of the content. This is particularly so since there seems to be no equivalent event for boys. Many girls, although they might assess it as a natural event, still felt that men-struation was unfair for this reason. For them, it is bleeding, secrecy and having to be careful that herald their entry into a new, more adult womanhood.

FORGETTING WHAT YOU KNOW

Returning to Gilligan, we could say that what girls encounter at adolescence is apprehended not just through what they *see and hear* of the contradictions of becoming a woman in a male world, but also, perhaps even more profoundly, through the unarticulatable experience of the *social embodiment* of these contradictions into who you are, your being-in-the-world. At adolescence the young girl looks both backwards, forwards and sideways in order to under-stand and evaluate what becoming an adult woman means. Looking backwards to childhood she sets the relative freedom of the imma-ture girl, or of the active tomboy who must become more restricted and careful once this change takes place. Looking ahead, she sees girls losing control, that the conditions of school, where she must spend a great deal of her time, are such as to render her maturing body as problematic, while judgements of its nature construct it as 'other', shameful, secret. Looking sideways she sees that boys, while they may have other dilemmas about the body, certainly have nothing like this. Worse, she sees that for a while at least, these changes work in boys favour, mobilizing the biological, giving boys embar-rassing and unchallengeable ammunition if they so choose to use it against girls.

To survive, girls must map a new embodied self against a gener-alized, fragmented, inaccessible and unarticulated sense of shame embedded in the very fabric of material and social arrangements. All girls must struggle to overcome them, and in that struggle many will fail to positively like, own and be able to accept responsibility for their new self. Their sense of the unfairness of some aspects of embodied value must be weighed against its positive attributes. In all of this they have to sort out what it means to be a woman and how some key aspects of being a woman, ones reproductive and sexual potential, are valued in relation to and by men. Echoes of these themes surface in Nielsen and Rudberg (1994) and more explicitly in Rudberg (1995), where she describes how the young women in her (Norwegian) research appear to want to deny their generative femininity, craving forms of disembodiment. For girls, she says, 'to forget the body is a powerful strategy to conquer the world' (1995: 37). In contrast, Prendergast and Forrest (1997a and b) and Hallden (1995, in a Swedish study) found in boys of the same age a prioritizing of growth, a pride in the capacity to use, develop and control bodily competence.

Bourdieu, in speaking of the power of embodied memory, remarks,

> If all societies and significantly, all the 'totalitarian institutions', in Goffman's phrase, that seek to produce a new man through a process of 'deculturation' and 'acculturation' set such store on the seemingly insignificant details of dress, bearing, physical and verbal manners, the reason is that, treating the body as a memory, they entrust to it an abbreviated and practical, i.e. mnemonic, form the fundamental principles of the arbitrary content of the culture. The principles embodied in this way are placed beyond the grasp of consciousness, and hence cannot be touched by voluntary, deliberate transformation, cannot even be made explicit . . . (1977: 94)

These complex practical, experiential and conceptual tasks of embodied mapping are not only done *par excellence* by adult women, but as we have seen, they have forgotten, or do not know, that they do them. Because of this they cannot easily be passed on to others. It is these tasks with which young women feel and often are most alone. Each girl learns that menstrual experience must be constantly present in their thoughts in order that it remains invisible to the outside world. This an exhausting and negative use of energy which contributes to no positive benefit to the self. This constant carrying of the body in the mind, and at the same time rendering aspects of the embodied self as invisible, the mindfulness of having to forget what you know, constitute an embodied mapping of gender itself.

Following the phenomenologists, I would make no distinction between the body and mind or body and 'self'. For children as for adults, the body/mind is the self, it is only through this embodied self that the world can be apprehended. Even today I still do catch like a boy and throw like a girl. This is not to say that anything is pre-ordained. In playing cricket or growing up the body offers us the ground of fabulous potentiality, drawn over by the mappings of a cultural biology on which we act as gendered individuals 'end-lessly becoming'. This is a paradox of both embodiment and childhood. If we want to discuss them we must, as Merleau-Ponty has said, become dizzy in our turning, possessing like the philoso-pher, '*inseparably* the taste for evidence and the feeling for ambiguity' (1988: 4)

ACKNOWLEDGEMENT

Some aspects of this chapter were presented and discussed at the Confer-ence *Children, Health and the Body*, Dept of Child Studies, Lindkoping University, Sweden, in April 1996, where a stimulating and useful discus-sion of some of the issues presented here took place (Prendergast, 1996).

NOTE

1. The three-year study was based upon fieldwork and an analysis of 74 interviews and 474 questionnaires from girls in ten secondary schools throughout the country. Full details can be found in Prendergast (1994). The research was funded by the Health Promotion Trust.

7 Re-presenting the Embodied Child: the Muted Child, the Tamed Wife and the Silenced Instrument in Jane Campion's *The Piano*[1]

Ronnie Frankenberg

In films, as in dreams, nothing is accidental, it is only awaiting the right interpreter.

> (Bergen Freudank, *When Truffaut Lied*, 1997)

I like young children a lot... I am extremely interested in the contrast between children and adults: there is a world looking at another world which is going downhill but this world does not yet know if its own fate will be the same ... The look of a child is always fascinating. It seems to be saying: is that what fate has in store for me, too?

The point is: are children really pure? I don't think so. The innocence they have will be destroyed. They are symbols of melancholy, not of purity. Children are usually put in pictures right at the end to show that a new generation is coming up. In my films I want to show exactly the opposite: I think it is the tragedies which are starting over again, always and always... (Douglas Sirk, in Halliday, 1971: 107)

The sign for silence is among the most fluid and beautiful of signs: both hands are held prayer-like over the mouth, then slowly and steadily spread apart and downward; a related sign is 'peace'. (Preston, 1994: 119)

THE POLYSEMIC PIANO

Over half a century ago in the early 1940s, the school music teacher, despite his best efforts, having failed to teach me as much as a single scale on the violin, I asked a school friend of the same age, to whom I was, to put it mildly, greatly attracted, to be my 'unofficial' piano teacher. We could thus legitimately spend time together alone in the music room, without raising the overt suspicions of pupils and staff about any friendship between an acknowledged swot and a distinguished sportsman; the chairman and founder of the Jewish Society and an evangelistic Christian protagonist of the Scripture Union: the school's only overt socialist and the scion of a family well known in national Tory politics. Indeed the association was commemorated in my final school leaving report by a tribute from a teacher to my progressive role in bringing together the two 'halves' of the school. It took that half-century, the cinema and art enthusiasms of a class on the cultural anthropology of the body, consisting mainly of women and teachers, who were also clinicians: doctors, midwives, nurses and others, Jane Campion's film *The Piano,* as well as 'the new musicology' (Kopelson, 1996; Leppert, 1993) to make me even remember these circumstances and to bring home to me that (as usual) I was not an original and radical innovator but merely a neutrino-sized participator in a European cultural tradition already two centuries old.

It is not, in fact, surprising that myth interprets the partially pragmatic and mainly legendary Victorian habit of covering the legs of the piano with frills to protect their veneer from the shoe-clad writhings of suffering unwilling child pupils as symbolic of sexual hypocrisy. A celebrated early twentieth-century pornographic print portrays this with total openness, contrasting the intellectual concentration of the calm, young woman, with upright head and shoulders and fingers placed firmly on the keys with the frantic, fleshly, oral activities of a young man hidden beneath the keyboard and her partially raised hooped skirt (Néret, 1994: 568). In one scene of *The Piano*, Baines places himself in a similar position, demands that Ada raise her skirt and we have a close up of a finger with a begrimed nail caressing white skin through a small hole in her stocking.

The film is a textbook representation of the unholy trinities, the eternal triangles, the unstable triads, which always divide eventually into two against one, theorized within formal sociological theory

by Simmel (1902) and Theodore Caplow (1968). The Piano as itself actor is, of course, the major filmic protagonist. In a scene cut
from the finished film, a blind piano tuner, doubting that Baines
will learn to play, but impressed by its rarity in the country, apos-
trophizes it: 'Well my dear Miss Broadbent, tuned, but silent'
(Campion, 1993: 48). A deliberate or unconsciously negligent slip
for the Broadwood label on it (see Wainwright, 1982, cited in Leppert,
1993: 36: 26).

The Piano is nevertheless the apex of most of the triangles and
of Jane Campion's desire to 'enjoy writing characters who don't
have a twentieth-century sensibility about sex. They have nothing
to prepare themselves for its strength and power' (1993: 135). With
now rare insight born, in her own view, of her national and home
experience and of her involvement in making, at the same time as
she was beginning work on *The Piano*, biographical films of New
Zealand life in the late nineteenth and early twentieth centuries
Campion brings to cinematic life, in an imperial, and in cultural
terms failed 'civilizing' context, the reality, more formally described
by Richard Leppert:

> To the Victorian bourgeoisie the domestic pianoforte was as es-
> sential as the dining room table – in an ideological sense perhaps
> more important; respectability demanded its purchase as a marker
> of family position and accomplishment. Indeed the history of piano
> design, manufacture and distribution in the nineteenth century
> serves not only as perfect metaphor of capitalist economic prin-
> ciples in operation but also as an agent of capitalism's political,
> economic, and ideological success, to the extent that these cat-
> egories of success may be understood as part and parcel of
> domesticity. Yet the socio-cultural organization of Victorian life
> was so new, conflicted, self-contradictory, and self-conscious that
> the preferred 'reading' of the sign 'piano' – like that of the sign
> 'music' – was unstable despite the centrality of its cultural semi-
> otics. *The piano seems to have been something of a floating signifier,
> a semantic pendulum that swung in an extreme arc.*
>
> Set up in the principal room of the semi-public portions of the
> home where guest as well as family members would gather, the
> piano bridged the gap between the public world and the private.[1]
> (1993: 153, my italics)

Indeed, the comparison with and metamorphic possibilities of the kitchen/dining room table is made in the film itself, two metonyms for one status, the docile suburban housewife (see below and Campion, 1993: 39) In sending to Scotland to acquire a wife and having a high-class piano thrown in, the ungrateful Stewart was thus getting two markers of respectability for the price of one.

In the bourgeois imperialist civilizing century and a half in which 'the devil was seen as making work for idle hands' and 'children [and especially female children] were to be seen and not heard', the piano and the piano lesson did in fact, and not merely in representation, subject children to a regulative discipline of body movement and provide them both with a substitute, less revealing and less threatening, voice and a symbolic training in the control of bodily self-awareness. At the same time it discreetly revealed erotic potential to both appropriate and inappropriate others as well as providing a point of weakness, actual or potential, in the armoury of patriarchal control by husband, father and possibly son (see Leppert, 1993, in general and especially his analysis of Tolstoy's Kreutzer Sonata, 153–87 from the opening of which the above quotation is taken. See also Wiltshire, 1992, on the body in Jane Austen).

While the embroidered sampler revealed, in quasi-religious disguise, what fingers had done (mnemonics of achievement in a dead past and directed towards eternity), piano playing showed them in motion (erotics of achieving in the living present). In the eighteenth century, as now, there is a widespread, implicit suggestion that the *real* body only exists in sickness. Wiltshire finds no direct reference in an age when the phallic guitar (for an early example of this see Frederic, Lord Leighton's magnificent painting, *Music*, reproduced in Leppert (1993: 225)) has replaced the uterine piano, to that which, like all lived culture, was so obviously natural to Austen's contemporaries as not to be worth drawing to verbal attention. (Mascia-Lees and Sharpe, 1995, in their discussion of *The Piano*, draw attention to the possibility of new media making this clearer.)

In Campion's film, the Piano is initially represented, unlike the emergent child, as person, heard but not seen, and while the fate of the child as actor is to be gradually faded out, the Piano is brutally drowned and fails, in its partially and ambiguously collusive attempt to take Ada, its betrayer, with it to its watery grave. Her fate, silence of protest transformed to silence of acceptance, of embraced defeat, is foreshadowed, and Baines warned unwittingly by the same blind but far-seeing piano tuner:

> My wife sang with a bell-clear tone. After we married she stopped. She said she didn't feel like singing, that life made her sad. And that's how she lived, lips clamped closed over a perfect voice, a beautiful voice. (Campion, 1993: 49)

CHILDHOOD, THE PIANO AND GENDER

My friend did not teach me to play music, but he did succeed in helping me to learn at least three other things. First that unexpected juxtaposition is often more enlightening than startling originality; second, that the world of relevant adults often overlooks, ignores or pretends not to notice the meaningful actions of the under 12-year-olds let alone even younger children; and third, that although there were many keys on the piano, in any performance or even practice scale there was a key of keys around which meaning was constructed. In this chapter, I do not suggest that there is only one thematic key to Jane Campion's richly textured film(s), but that childhood is certainly central and profitable to explore. Most critics and perhaps the general public failed to perceive them in *The Piano*. Writers in the *American Anthropologist* (Mascia-Lees et al., 1995: 765), in an interesting but perhaps over enthusiastic attempt to claim Campion for postmodernist anthropology (overlooking Hollywood directors like Altman), read Flora 'as a miniature visual echo of herself [Ada]'. failing to consider the dialogic/dialectical reciprocal possibilities. Even the videocase notes talks of three protagonists only, its grammar leaving it to us to decide whether the third is her husband or her daughter. The film, in fact, shows Flora as (a sometimes but by no means always involuntary) actor in her own life and in the lives of others. At the same time her attempts to act in order to structure her own life are usually frustrated by at least the *pakeha* (Maori term for European) protagonists of the film, for the same reasons as audiences fail to perceive what they are seeing: the threat of a consciously desire-driven child body. Even Freud took refuge in a latent period between the erotic polymorphous perversity of infancy and supposedly normal post-pubertal focus of desire.

Obviously, I did not arrive at the considerations below at the first or even the second viewing, but I was convinced by what I then remembered as the opening (pre-credits) sequence that one significant way in which one was led to read the film was that it was concerned with childhood and indeed the child as actor. This was in contrast to what had been said by most critics, and to how it was seen by members of the class, even those who were themselves mothers, paediatricians or otherwise closely concerned with children. (Both Pia Christensen and Alan Prout, with whom I discussed it at the time, had also been sensitized by their studies to see it as I did.)

WHEN SPEECH IS SILENCED, THE BODY'S VOICE IS HEARD

The unity of its apparently very diverse incidents and the emotional experiences from which it may emerge are hinted at as the film ends with a spoken quotation of part of a sonnet by Thomas Hood:

> There is a silence where hath been no sound
> There is a silence where no sound may be
> In the cold grave, under the deep, deep sea,

followed by the dedication to Campion's stillborn, but named, child in the last written but silent words of the film (not reprinted in Campion, 1993):

> For
> Edith

Hood's poem is one of two (see Roberts, 1938) in which the first suggests that 'natural' silence is, so to speak, neutral, asocial and acultural; the silence that is felt, that hurts or exalts, is embodied. It is present because it is the partially erased memory of a now absent past. The second speaks similarly about death. Being in the grave is 'natural' and possible to contemplate as part of one's future. The real death, which is unimaginable, is no longer being part of the embodied actions of the living. Campion's film replaces what might have been Hood's third poem. She pairs the bodily experience of mother and daughter, adult and child and draws attention to a third antithesis. 'Natural' innocence which becomes real chosen and felt innocence through the creation of a past; know-ingness in fact (cf. Sirk epigraph above). She re-presents for us, who reject as intellectually and emotionally maimed and maiming the reductionism of cognitive, socialization and social constructionist views of the child, the unity across age of lived bodily experience. In both method and in her practice of it, she helps us to find ways to argue against the fallacy of the excluded middle (age) in which, as Hockey and James (1993) suggest, the experience of the old and young are glossed as different in kind from general human experience and are seen as inherently, rather than socially, vulner-able, handicapped, inadequate and lacking autonomy.

I failed to notice until much later that the main part of this opening sequence was preceded by a momentary vision suggesting that it was being seen by an eye peering through the fingers of both hands, seeing in fact not just by and through the eye, but perceiving at the same time, in the only physical way possible, through and with the body. Campion also uses this device near the beginning of *An Angel at My Table* (1990), the film trilogy in which she re-presents the verbal autobiography of Janet Frame. As a child, she is por-trayed as peering through her fingers out of a train window and frames through them a bodily representation of mental handicap or disorder which presages the eight years of her later life when she is similarly perceived and persecuted.

INNOCENTLY KNOWING TO KNOWINGLY INNOCENT: A CASE STUDY

What the eye at the beginning of *The Piano* sees, and the fingers bring into frame, is first, Flora (Anna Paquin), provisionally ident-ified in the voice-over as the daughter of Ada (Holly Hunter), the silent heroine, seated on a pony which an unsuccessful attempt is being made to pull along in the grounds of a Scottish mansion. Ada holds herself apart at a distance, under a tree. The scene quickly changes to Flora's rapid progress on roller skates along a corridor and cuts to her sleeping in bed, her protruding feet still wearing skates. Ada enters and cuts off the skates. She moves to, lovingly fingers and plays the Piano for the first time, but stops dead and emotion-less when she notices she has an audience, even though this is only an elderly maid. Clearly she plays (for herself) rather than performs (for an audience even of one other) (see Barthes, 1977: 149 et seq).

We are instantly under the sea with a longboat above us off a wild New Zealand beach to which Ada and Flora are immediately carried. A voice says with irony as they land 'Here we are at Paddington Station' (not in Campion, 1993). Fearing that their passengers will not easily be picked up from this remote beach in bad weather, the sailors suggest in a dialogue, notionally with Ada, but conducted through Flora, that they will take them on to Nelson, which, at the end of the film turns out in truth to be her ultimate destination. The sailor verbally as well as physically recognizes, for the first time, the possible autonomy of Flora (Campion, 1993: 16):

> SEAMAN: (*Stunned*) You be damned fortune I don't smack your puppy gob, missy.

We have already been told by Ada, 'The voice you hear is not my speaking voice but my mind's voice', that she does not speak.

> I have not spoken since I was six years old. No one knows why, not even me. My father says it is a dark talent and the day I take it into my head to stop breathing will be my last.
>
> Today he married me to a man I've not yet met. Soon my daughter and I shall join him in his own country. My husband said my muteness does not bother him. He writes and hark this: God loves dumb creatures, so why not he!
>
> Were good he had God's patience for silence affects everyone in the end. The strange thing is I don't think myself silent, that is, because of my piano. I shall miss it on the journey.
>
> (Campion, 1993: 90)

It is not only the Piano that breaks her silence, of course. Those present in the cinema or who place themselves before the video screen are privileged sometimes to hear Ada's mind, an echo of the chorus in Greek tragedy, something emphasized in the later radio adaptation. To most of the protagonists she communicates, through her hands and fingers. An exception is reported by each of her 'lovers' about two highly sexually charged occasions when she is said to have communicated in unspoken words, mindful body to mindful body by and with Baines and Stewart. Stewart had, much earlier in the film, told Baines, in a polysemic warning full of unconscious dramatic irony, when he was overseeing the arrival of Flora and Ada to give the first lesson:

> Flora will explain anything Ada says. They talk through their fingers, you can't believe what they say with just their hands.

She uses her hands to write on a pad, but most overtly her fingers, to speak with her child, at first to caress the Piano, to caress (somatically and reversing power relations) the bodies of Baines and Stewart, to express love for Baines and finally, as she leaves, to caress the sea, about to become the Piano's final home. The everyday utilitarian use of Sign through Flora as interpreter, is one of the means through which Campion reveals the power of child as actor. (Mascia-Lee et al., 1995, draw attention to a virtual epidemic of Sign as sign in recent cult movies, although their interpretation is different from mine. For me the arbitrariness of the sign means that 'White man speak with forked fingers.') She and Stewart (in contrast to the Maori, who are more sharing and less exclusive, as is shown in their relations with Baines) are overtly portrayed as at pains to deter Flora acting more freely with her fingers or other parts of her body. The continuation of the bodily freedom of Stewart and the bodily liberation of Ada is to be achieved by their control of Flora's body.

Paul Preston (1994) wrote *Mother Father Deaf,* a study of others in the same position, as the anthropologist child of signing parents. In it he discusses the implications of a child role as simultaneous translator in which one is heard as an other but not seen as a self. When he first presented his work, one eminent anthropologist was shocked that he must have known things about his parents which no child *should* know (my emphasis).

Flora, then, is torn away from her familiar Scottish context, separated from her, in its turn, obstinately autonomous pony; cut off (shades of castration) from the extended powers of autonomous movement and action represented by her roller skates, transported like a felon across stormy seas to the Southern Hemisphere. At significant moments, she reverts to a more marked Scottish accent and to singing Scottish songs. The Holly and the Ivy in the script is substituted by Barbara Allan in the film. Nyman, who composed the film's music, reports that he deliberately chose Scottish folk themes (Campion, 1993: 150). Flora's first foregrounded action in the moment of her rebirth within a New Zealand frame is the most dramatic noisy and visible sign of unspoken rejection possible through bodily a-voidance, she is violently sick.

They spend a full day on the beach alone with the Piano and the sea, and recognize and partially defy a shared powerlessness against a new natural, and by implication, cultural environment. Ada begins to make contact with the Piano after the deprivations of the voyage. Flora speaks her first autonomous words in the film while still, within the as yet relatively undisturbed triad: Ada, Flora, Piano: Mother, Childvoice, Piano. They are preceded, continuing and contextualizing the identification with her mother of the words she had spoken for her the day before as Flora's first words in the film, by a statement in Sign,

'Mamma. I am thinking.'

She interrupts the bedtime story Ada is telling her, seen, according to the published script, by viewers as an 'odd shadow play' within an improvised tent, a hooped petticoat, illuminated by eerie oil lamps within. Here they symbolize their biological oneness; even the Piano is outside and at a distance. They have symbolically marked off their separateness by making a decorative boundary of seashells around their shared temporary home. Ada pauses to listen and Flora continues speaking aloud:

'I'm not going to call him Papa. I'm not going to call HIM anything. I'm not even going to look at HIM.' (Campion 1993: 17)

For the viewer a few seconds later, for the protagonists after a night has past, a liminal phase is over, a new set of social and cultural relations within a new natural environment is about to begin. Enter, still in *their* liminality, the forest, the Maori *people*, men and women not so fundamentally separated by sex, by gender or by generation as are *pakeha* New Zealanders; and a *man*, Stewart (Sam Neil), the husband, tall and dignified, already married by proxy. Baines (Harvey Keitel) is sited socially between them, marked by his shyness, his poverty, his incomplete facial decoration revealing his albeit partial knowledge of Maori language and culture. He is socially inferior and partially feminized. Just as his facial markings indicate blurred boundaries, so do the mixed European/traditional dress of the Maori. Baines is asking in vain for instructions as to whether or not to tell the Maori to stop. Stewart looks at a small glass-covered framed picture of Ada, in the film he sees himself reflected therein, and takes the opportunity to comb his hair. (There is a different and much weaker description in Campion, 1993: 19.) In this and in his later comments on his wife's stuntedness he suggests an intention and desire to outcreate God, and not merely to create Ada in his own image, but to incorporate her as part of his own. (See Marcia Pointon's (1990) discussion of the Pygmalion myth in nineteenth century art and literature. On page 15 she even draws attention to Henry James's *Portrait of a Lady*, destined to be the basis for Campion's next film.) It is some time before he becomes (always only) partly aware of the existence of the Piano and of Flora as potential allies or enemies of this ambition.

The reception party arrives at the beach, Stewart puts on his smart top hat in contrast to his muddy clothes. A tell-tale foot reveals that the women are hidden under the hooped petticoat and when the feet of both are revealed, a Maori cries that feet so small must belong to angels presaging a symbolism to come which will point up *pakeha* attitudes to children and to nature, once again by juxtaposed difference from the Maori.

Like Walter Benjamin, in his symbolic use of Klee's Angel (Scholem, 1991 see also Sirk epigraph, above), Campion recognizes the different combinations of innocence and knowingness that the status of angel simultaneously implies, as well as the Victorian and earlier use of the piano as a boundary marker between the supposed domesticity of innocence and the alleged outsideness of the worldly wise. In those days it was the *haute bourgeoise* maiden who came out and the piano that helped her to do so. (Compare for a queer postmodern explanation of both, Kopelson, 1996.) The cultural capital implied in knowing cannot be invested in each and every market. Confusion of markets negates knowing; knowing markets may destroy innocence. Throughout the film each protagonist is to learn this, until the Piano, through which mainly the learning is mediated, marks the closure of this set of apparently diverse but emotionally unitary episodes. Its death by drowning and the fact that Ada does not die with it creates a liminal space for the others, and the closing sequences in the town of Nelson, at last reached in knowing after having been initially rejected in innocence, suggests an emergent structure and future. This is spelled out only for Ada now united with Baines. It is in fact a realistic, even naturalistic, conventional Victorian ending rather than the romantic sell-out of which Campion has been accused. Victorian women piano players did became housewives: Victorian piano players of talent did become teachers. Ada became both. Aunt Morag's insight, conveyed to Nessie, at a moment when her body, peeing in semi-public, was unusually open to unconventional truth. 'She does not play the piano as we do' is no longer true.

In the sequence that follows landing and discovery on the beach, some of the Maori continually mime the actions of the *pakeha* and especially Stewart and Ada behind their backs suggesting by reducing meaningful incarnate action to mere somatic movement the essential meaninglessness of their exchanges. The central lack of understanding which is to come is signalled first by the formality of Stewart's self-introduction, then by his adverse comments on her size and the general lack of emotional affect until the crucial issue of moving the piano is raised. When asked what is in the very heavy box, Flora replies 'It's my mother's piano', when it becomes apparent that it is to be left behind, Ada writes on her pad 'THE PIANO' and then 'I NEED THE PIANO' and Flora reinforces, prompted by her mother's signs. 'We can't leave *our* piano' (my emphasis). The argument continues and is joined from without by the Maoris through mockery, by disquieting mimicry and, to most of the whites unintelligible speech (a subtitle reveals 'Watch it! Dry balls is getting touchy'). Through classical English root metaphors related to travel (Lakoff and Turner, 1989, but foreign to the Maori in turn, see Salmond, 1982) the men telegraph their later paradoxically co-operative roles:

STEWART: I suggest you prepare for a difficult journey. The bush will tear clothes and the mud is deep in places.

And:

BAINES: Mr Stewart asked if I might show you to the path . . . May I carry something? (Campion, 1993: 26)

The mutual strangeness, alongside the interweaving of the two cultures is further demonstrated in the sequence of the journey from beach no man's land through Maori bush. They stop to argue over the route; Stewart sees them as making difficulty in order to slow down and earn more money for their lost time. Baines explains that they are saying they want to avoid disturbing the dead buried underneath.

ADA *and* FLORA *sit watching, out of breath. One of the* MAORI
women *sits close to* ADA *apparently not looking at her. Slowly she
draws the scarf that is in* ADA's *lap into her own. Defiantly she
puts it on.*

*Meanwhile another woman makes a very dignified attempt to wipe
the freckles from* FLORA's *face.* (Campion, 1993: 29)

They eventually arrive at civilization, a *pakeha* domestic interior,
even if this, in colonial New Zealand, has not the protection from
the rain it was afforded in Scotland. As is still, perhaps increasingly, the case, the wedding and the hoped for domesticity have to
be represented photographically to be made real.

There follows the preparation of the taking of The Photograph
which is to stand in for a marriage ceremony. This introduces a
conventional *pakeha* family including the Reverend, indulging in
practical jokes and horseplay with the latter wearing the 'wedding
dress' which, since it is only to be used for a photograph taken
from the front, is itself only a façade. Unable to get herself included in the enduring photographic record which is intended to
crystallize, reify and distort this particular present, Flora nevertheless uses the opportunity to improvize her own highly memorable
myth of the lost family past. To do this she has to overcome the
mud and rain within the house, her mother's Signed rebukes, down-
to-earth interruptions by Aunt Morag (Kerry Walker) and Nessie
(Genevieve Lemon) involved in the transfer and pinning of the
dress and the departure and return of the 'wedding' party as well
as Stewart's illusion that he is taking part in a real wedding to a
beautiful bride. Flora's fantasy is clearly a fanciful, enjoyable, la-
ment for a lost romantic future intended, nevertheless, further to
subvert, both the present progress and the future memory of the
already chaotic and unintentionally comic now.

'My REAL father was a famous German composer. They met
when my mother was an opera singer . . . in Luxembourg . . . Well
yes in Austria, where he conducted the Royal Orchestra . . .'
(And where did they get married?)

In an intensified Scottish accent, Flora continues:

'In an enormous forest, with real fairies as bridesmaids each holding
a little elf's hand.'

(Morag shows disbelief, disapproval and disappointment)
'No! I tell a lie, it was in a small country church near the moun-
tains . . .'
(Which mountains are those dear?)
'The Pyrenees.'

(Campion 1993: 31 says the slightly more plausible Alps!)

'Mother used to sing songs in German and her voice would echo
across the valleys . . . That was before the accident.'
(Oh! What happened?)

Flora continues with total conviction over a very brief cartoon sequence (like comic strip and interactive computer game for rebellious
youth, a metaphor for children's public cultural expression of meaning; see for a fictional example of the former, Brite, 1994).

'One day when my father and mother were singing together in
the forest, a great storm blew up out of nowhere. But so passionate
was their singing that they did not notice, nor did they stop as
the rain began to fall, and when their voices rose for the final
bars of the duet a great bolt of lightning came out of the sky
and struck my father so he lit up like a torch . . . And at the
same moment my father was struck dead my mother was struck
dumb! She–never–spoke–another–word.'

Morag now expresses sympathetic and total belief, as the 'Wedding' party return 'dripping wet, exactly as the couple in the story'
(Campion, 1993: 32). Ada violently tears off the wedding gown,
and reinforced by an change in tempo and loudness in Nyman's
score turns to the window thinking of her piano in the rain which
is now shown 'small and embattled on the dark rainy beach'
(Campion, 1993: 32).

Flora has stated her allegiance for an imagined past and secured
for it a sort of legitimation; Ada, her fears for her own future and
that of the Piano.

THE PIANO, PICTURED, EMBODIED AND AT HOME IN A STRANGE LAND

Having ritually secured his prize, Stewart now removes himself from the action to follow 'business as usual' and acquire land from the Maori. The stage is set, at first just outside his house and then on the distant beach, for a new triad. Baines, Ada/Flora speaking as one in a symbolic and actual duet in Piano and Sign (broken by Baines's intervention and Ada's regression to conventional child-ish games, making a seahorse of shells in the sand and turning somersaults) and the Piano's emergence from first the liminality of its temporary (natural = non-cultural) existence on the beach and still partially enclosed in its packing case. Its renewed state is made possible by Baines's full and Stewart's partial collaboration and it is to be liberated, despite her resistance, from Ada's exclusive power: she will no longer be able either to exclude others with it nor to exclude others from it. Ada's use of both her daughter and her Piano as combined instruments of her will become less and less effective until the Piano's story ends on the way to Nelson and domesticity, and Flora's becomes irrelevant because it is either autonomous or the start of a new cycle.

Stewart's return is buoyed by false hope and by suspicion of si-lent deceit since before entering the house he mistakes Flora's singing for Ada's. Both emotions turn to bewilderment when he discovers that Flora is accompanied by Ada playing on a silent piano with mock keys carved into the kitchen table. He explores their feel under the cloth. We cut once more to the scene of the wedding photographs, the kitchen of the mission crowded with conventional and unconventional *pakeha* and seeking, with apparent unsuccess, to freeze 'natural' Maori into a less expressive culture of civility and bodily distance, although Morag does suggest that Stewart's continuing and unusual hair combing has been excessive (perhaps because it has been improperly public. Rehearsals are (mysteri-ously to cinema audience and to Maori both at this stage) in train for a celebratory entertainment which the missionary has devised. This is based on the story of Bluebeard who will apparently be seen as a shadow behind a curtain beheading his disobedient wives with special effects of spurting animal blood. A chorus of innocent child angels are also to take part. The whole symbolic scheme is curiously reminiscent and roughly set contemporaneously with Burne Jones's decoration of the domestic upright piano donated by his aunt as a wedding present to his wife who regularly played it (for description see Leppert, 1993: 145–7).

In Campion's film version, the girls are dressed as angels, the boys symbolize the clouds on which they are carried.

Stewart's conversation during the early stages of discussion of the play is to recount the incident of playing the kitchen table, the conclusion is reached that she is certainly odd, perhaps even mad, but that she may become affectionate in time. It is left to the garrulous Morag to confirm Stewart's view that there is virtue in silence and to fulfil Ada's prediction in her very first voice over.

> AUNT MORAG: Certainly, there is nothing so easy to like as a pet, and *they are quite silent*. (emphasis in original Campion, 1993: 40)

Ironically, the dog that noisily licks Stewart's hand while he observes his wife make love to Baines is far from quite silent.

Well directed film (like mediaeval paintings of the Nativity which portray the holy family as sad and the infant's swaddling clothes as shroud-like and thus condense linear time) often refers to the recent future, and the significance of some scenes is only fully appreciated (a day or two?) after the closing credits. Baines opens his negotiation to swap the Piano for a piece of land in Stewart's woodyard where the latter is showing off his skill. Flora is watching and stacking the fallen timber. She flinches as the axe hits the wood but scurries in to pick up the timber.

It is however in the kitchen that Stewart seeks first to persuade Ada to yield the piano and, adding insult to injury, to teach Baines to play it. When he fails to persuade, he orders her to obey. The first act of violence in the film is from Ada who hurls a plate at his departing back.

During their first reluctant visit to Baines's hut, Flora and Ada find the Piano is the only clean object in it (in the text even Stewart admires its beauty). Ada's objections continue, however – Baines is too dirty, he is illiterate, his hands are not merely dirty but uncleanable and in any case the Piano is untuned and therefore unplayable. Stewart has suggested a solution on the way there which groups together, Ada, Flora and Baines as child-like and feminized:

> 'Just encourage him, no one would expect him to be good.
> I'd try children's tunes, nothing more complicated . . .'
> (inverted order of sentences in Campion 1993: 43)

Visits are intercut by the incident with the blind pianotuner already described in part and by Baines's naked interaction with the Piano by which he too is tuned as – a yet to be embodied – love, as opposed to sex, object. The visual images recall the homosociality of the celebrated wrestling scene in Russell's *Women in Love* and foreshadow the later complex homosocial relationship of Baines and Stewart as well as the bargain being struck between Baines and Ada (on the general issues, see Sedgwick, 1985 and 1990 passim, and as cited in Kopelson, 1996, Chapter 6 on Liberace). On the second, still reluctant visit, Ada stays outside while Flora goes in alone and engages in conversation which combines a simple level of technicality with emphasis on the importance of clean hands. This is the high point of her single-handed attempts to defuse events around the Piano and to maintain her relationship with her mother unchanged. Despite Flora's ironically prophetic remark 'Everyone has to practise', Baines indicates that he wishes to learn piano by observation rather than by participation. In the next scene Flora tries once more to anchor her mother to the past with a more realistic but only partially shared fantasy of life and Ada's at first ideal communication with Flora's father and her original lover. A brief attempt by Stewart to replace the latter in the triangle fails despite the advantage (?) of his being present.

A GAZE FOR A GAZE, A *TOUCHE* FOR A TOUCH, AN EYE FOR A BARGAIN

Soon we see Flora in the pouring rain on Baines's verandah locked out with, and like, Baines's dog (Flynn) which she first ruthlessly torments and later, after we have seen the bargain struck, cradles in her arms. The bargain is that Baines will 'sell' back the piano, piecemeal, black key by black key (*touches noirs par touches noirs* in the French subtitles to the film) in return for piecemeal contact by glance, and then by touch) with her body. Ada is portrayed as not seeing initially that just as the keys will eventually add up to her possession of the whole piano, so revelation of parts will lead to his possession of her body. When his feelings for Ada are transformed from corporeal lust to incarnate love, partly through the agency of his Maori *alter ego* and name, Peini, his self-image derived from the Maori in general and especially from Hira (Tungia Baker), he realizes the enormity of his use of power to deceive Ada and himself. This will lead him to abandon the bargain, and to return the Piano, still only part-purchased, to Stewart's household. By this time they have shared knowledge of each other's nakedness without consummating what we suspect is now a growing and shared desire (see directions Campion, 1993: 62).

During this whole process Flora tries desperately to be included within, if only as a spectator, as she has also begun to be from outside, Baines's hut. When she has clearly failed to establish this new group of three, she attempts to achieve another by alliance with Stewart.

The events within Baines's hut are intercut with the major *pakeha* community event of the film; the performance by the children as a choir of winged angels and of the Bluebeard shadow play to which I have already referred. As the audience assembles, Baines is seriously invited to play a tune, to turn pages for the pianist and teased (ironically) for the suggested loss of virility involved in learning music. He also unsuccessfully attempts to claim his place by Ada and is told it is reserved for Flora (!) when her part in the performance is over. The Maori in the audience are stimulated by the realism of the performance of Bluebeard to intervene to save his remaining wife and the *pakeha are* forced to reveal that their cultural performance like their performance of their culture is fraudulent and hypocritical, and especially that their overt attitude to sexuality does not reflect their actual practice. We see the Chief and his followers being shown backstage the theatrical devices; the blood-bucket, the paper axe, the splits in the sheets, and we hear a voice say 'It's all pretence you see'. The overquiet singing of the angels reveals that even as angels *pakeha* children are to be seen rather than heard and, in a cut scene, their corporeality is marked by one pissing on the stage.

The scene is followed by Baines's and Ada's first forced, passionate kiss: Baines is now overtly jealous of the Piano. Ada is now more knowing of her own power, but still sees it as tied to the Piano and is still justly resentful at both his forcefulness and the partiality of her desire to resist. Another scene shows how Stewart's need to acquire land overrides both other aspects of his own culture and any respect he might develop for that of the Maori. Indeed, to him the Piano and its fate is still seen as most closely related to his ability to get land. He seems much more concerned that Baines's return of the Piano will sabotage this than to perceive any significance for the future of his marriage. Most pointedly and sharply, the contradiction within and the clashes between cultures are shown some scenes later after Flora has observed through a hole in the hut Ada and Baines lying naked together, when Stewart finds Flora with the Maori children and in view of Maori adults simulating sexual intercourse with tree trunks and makes her, to the incredulous amusement of the Maori, purify the tree trunks by washing them. Baines is also present as interpreter of culture and language during the negotiations with the Maori and Stewart. His suspicions perhaps aroused by the by-play at the concert, Stewart takes the opportunity to question Baines about his progress at learning to play the piano.

THE INSTRUMENT OF EXCLUSION: A PIANO AND ITS PLAYERS METAPHORICALLY AND LITERALLY DISMEMBERED

There now continues what in retrospect we can see has always been an uneven and faltering process of rejection of the Piano as such, which began with the action of Ada's grandfather (never seen in the film although an actor, George Boyle, is credited with playing the part in the titles) in expelling Ada from his home and from Scotland. In film drama as in ethnography the actions and meanings of crucial actors often have to be inferred from the specific nature of their absent presence.

While she is engaged in washing the trees, made doubly futile by the fact that it is raining, Flora avenges the triple betrayal of her exclusion from the activities of Baines and Ada, being led by the Maori into disapproval of Stewart and Stewart's vehemently imposed punishment, by revealing about Ada's 'lessons' that 'She just plays whatever she pleases, sometimes she doesn't play at all' (Campion, 1993: 73), and in answer to Stewart's question says that the next lesson is tomorrow.

The next day brings a dramatic reshuffling of all the protagonists. The Piano is expelled by Baines, mishandled and manhandled by the Maori, and rejected by Stewart before it is reinstalled in his house. Ada, however, at first refuses either to play it or even to remain in the same room or inside the house at all. Stewart demands that Flora play a jig which she evades by asking Ada if she knows one; she agrees finally to play, and plays and sings a traditional Scottish song. It is at this point that Ada goes outside and Stewart marks his alliance with Flora, the Piano and reason and his frustrated anger by beating time on the lid of the Piano. In the next internal shot Ada is back inside and at the Piano, which she is caressing sensually all over with the back of her fingers. She lifts out a key which has burned on it a love message: A, a pierced heart, and then a D. She has been here before. She plays her theme loudly but stops, thoughtfully, with her hands on the keys. We next see her striding up the hill, with Flora trying to keep up, but she peremptorily and brutally sends her away and infantilizes her. 'Go back to your lessons!' Flora resists hysterically and passes Stewart while cursing as badly as she knows how. Stewart asks where her mother is: 'Where has she gone?' 'TO HELL'.

We now follow Ada to her arrival at Baines's home and a sequence which, beginning with an enquiry about the welfare of the Piano, moves through incomprehension, anger, a violent attack by Ada on Baines, recognition of love, a slow undressing, by now watched by Stewart, and passionate coupling, with piano over. Afterwards there is shared confusion and sadness. What now? During the process of dressing again, Ada loses a button which falls through the floor onto Stewart hiding underneath – part of a series of events in which buttons unite and divide across class, race, generation and gender, which I have not had space to explore. There is again a Sirkian use of mirrors to indicate subjectively experienced relational change. (Halliday, 1971: 79).

Within Stewart's household, relationships between Ada and Flora have apparently become more relaxed and they play together on the bed, Ada's hair now totally loosened but also tangled, watched by an excluded but tense Stewart. Next day Ada sets off alone to visit Baines again as promised. Stewart attacks and attempts to rape her on the way as simultaneously Maori break into Stewart's house and 'rape' the Piano. Stewart's attempts are interrupted by the arrival of Flora, dressed as an angel but with twisted wings, calling 'Mama! Mumma! They are playing *your* piano!'

FLORA: CHANGING ALLIANCES

Later again, Stewart, with Flora's help, is boarding up the house to imprison Ada and Flora within. Flora reproaches Ada in the name of Stewart whom she now calls Papa. Ada's relationship with the Piano is changing: she plays harsh chords, she abandons it in mid-tune, she plays it unconsciously in a sleepwalking incident during the night. Ada and Flora wash clothes with Flora leading, under guard by Stewart. Campion's notes tell us that Flora's beaming arises because '... *she is enjoying the feeling of having a family of which she is now the boss*' (Campion, 1993: 89).

Ada has rediscovered not only her power of love, released both for Flora and for Baines, but also the power of her sexuality, like Catherine in *Jules and Jim* (and her namesake in *Wuthering Heights*), which she now exercises on Stewart without permitting any reciprocity from him. (Campion acknowledges *Wuthering Heights* (1993: 140) as an influence on *The Piano*, as Q.D. Leavis argued long ago (1969) it might have been unconsciously on the former film and Roche's novel on which it was based (see also Frankenberg, 1978).

In a semi-comic interlude, dampening down the emotional intensity between the two great climactic events of the film, Morag and Nessie reappear, assuming that the barricades are to keep the Maori out and, unconscious of either colonial or sexual irony, they reproach Stewart for barricading the doors on the outside. They announce Baines's imminent departure and attribute it to the fact that 'He has got in too deep with the natives'. Nessie, Morag says, has also formed an unsuitable attachment to him. Stewart, however, like the male protagonists in Campion's other works, assumes that since Ada is now paying him some sexual attention, all is going to be well. After extracting apparent promises from Ada that she will stay away from Baines, he relaxes his guard and removes his barriers. She keeps her word, but removing a key from the Piano, she fire-engraves on it in a fine Victorian hand: 'Dear George, you have my heart, Ada McGrath.' She seeks out Flora and finds her still wearing Angel's wings, playing at housewife doing the wash. Ada sends her off reluctantly with the key wrapped in cotton, despite Flora's significantly plural protest 'We're not supposed to visit him.' On the way Flora changes route, goes along the side of the unfinished fence on which Stewart is working with Maori attendance and sometimes assistance, singing 'The Noble Duke of York' as she goes, and delivers the little parcel to Stewart instead: 'Mama wanted me to give this to Mr Baines ... I thought maybe it was not a proper thing to do ... Shall I open it?' He drops the key as he rushes off after opening the packet and a Maori complains, 'It will not sing, the Piano has lost its voice.' Stewart returns to his hut where he finds Ada at the Piano which he strikes viciously with an axe. He drags the still silent Ada, out into the woodyard, where the rain is now pouring heavily, forces her hand on the block and with the axe cuts off one of her fingers to the sound of Flora's anguished screams. Ada sinks into the thick mud and Flora's wings and clothing are bespattered with mud and blood. Stewart wraps the finger in a white handkerchief and says to Flora 'Take this to Baines. Tell him if she ever tries to see him again, I'll take off another and another' (scenes 120–8 inclusive; Campion 1993: 104–10 in which the Maori pay a farewell tribute to Baines and Baines gets the schoolchildren to read him Ada's message and returns to his hut are not on the video version). We see Flora arrive at the hut and eventually showing the severed finger and reporting: 'He says you're not to see her or he'll chop her up.' There is anger and confusion which Hira eventually calms down and the film cuts to Stewart first singing 'Some enchanted evening' to the sleeping Ada, then undressing her and himself and preparing to make love to her. She wakes and looks at him. He retreats and we see him out-doors, armed with a gun, making his way to Baines's hut. He negotiates his way past the sleeping Hira and Flora's washed clothes to point the gun at Baines whom Flora is now sleeping beside. Baines wakes and a conversation follows, prototypical of this kind of dramatic situation, in which the two men are united and recon-ciled through their shared love of Ada. Stewart reveals that Ada has spoken directly to his mind. She is afraid of her will and Stewart must release her to go with Baines. Campion's late modernist twist to the story, although we don't yet know this, is that Ada is going to survive at least physically (cf. Bronfen, 1992). Flora's last au-tonomous act is to wash her Angel's wings in the stream. In the closing scenes we see that the Piano does not survive. As it sinks, accompanied by a rare burst of orchestral music, a Maori declares: 'It is a coffin, let the sea bury it,' indicating that it takes with it the Ada and Flora with whom we have been concerned. The future, as we are soon told, perhaps with aporia (see Sirk's comment on the happy end in Halliday, 1971: 132) suggested by Ada's having her face covered with a black headscarf, is suburban domestic bliss but not without passion. Flora's last appearance is prototypically child-ish, she is doing somersaults on a suburban lawn and her image is appropriately blurred.

UNA COSI DETTA CODETTA

Jane Campion was born in New Zealand and lived there, in Australia, in Paris, in England. At some time she thought of making a film like *The Piano*. She mobilized resources and locations and, in co-operation directly with several hundred other people and indirectly with thousands more, she succeeded in causing to be created and distributed a work of that name of which she could claim, in some sense, authorship. The resultant film could be and was projected to millions in cinemas and other public buildings and on semi-private video screens. She could not predict (or even care perhaps) that amongst these millions would be students of anthropology concerned especially with the lives and deaths of children and with the experience of bodily change in general. She could certainly not dictate how we ought to read or experience it. My point is to show how anthropologists might add, even indirectly, to the resources with which they seek to understand the situations which confront them by influencing the questions they pose and the problems they perceive. The arguments for focusing on the particular themes of 'childhood' and the 'body' are twofold. First, as I have tried to indicate, because there is, at least in Western tradition, a bias against paying undue attention to each, either separately or in conjunction; second, it is not just that interesting phenomena in themselves are thereby neglected but also that the general analysis and understanding is totally impoverished.

I also wanted to show that one of the reasons that Campion's film had such wide emotional and intellectual appeal was precisely because it presented experience in nineteenth-century New Zealand as at once very specific and as giving rise to the possibility of much more general empathies and intuitions. Certainly Campion reminds us visually quite often of the importance of metonymic or metaphoric mirrors in defining ourselves and the transitions backwards and forwards between them. It is also interesting, and underlined by differences in the order of scenes between book and film, that she is able in the medium of film to recognize the complexity of temporality in real life, in a way that both novelists and anthropologists find much more difficult in narrative prose. Whatever the order of events in the past, they are now simultaneously present as, of course, may be future expectations.

Finally, and perhaps most importantly, I think her film helps us to see the relationship between events in the world at large (the rise of capitalism, colonialism, the interaction and merging of cultural forms) which are relatively (*relatively*) easy to describe and document and events which directly invest our personal lives and experiencing bodies. Film makers, authors, visual artists and poets have always been much better at doing this than social scientists or cultural analysts and infinitely better at doing so than politicians and statesmen; clinicians, educationists and 'responsible' adults. Revolution and health education both, may be argued with objectivity and impeccable, irrefutable scientific rationality and still be totally meaningless and counterproductive as an explanation or as a guide to action at the level of the practising subject. I have tried to show by partially contextualizing one film the ways in which, consciously and unconsciously, within the text and by external resonance, some works of art may reveal what works of regurgative (rather than creative and imaginative) science reductively conceal. Postmodernist critique of anthropology and denial of metanarrative may sometimes be overstated to the point of absurdity, the tragedy of the so-called scientific backlash may be the apparent belief that to be accused of writing fiction is not the praise intended but to be called a liar and a cheat.

NOTE

1. The framework and basic ideas of this chapter were presented to and benefited from a seminar at Keele in 1993 organized by the editor under the auspices of the ESRC. It was originally suggested by and had already benefited from discussions with students and colleagues at Brunel. Ideally, the reader who is not familiar with Campion's work should watch a video of *The Piano* before, or even perhaps instead of, reading the chapter. If the spirit nevertheless moves to read the chapter, it might then be a logical outcome to watch the video again afterwards. I thought it appropriate to allow the general lines of the plot to emerge from my meta-narrative rather than to present an, inevitably inadequate, summary. Should Anne Mobbs or Colin Macarthur happen to read it they might either be surprised that their influence has lasted so long or dismayed that it has been so misconstrued. The latter, at least, might applaud my recognition of non-diegetic syntagms. I am also grateful to Annelise Middelthon who, with difficulty, forced me to recognize that metonym was at least as important as metaphor.

8 Faith in the Body? Childhood, Subjecthood and Sociological Enquiry
Nick Lee

INTRODUCTION

This chapter concerns a recent change in the status of child witnesses in criminal trials in England and Wales. Adult witnesses have long enjoyed the dignity of being treated as 'speaking subjects' capable of more or less accurately reporting past events. Children's ability to perform as speaking subjects in court and thus their ability to report past events accurately, has been in question. Since in cases of sexual abuse the child may be the only witness to the alleged crime, this has presented difficulties in procuring convictions. Because of the question mark over children's subjecthood, evidence abstracted from the bodies of children has been understood as more reliable than their spoken testimony. This has been complicit with the view that since children are closer to 'nature' than adults, the most reliable forms of knowledge of them are to be found by investigating them as 'objects'. As Morss (1996) argues, this view has, in the past, led developmental psychology to view processes of development as natural, quasi-biological processes. The truth of the child is to be found in her physical body. In the case of legal rather than scientific debate and evidence, this 'faith' in the body has been just as pronounced.

The provisions of the 1991 Criminal Justice Act allow children to give their 'evidence-in-chief' to the court through the medium of pre-recorded video-taped interviews with them. I will argue that the video medium enables children to perform 'subjecthood' in court. The questions I will address are those of how and why this change in children's status as witnesses has occurred. These questions are about changes in children's status as subjects. My inquiry, then, is based on the contention that ontology is malleable, that 'subjecthood' in court is not to be understood in terms of a determinable relationship between a person's rational faculties and biological make-up, but as the emergent product of variable interactions between persons, modes of evidence making and mediations between past and present.

This starting point, so necessary to the questions at hand given the variability of children's subject status, raises a problem of sociological explanation. Studies of social change often attempt to explain change by positing agents, themselves immune to the change they control, that stimulate observed change (Boudon, 1986). Candidates for this agentic role may include Government, pressure groups, public opinion or even, as we shall see, ideologies. Each of these agents may dictate that change occur. Though their will for change may be interrupted, confounded or supplemented by other factors, these agents operate in many sociological narratives as the originators of change. Sociological explanation, then, is often founded on the instruments and faculties of subjecthood (Game, 1991). But the conditions of applicability of the notion of subjecthood is precisely what children's changing status calls into question. Thus the task of accounting for change in children's subject status is immediately complicated by the fact that sociological accounts of change explain by performing their own distributions of subjecthood. So, if I want to explore the notion that subjecthood and objecthood are malleable, as the question concerning children's status demands, I will be unable to rely on sovereign centres of subjecthood in my account of change. In other words, since children's subjecthood is variable, any consideration of children's status poses a problem for forms of sociological explanation which depend on apportioning commanding subjecthoods. In order to give this important matter the treatment it deserves, I will spend some time arguing against the notion that the change in children's status is the result of a prior change in beliefs concerning the ontological status of childhood. I want to ward off 'beliefs' and idealist treatments of discourse and ideology first, because they are rooted ultimately in subjecthood, and second, because the notion that 'beliefs' rather than 'facts' govern our treatment of children forms the basis of a relativizing strategy for the study of child-related policy which promises to give academic commentators both a power to comprehend such policy and an insensitivity to what I will call the 'practical difficulties' of child protection work.

I will argue that children's ability to perform as speaking subjects is the result of the development of new practices of 'mediation' between child and court. The development of these new practices was called for by practical difficulties of abstracting evidence from children's bodies encountered during the Cleveland Crisis. It was these practical difficulties that stimulated the change in children's court status.

By developing an account that does not ultimately rely on belief or any other faculty of a stable subject as its motor of change, I hope to move some way towards a form of sociological analysis that does not require us to decide ontological matters before we can do anything else. The aim, then, is to develop a way of thinking about children that does not requires us to decide whether they are really incompetent as subjects or not, in other words, to challenge the primacy which that complicitous pair, 'nature and culture', have achieved in our understanding of childhood.

Since the new practices I will refer to involve video technology, they may be understood as untrustworthy artifice. So, first, I will argue for the view that all evidence, whether bodily or verbal, attains credibility only through the application of technique and artifice. In order to avoid the pejorative implications of the word 'artifice', I will use the term 'mediation' to describe these matters.

EVIDENCE AND MEDIATION

Evidence of past events comes in two forms: physical, material traces and linguistic traces carried by human witnesses. These are, respectively, the evidence of objects and of subjects. Many children are capable of carrying both sorts of evidence.

Each form of evidence has its own claim to credibility. Leaving aside for a moment the issue of the credibility of any particular witness, the testimony of a subject depends for its credibility on a commonly attributed faculty of the subject – the ability accurately to preserve a memory trace, and to report on that memory trace without distorting its content. If a witness is incapable of these functions, their testimony will not merit attention. Leaving aside for a moment the issue of the interpretation of physical evidence by expert witnesses, the testimony of the object depends for its credibility on the object's ability to carry traces of past events, and its inability wilfully to distort that record. Both forms of evidence, then, would appear to depend for their credibility on being a medium which is at least capable of bearing and delivering a trace without distortion. By these faculties evidence can be held to connect the past with the present.

Let us now consider the issues of credibility and interpretation which we temporarily shelved. The human witness, equipped with a voice of her own would seem, at first glance, to deliver an unmediated account of past events, while speechless material traces require the mediation of an expert to grant them the power of speech. Both sorts of evidence, however, require mediation of some kind to be credible in court. For example, in court cases which involve the testimony of witnesses, practices of swearing in and laws of perjury have been put in place in an attempt to guarantee that witnesses' memory be converted by them into spoken testimony without distortion. The witness is enjoined to report events as he saw them without allowing lies or fear of, or favour towards, the accused to stand between memorial record and utterance. Just as the physical trace must be mediated to become evidence, so human testimony must similarly be mediated by a passage through court techniques in order to pass as evidence. In the English judicial system, as in many others, a premium is set on unmediated verbal reports, but certain techniques or mediations must be employed to demonstrate that these reports are unmediated or undistorted. Before the past and present may be linked, before testimony can be given, a mediation must first testify that it is possible to consider the testimony which follows as a record of the past. An artifice is required to vouch for the good faith of physical or verbal evidence.

In the case of physical evidence, prosecuting and defence counsel must demonstrate that although their evidence is necessarily mediated by an expert interpreter, the interpreter has restricted herself to those forms of mediation that allow the physical trace to 'speak for itself'. The expert's performance under cross-examination, along with other demonstrations of her expertise, is one of the means by which the appearance of unmediated evidence may be engineered. Once again we find a premium set on the production of reports that can pass as unmediated – once we find the expert credible, we can safely forget their intervention and treat the physical trace as if it speaks for itself.

Good evidence, then, like good photo-journalism, becomes 'good' by effacing the mediations, artifice or effort that have gone into producing the effect that it can be read as unmediated. The evidence maker, like the photo-journalist must be able to manage the unsolvable antinomy between the artifice of their product and the occurrence of the events their product records. They must manage mediation so that when their product is used, the significance of the artifice involved is minimized.

As we have seen this holds for spoken testimony just as it holds for physical evidence. There is, for example, a fine and moveable line between 'coaching' and preparing a witness to give testimony. Where a witness is deemed to have been 'coached', mediation has failed to efface itself. An example of this can be found in the 1980s controversy over the acceptability of records of 'disclosure' interviews between therapists and children as evidence in court (Butler-Sloss, 1988: 206–9; Stainton Rogers and Roche, 1994: 101). Much dispute over evidence in the courtroom takes the form of attempts to expose the mediated nature of evidence to view and thus to render it unreliable as a record of past events.

These preliminary comments do not indicate an indiscriminate scepticism on my part with regard to the occurrence of past events. Instead, I am suggesting that it is difficult to connect the past with the present because such a connection must follow a forked and crooked path and yet appear straightforward. The way in which those connections are established and challenged within our courts (swearing in, cross-examination, etc.) characteristically involve evidence makers in the management of mediation to produce the appearance of the unmediated. In other words, though court proceedings put a premium on the unmediated, the passage between past and present that is represented by credible evidence, cannot be secured without the application of technique.

MEDIATION AND THE CONDITION OF CHILDHOOD

I have so far suggested that evidence, whether verbal or physical, can be understood as neither a straightforward, unmediated record of past events, nor can it be understood as simple fabrication. The skill of producing evidence that will pass as a straightforward record of past events is the skill to mediate in such a way as to conceal the necessary mediation. Turning to the question of child abuse, a child's body can be seen potentially to offer us two sorts of evidence. On the one hand, as a physical object, the body may carry non-linguistic traces of past abuse in the form of bodily marks and reactions (see Swann, 1993). On the other hand, if the child can speak, she may carry memory traces deliverable through language.

The general requirement that evidence be mediated in such a way as to appear unmediated holds for both these sorts of children's evidence as it does for that of adults.

My focus on mediation is intended to divert our attention from what often seems to be the most pressing question concerning children; that of whether they are really incompetent or not, whether, for example, any quasi-biological factors may prevent some children from being able to act as witnesses. As you may have noticed, I have given very little direct attention to this issue, even though it may be argued that any consideration of children's treatment in court must base itself on such a determination. Thus, I have offered no account of why children should pose a problem for legal truth regimes in the first place. I have instead adopted a strategy through which childhood and materiality may be considered together without lapsing into a quasi-biological determination of children's status. Since the testimony of both adults and children relies on mediation, to analyse evidence making in terms of mediation is to explore a plane of analysis that is beneath that plane on which attributions of subjecthood and objecthood, and discriminations between adults and children occur. The events and processes I will identify and discuss, then, take place before subject/object discriminations have been made and are thus in a position to inform such discriminations. Therefore any attempt on my part to decide whether children are really competent or not would be premature.

There has been long-standing doubt over the credibility of children's spoken testimony. This amounts to doubt over children's ability to 'speak for themselves' and thus over their ability to speak authentically. Because of various notions of the psychological constitution of children (see Walker Perry and Wrightsman, 1991), prior to the 1991 Act, the available courtroom techniques for producing unmediateness were inadequate to the task of allowing children to be seen as 'speaking for themselves'. Prior to the 1991 Act, courts had no techniques of mediation suitable for such problematized witnesses.

Until recently, then, children's ability to act as sources of credible evidence in court cases concerning their own alleged abuse had been skewed toward the mute testimony of their bodies. Physical evidence from a child's body could be more easily rendered credible than the child's verbal testimony. Children were more credible when consulted as objects than when consulted as subjects. Despite the likelihood that the criminal sexual maltreatment of children has been experienced, remembered and spoken of by children for many years, it took the clinical identification the 'Battered Child Syndrome' (Kempe et al., 1962) to make it officially visible. In a continuation of this trend, the responsibility for the production of reliable evidence of child abuse has involved medics (specialists in the body), rather than therapists (specialists in the word). Clinical expertise has been required to draw marks and non-linguistic responses through the crossing of mediation and unmediation. Each of these marks and behaviours has required the intervention of an expert medical interpreter to allow it to appear to 'speak for itself'. The child's voice and memory have thus been sidelined as sources of evidence.

Attempts have more recently been made, however, to work on the conditions in which children speak so as to change this situation. The technique of the 'disclosure interviews' used by therapists in the 1980s was an attempt to match any pressure on children from putative abusers to remain silent with pressure from the therapist to disclose their putative abuse. In this case a silencing mediation was countered with the therapists mediation, to reveal the putative unmediated past event of abuse. The 1988 and 1991 Criminal Justice Acts also made attempts to change the conditions under which children spoke in order to allow them the possibility of credibility. Two of these strategies, the 'disclosure interview' and the provisions of the 1988 Act, were based on attempts simply to remove mediations to expose the unmediated. I will shortly describe the relevant provisions of the 1988 Act. The relevant provisions of the 1991 Act, however, employed a different strategy. They allow a new supplementary layer of mediation to come between the child and court – the video record of an investigative interview between child and a two-person Police and Social interviewing team. As I will argue, the 1991 Act was inspired less by a belief or disbelief in children's competence as witnesses and more by the events of the Cleveland Crisis (Butler-Sloss, 1988), which gave an example of the failure of bodily evidence to display itself as unmediated.

If, as I have argued, the testimony of a human is dependent on the testimony of a mediation, this allows us to refine the question of why children's voices are now more easily acceptable in court. Credibility of evidence can be seen as no longer dependent merely on our judgements of the person giving evidence. It also depends on the ability of the mediations secretly to vouch for the human. Our belief in testimony is a matter of mediation, technique and artifice as much as a matter of judgements concerning witnesses status with regard to subjecthood. So rather than ask what beliefs we must have in order to hear children as 'speaking for themselves' I will ask what problems and solutions in the practice of evidence production have made it possible. Rather than account for change as the result of a prior increase in children's credibility as subjects – a change in beliefs about children – I will argue that it is the result of a decrease in the credibility of the physical trace and a subsequent application of new sophisticated techniques for the management of mediation in the case of children's verbal evidence. A change in beliefs about children's credibility, then, was not the sponsor of changes in policy, but, where a change in the conditions of possibility underlying the credibility of children has occurred, it is the result of the application of new techniques of mediation. 'Beliefs' were no doubt involved in this policy change. It would be absurd to call for the censorship of all analytic concepts redolent of taken-for-granted attributions of subjecthood. The issue here is not whether 'beliefs' are to be believed in or not, but how to avoid the confusions that would attend any attempt to account for shifting ontologies in terms of an ontology that is presumed to be static. If indeed we can find a role for 'belief' once our non-subjectivist account is in place, so much the better for that account. One thing is certain however; this account will have no place for 'belief' as long as 'belief' insists upon its erstwhile narrative rights to autonomy and to a position of ultimate control over events.

CHILDREN 'SPEAKING FOR THEMSELVES'

One attempt to allow children to be treated as subjects and to 'speak for themselves' in court involved the abandonment of a standard court technique for managing mediation. The Criminal Justice Act 1988 reformed the law by allowing a court to convict on the uncorroborated evidence of a single unsworn child (Stainton Rogers and Roche, 1994). Since questions might have been raised over a child's ability to comprehend the obligation to tell the truth in court, the swearing in practice was deemed irrelevant to some children and was thus waived. Dropping the requirement that children's testimony could only be credited if accompanied by corroborating evidence, similarly seems to open the way for children to speak for themselves. But the lifting of such mediations was not to be understood simply on the model of lifting barriers to allow the free flow of children's memories. When it comes to evidence, the unmediated heart of significance is a fantasy. As we have seen, mediation has a dual function, at once allowing testimony to be discredited as evidence and allowing testimony to stand as evidence. To remove certain mediations can get us no closer to the 'unmediated' since 'speaking for oneself' calls for mediation. To remove barriers is to remove practices by which the credibility of evidence can exhibit itself, thus, the removal of swearing in is the removal of a technique that vouches for the witness. Further, since witnesses who make unsworn statements are not subjected to cross-examination (King, personal communication), the removal of swearing in also removed this second practice through which children may have become potentially credible.

The 1988 Act was followed by new provisions for child witnesses with the publication of the Criminal Justice Act 1991 and its companion guidance document the Memorandum of Good Practice on Video Recorded Interviews with Child Witnesses for Criminal Proceedings (Home Office and Department of Health, 1992). The Sloss Report on the Cleveland Crisis (Butler-Sloss, 1988) was published between the two Criminal Justice Acts. The significance of the Report for changing legislation will shortly be explored.

Children in England and Wales were given a new role by the 1991 Act and a new way of giving testimony in court cases concerning their alleged abuse. Across the country, in accordance with the Memorandum, special interview rooms, arrays of video and audio equipment and styles of questioning were developed to allow children to speak of their past experience. If investigation led to a prosecution, then the video record of an interview with a child was admissible in court as the child's evidence-in-chief in the prosecution case. They need only be present in court for cross-examination based on this initial testimony (see Stainton Rogers and Roche, 1994 for full details of the conditions surrounding the use of video recorded interviews). Over recent years, then, we have been presented with two changes in the distribution of rights to testify, the first (1988) which aimed at 'barrier removal' in an attempt to reveal the unmediated truth of the child's experience, and the second (1991) which has taken place through an extension of the techniques for the management of mediation, both in its obvious form where it corrupts evidence, and in its tacit form where it presents opportunities for evidence to become credible. The 1991 Act created a path that children could follow to reach the self-presence of subjecthood or the ability to be understood as 'speaking for themselves'. But the path to self-presence wound away from the imagined unmediated heart of significance and through mediation and technique. These apparent detours were in fact necessary given the problematic relationships between past and present as analysed above. So, when the recommended approach to interviewing children is used (Home Office and Department of Health, 1992: 15), mediation in the form of 'leading questions' is minimized, allowing us to hear the child's words *as if* they were unprompted. When interviewers build a rapport with the child (Home Office and Department of Health, 1992: 15), mediation in the form of the child's anxiety is minimized, allowing us, and hopefully the child, to *forget* that the interview is not a naturalistic situation. When two cameras are employed to record the interview, one focused on the child, one on the whole room (Home Office and Department of Health, 1992: 48), mediation in the form of editing is minimized, allowing us to forget that the record has been produced through technological devices.

Though the mute body of the child is still consulted in investigation, the child's own voice and memory have been activated as potentially reliable sources of evidence concerning past events. Rather than attempting to achieve this along the lines of the Criminal Justice Act 1988 by simply removing a layer of mediation, this strategy relies upon creating new forms of mediation and new techniques for managing mediation. The child's voice and memory have thereby been rendered testable in courts, thus providing the conditions of possibility for children to enjoy 'subjecthood'. Where once the child's voice was treated as beyond the question of its trustworthiness or untrustworthiness, delivered as it was from a suspect subjectivity, it can now be subject to that question, and thus play a part in a court case. The child as a material body or 'object' has always had a place in the 'truth regime' of criminal justice, but now the child as memorizer, speaker or as 'subject' has also been brought into that truth regime. As a complement of this shift, as I will argue more fully later, clinical expertise, concerning physical symptoms has been pushed to the sidelines of investigation into allegations of child abuse, making way for the Police and Social Work joint investigative team. Before I give my account of this shift, I will first discuss approaches to this question which would account for it as the result of a prior change in belief about children's status as subjects.

GENERAL CULTURAL CHANGE?

If, as I have suggested, sociological explanations of change often depend on agents such as pressure groups, ideologies, governments, etc., which derive their explanatory powers from their resemblance to 'subjects', the notion that changes in children's treatment are the result of 'general cultural change' is at once the most powerful and the weakest of explanations. General cultural change gains explanatory power by a treatment of 'culture' as an homogeneous super-subject. When 'the culture' changes its mind, everything changes. But there is no analytic gap to separate general cultural change from the matters it is supposed to influence. There is no room in such an account to specify 'mechanisms' of change. To resort to 'general cultural change' is to refuse the complexity of the social and to refuse the task of analysis and explanation, thus, viewed in terms of the task of sociological analysis, it is a tautological excuse for ignorance. It is hardly surprising that 'general cultural change' enjoys little currency amongst academic commentators. In some circumstances however, a currency is enjoyed by figures that are similar to 'the culture' in scale, in totality of self-governance and in explanatory power. Jenks for example, mobilizes the notion of 'the public' (Jenks, 1996: 191) as a homogeneous subject in a discussion of 'violent children'. Though the limitations of the notion of 'general cultural change' are clear, it seems that a paradox, best exemplified by the simultaneous weakness and strength of 'general cultural change', haunts the logic of sociological accounts. Absolute explanatory power meets absolute explanatory ineffectiveness in the figure of general cultural change; it says too much and too little. The more we grant one agent autonomy and control in our accounts, the less sensitive we are to complexity and to the demands of analysis and explanation. It is because of this that I find the use of other subject-related explanatory terms, like 'belief' and 'ideology' to underestimate the complexity of the means by which child-related policy changes. Were we to adopt a subject-based vocabulary, then the subtle changes in the status of children which we intended to examine would be drowned out by a cacophony of adult beliefs, ideologies or discourses. Once we had granted that the field of inquiry was dominated and controlled by such ready-made autonomous agents we would lose any sense that the production of evidence might be conditioned by unpredictable events beyond the influence of such agents, and thus lose any ability to recognize and to take seriously into consideration that the production of good evidence and the production of workable policy is difficult.

RELATIVISM AND THE EXPLANATION OF POLICY CHANGE

Since matters of the 'general culture' might be boiled down to matters of shared belief, is it possible that more sophisticated accounts of the treatment of children, which depend on notions of shared belief, share some of the problems we have identified with our 'general culture' account?

If we are to account for children's treatment (say, the exclusion of their verbal evidence from the courts of yesteryear), to bring it into question in any way, then we are likely to relativize the rationale for that treatment, to question the factual bases of the authoritative knowledges that inform that treatment. We would seek to approach 'statements of fact' about childhood as if they were 'statements of belief', or excavate beneath those 'statement of fact' to discover the values and beliefs they are built on. To do this would be to claim that those treatments are the result of 'social constructions', 'beliefs' or 'ideologies'. To those who would explain the exclusion of children's verbal testimony as a rational response to their real incapacities, we could reply that that characterization of childhood tells us more about adults and their beliefs than it tells us about children.

Having thus severed a policy from its basis in fact and rationality, having converted every question into one of more or less shared belief, what resources are we left with when we come to the task of explaining changes in practice? We have little but ideas and beliefs that have changed according to some unspecified principle, and now are sending their influence over practice as a dropped stone sends ripples over the surface of a pond. One dominant set of beliefs has been replaced by another, one dominant discourse by another.

It seems that nothing can be said about the reason for the change of belief. There is nothing to account for the movement over time from one dominant construction, discourse or set of beliefs to another, save reference to the winning of a battle between them. Once understood as the becoming-dominant of a dominant set of beliefs, the emergence of new policy is given no explanation other than the becoming-dominated of another set of beliefs. For example, when Freeman (1992) debates the reasons for the emergence of the Children Act 1991 with Fox Harding (1991), it is in terms of which 'value positions' the Act reflects and is governed by. We are really not so far from calling on 'general social change' to cover our embarrassment – perhaps a set of beliefs in operation in a relatively small arena gain strength from the unaccountable triumph of a set of beliefs in operation in a wider context. If we rely on 'beliefs' in this way, we will surely end up 'begging the question' of change and will gain no insight into the conditions under which children may enjoy the benefits of, or be exposed to the rigours of, 'subjecthood'.

If we require a more thorough understanding of the emergence of children's spoken testimony, we might turn our attention away from explanations based on 'belief'. We might reason that 'beliefs' and the particular relativizing strategy they rely on for their identification by the analyst deny the possibility that some practical difficulty might have informed that emergence. Here I have in mind not the practical difficulties attendant upon some quasi-biological limitations that are peculiar to children, but those difficulties of mediation-management encountered by evidence makers as they attempt to connect the past and the present. Once we see things in terms of belief, we will see nothing but groups of people who share certain beliefs about childhood, and the ultimately senseless conflict between such groups. We will see the emergence of policy as nothing but the settling of dust after the battle of beliefs has been won, and the policy itself as nothing but a reflection of the new 'dominant discourse'.

We stand in danger of writing as if belief precedes and governs practice without respect for practical difficulties. One reason to be suspicious of this is the ease with which such work could occupy the seat of judgement over the conduct of policy-makers and evidence makers. We might develop a mode of study that edits out any practical difficulties that may be encountered by finite, temporal creatures like us when we attempt the tricky task of linking the past with the present. Only entities capable of the pure abstractions of idealism could ever be free to simply ignore the passage of time. In sum, we will have ignored the limitations experienced by people as embodied creatures.

Given this unexpected consequence of relativism – to lead researchers to ignore the real and practical difficulties of converting traces into evidence – it is surprising that it has now become the industry standard of social research into policy concerning children (Hallett and Birchall, 1995; Wattam, 1992). It is now a matter of record that different people hold different beliefs about childhood, and that this may be significant in the development and implementation of policy. No doubt this is the case. But if we allow that 'belief' governs practice in this fashion it is a short step to concluding that the adoption of good beliefs and the rejection of bad beliefs will suffice to guarantee well-made policy and proper implementation of that policy. This bears on the political issue of the relationship between academic inquiry and those who perform child protection investigations. Through the systematic exclusion of the inherent difficulties of evidence production academic commentators risk becoming little more than the police of belief.

A STUDY OF MEDIATION IN EVIDENCE MAKING

Let us now return to the question of how children's courtroom status has changed. It is possible to account for this change in the treatment of children, this redistribution of speaking rights, in a way that undercuts the over-publicized procession of beliefs and, by doing so, attends to the practical problems of evidence-making. The practical problems I point to here result from the general problem of evidence and mediation referred to earlier. To restate this: We can rely on neither human witness nor physical evidence to be simply unmediated; whenever a human or object appears to speak for itself in an unmediated fashion within court, we can be sure that this appearance is achieved by the careful application of mediations. On this view, the oath taken by witnesses in criminal trials is not an assurance that the witnesses' testimony is unmediated by deceit, but a device that vouches for the status *as testimony* of what they go on to say.

If we take this approach, then, we will circumvent both the question of which beliefs about children's subjecthood are correct and the analytic limitations of relativism. We will attend to the management of the necessity of mediation in the production of passable children's evidence instead. Once this path is taken we may formulate our question of why children's voices have now come to be heard in court in terms of earlier problems encountered in managing that common problem of evidence-making – making the mediated seem unmediated.

My argument is that the mediated/unmediated problem was revealed as in need of attention when a single physical sign was used as if it were an entirely unmediated and sure record of past abuse. Once faith in the object was questioned, the necessary element of artifice in all evidence became clear. This allowed the development of new techniques of evidence production (video testimony) to seem both acceptable and necessary. I am concerned here with the physical phenomenon 'Reflex Anal Dilatation' and the role it played in the Cleveland Crisis. I will argue that the emergence of children's voices in court is not to be attributed to a prior cultural decision to have faith in children's subjecthood, but as a reaction to a clear demonstration of the limitations of evidence yielded by children in their role as physical objects. When children's bodies became patently unreliable, the mediations necessary for their treatment as speaking subjects were developed.

Before I turn to my account of the emergence of children's testimony, I would like to summarize the distinctive features of the approach I develop here. Instead of postulating a number of belief-sets and accounting for policy change in terms of their interaction, I will focus on the gap between past and present that cannot be filled, but is open to management. In place of the contest of beliefs and ideologies, I offer a 'material semiotics' (Game, 1991) of evidence making which follows the conversion of traces, bodily and linguistic, through various forms of mediation into a state of 'speaking for themselves', that they may stand as evidence.

THE CLEVELAND CRISIS

Between February and July 1987 in the County of Cleveland, 125 children were diagnosed as sexually abused by local paediatricians. As the number of diagnoses increased, questions were raised over the accuracy of the diagnoses. A particular concern was the use of Reflex Anal Dilatation (described later) as a diagnostic sign of abuse. Arguments over the utility of this sign and over the separation of children from their parents were fierce and occasioned hostility between representatives of the Health and Social Services on the one hand and police on the other.

The Cleveland Report cited failures of communication and understanding and 'differences of views' (Butler-Sloss, 1988: 243) between Health, police and Social Services as causes of the Crisis. Amongst these, there was a 'difference of view' between a paediatrician (Dr Higgs) and a police surgeon (Dr Irvine) concerning the utility of 'Reflex Anal Dilatation' as a diagnostic sign of past sexual abuse. The Report charges that the failure of the agencies concerned to prevent this difference from producing warring factions amongst Health, police and Social Service employees lay at the heart of the Crisis. The controversy was over how much faith could be placed in the behaviour of children's bodies as a record of past events.

WHAT IS REFLEX ANAL DILATATION?

RAD is a putative indication of a past episode of buggery. The Report did not use the term 'Reflex Anal Dilatation', reserving judgement over the reflexive nature of the response, but described Anal Dilatation as follows:

> when the buttocks are separated, the external sphincter and then the internal sphincter open so that the observer can see through the anal canal into the rectum. (Butler-Sloss, 1988: 190)

Since a similar response to buttock separation had long been observed in what the Report quaintly describes as the 'passive homosexual', and since some medical literature (Hobbs and Wynne, 1986) had reported 'dilatation and reflex dilatation' as occurring amongst a host of other anal features in children who had been buggered, the consultant paediatrician, Dr Higgs, found reason to use RAD as evidence to support 'diagnoses' of sexual abuse. Over 100 children were diagnosed as sexually abused between February and July 1987 by Dr Higgs and her colleague Dr Wyatt. Many of these diagnoses were supported by their detection of the RAD phenomenon. Over the following months, in most cases, allegations of abuse were subsequently dropped.

Although Dr Higgs told the Inquiry that her diagnoses were not based on RAD alone,

> The children in which I thought there were signs of sexual abuse I felt were children that needed to be examined in that way for a *variety of reasons*, as well as having *referrals from other agencies* such as social workers . . . (Butler-Sloss, 1988: 141: my emphasis)

the report concluded that in Dr Higgs' and Dr Wyatt's work, 'The presence of the physical signs was elevated from grounds of "strong suspicion" to an unequivocal "diagnosis" of sexual abuse' (Butler-Sloss, 1988: 243), and that, 'The medical diagnosis assumed a central and determining role in the management of the child and family' (Butler-Sloss, 1988: 243). In other words the Report concluded that Drs Higgs and Wyatt had on occasion treated RAD as so compelling a piece of evidence that it could 'speak for itself' as a record of past abuse apparently without the need for mediation. Drs Higgs and Wyatt treated RAD as a 'breakthrough' in the detection of child abuse. They treated it as a direct indication that a specific injury had been done to children. It was, in their view, such a strong indication that it was able to cut through all indications that nothing untoward had been done to the children. As the Report states, in some cases Drs Higgs and Wyatt gave, 'a firm diagnosis of sexual abuse without other grounds of suspicion, no prior allegation or complaint by adult or child and no social family history . . .' (Butler-Sloss, 1988: 144).

If children were not complaining of abuse, despite exhibiting RAD, this was due to the distorting mediation of the abuser, silencing the child through threats or shame. RAD was able to cut through those mediations, connecting the past with the present in an unbroken line to reveal the unmediated truth of past abuse. The value of RAD was that since it was beyond the influence of the abuser, the response of a child's anus to buttock separation constituted an indelible trace of abuse. RAD made up for children's inability to report abuse, and compensated for their inability to speak for themselves. As an autonomous response of the child's body RAD also seemed to dispense with the possibility that Drs Higgs and Wyatt played any mediating role in the passage between past and present. Dr Higgs had faith in the body, in the trustworthiness of materials, in the patent inability of objects to lie or to conceal as opposed to the ability of the speaking subject to do so. RAD led to the imagined heart of unmediated significance that I have previously noted. Because RAD partook of the supposed faithfulness of physical traces, Dr Higgs could also understand the failure of other professionals to find her diagnoses credible as the result of a mediating confusion on their part which concealed the unmediated truth of past events. Amongst the forms of mediation that Dr Higgs could 'break through' using RAD was the 'state of denial' that other professionals exhibited when presented with the 'evidence' of past abuse.

THE FAITHLESS TRACE

It would be easy, with hindsight, to localize blame on individuals and conclude here that Drs Higgs and Wyatt were simply wrong in their 'diagnoses' of sexual abuse, and easier still to aver that they were driven into questionable practices by their conviction that abuse was widespread, and thus, that the seeds of the Cleveland Crisis lay in their 'beliefs' or 'ideologies'. But that would be to ignore the fact that they shared a problem with anyone who attempts to diagnose, to read bodily traces as signs of causal agents. Physical traces never speak directly for themselves, they can only be made to appear to do so. To make physical traces into credible evidence of some past event would require us to manage mediation rather than attempt to abolish it. The paediatricians' only problem was their faith in the possibility of reaching pure unmediatedness, their failure to recognize that mediation cannot be avoided, and is essential to the production of credible evidence.

Against Dr Higgs certainty over the significance of RAD, specialists consulted by the Inquiry were able to muster a range of potential non-criminal causal agents of it. These included 'forceful separation of the buttocks', 'constipation', 'megacolon' (the result of very prolonged constipation), the 'presence of threadworms', the use of 'bronchodilator medicines' and 'fear' (Butler-Sloss, 1988: 191). The possibility was also raised that RAD is a 'normal phenomenon' (Butler-Sloss, 1988: 190). These alternatives tell us that RAD may either be the trace of something non-criminal, or if it was a normal phenomenon, the trace of nothing significant except the practices adopted in medical examination. This possibility suggests that RAD could never stand as an unmediated record of an unmediated past event since it indicates the involvement of the examiner in the production of the response. As the Report notes,

> There were occasions when Dr Higgs and Dr Wyatt elicited anal dilatation at a time when Dr Irvine and Dr Beeby did not. Likewise Drs Paul, Roberts and Clarke did not to our knowledge demonstrate anal dilatation in any child they examined in Cleveland. (Butler-Sloss, 1988: 193)

This suggests not only that the mediation in the form of 'interpretation' can never be simply abolished, but also that the specific conduct of the examination by the examiner constitutes an irreducible mediation. Without the mediating practice of examination, RAD would never exhibit itself, whatever it may mean. None of this should be taken to suggest that RAD is or is not a sign of buggery, but that the connection between past and present is never so straightforward as to allow evidence to be treated, *ab initio*, as unmediated.

Drs Higgs and Wyatt tried to do for a bodily trace what the 1988 Act tried to do for children's memory traces – to find a way to break through deception or break down barriers, to dispense with mediations on the understanding that they prevent access to the unmediated heart of past events. Where the 1988 Act dispensed with swearing in in an attempt to liberate the flow of children's verbal testimony, to allow an imagined uninterrupted passage from the past to the present, Dr Higgs, in the faith she displayed in the incontestable nature of a bodily trace, dispensed with other potentially contradictory traces, in the hope of creating a similar straightforward passage between the past and the present. But, as we have seen, the passage from past to present can never be straightforward. Sharing the goal of the purely unmediated, both strategies encountered the confounding result that the 'breakthrough' or breakdown of barriers led them further from credibility rather than bringing them close to it. Thus the trenchant opposition Dr Higgs found in Dr Irvine the police surgeon.

These disappointments did not arise by accident, nor by misguided zeal alone. They are the result of the feature shared by all forms of evidence; they gain the appearance of unmediated truth not by the demolition of mediations but only through the careful addition of mediations that are contrived in such a way as to minimize the significance of mediation. This episode dramatized the necessity of careful engineering of the mediation of physical evidence, and that the path from the past to the present was not a straight line but was drawn through many points of mediation. Bodily evidence could never speak for itself without the contrivance of mediators. Since it had now been patently demonstrated that the body's evidence was credible only on the similar conditions as verbal evidence, there was reason for what we might term a decrease of 'faith' in the body.

It is important to emphasize that the Report came to no decision as to whether RAD was a sign of buggery or not. Neither the view that it was such a sign, nor the contrary view can be deemed to have triumphed. Instead the Report revealed the irreducibility of the gap between past and present and the impossibility of direct, unmediated access to past events, even through the testimony of objects. The significance of these events for the present argument does not depend on establishing whether one view of or 'belief' about evidence triumphed over another, but on the degree to which they exposed a general and practical problem, that attends evidence making no matter what the 'beliefs' of those concerned may be.

THE CONSEQUENCES FOR THE VOICE OF THE CHILD

As I have argued above, both physical and linguistic types of evidence have their claims to credibility. For many years, the status of children with regard to subjectivity has been in question. Their ability to separate fantasy from reality, to remember and to give accurate account of their memory have all been under suspicion. This has had the effect of compromising the credibility of children as court witnesses to their own abuse. Incredulity towards their testimony has been justified on the grounds that because of the deficits of their subjectivity they are unable to forge acceptable links between past events and the present. Thus the evidence they can provide as objects, in the form of physical traces has had an easier passage through courts, shepherded by experts on the interpretation of bodily marks and responses. Until the Cleveland Crisis, it was relatively easy to forget the mediating role of the physician in producing physical evidence and to have that 'faith' in the body that allows us to read bodily signs as an unmediated connection of the past to the present occurring spontaneously and without artifice. But the mismanaged mediation concerning RAD has shaken the grounds for that faith and revealed the involvement of skilled mediation in the production of the appearance of the unmediated even in the case of the object. In this context, the otherwise dangerous artifice of the video-recorded interview, with all the potential it carries for the interviewer to lead the witness into false statements, can be seen as yet another form of mediation that requires no more caution in its use than does a photograph of a body's response to examination. The precise management of this new video medium takes a different form from the management of an expert's mediation, since the medium is different. As we have seen above, the video images alone are not enough. To make the video into a record of past events, it must be produced in such a way that the mediations it involves can efface themselves. The interviewers must not be seen to lead children to make statements; the tape must pass as unedited; and, a rapport must be built with the child so that the 'artificial' nature of the interview situation may be discounted. But video-recorded evidence is essentially no more and no less fallible than the testimony of a medic.

Perhaps the clearest token of the shift from body to voice can be found in the arrangement of the personnel involved in today's formal procedures for the investigation of allegations of child abuse. Police and Social Workers, experts on the voice, have been drawn into the co-operative compact of Joint Investigative interviewing. The expertise over the body, which played such a crucial role in the Cleveland Crisis is still called upon, but medics now form a satellite of the central police and social work team.

CONCLUSION

It might seem that my arguments have been based on an assumption that the 1991 Act has succeeded in making all instances of children's video testimony eminently credible in court. On this understanding, the sceptical reader might expect me to have produced statistical evidence to back this up in the form of a decisive increase in conviction rates in child abuse cases following the implementation of the new video techniques. As I outline my conclusions, however, it should become clear that far from rendering all children immediately credible, the supplementary mediations represented by the video interview do nothing more than raise children's testimony to the level of acceptability within court hitherto enjoyed by physical evidence mediated by an expert. There now exist mediations that will vouch for children's reports *as testimony*, as instances of children 'speaking for themselves'. This means that children's testimony has been rendered accessible to the same processes of disputation that have always surrounded physical evidence. Defence counsel will be able to challenge the management of mediation involved in producing children's video evidence, to try to expose that mediation and thus spoil the unmediated impression that prosecuting counsel will have produced for it. The success of the provisions of the 1991 Act and the Memorandum, are not therefore measured in terms of conviction rates, but in terms of the parity of courtroom utility that now exists between children's bodily and verbal evidence.

I have argued that rather than being the result of a general change in belief about childhood competencies, the achievements of the 1991 Act are the result of the exposure of the mediations involved in the production of physical evidence, and the subsequent development of self-effacing styles of mediation between child and courtroom in the video interview procedure. If it is now easier for a child's evidence to be considered by a court, and if children seem to have made a leap between being poor testifiers or poor subjects and adequate testifiers or adequate subjects, any change in belief concerning children that we might read into this is the result of technical supplementation which makes good their otherwise untrustworthy status. The burden of my argument has been that practical problems of the production of evidence come first, and changes of believability come second and that changes of belief are not adequate to the explanation of changes in the treatment of children.

On my account, then, it is not necessary to call upon a prior, commanding and decisive shift in belief about children to understand the emergence of their voices in court. To put this another way, children have not shed their ascribed deficiencies as subjects, but the conditions are now in place for children to perform as subjects as well as objects when called upon to provide evidence for the court. The difference between adult and child with respect to the court is that the mediating techniques that allow adults to perform as subjects are very old and those techniques that allow children to perform as subjects are very new.

The case I have made is clearly 'constructionist' (James and Prout, 1990). It depends on the argument that evidence is made rather than found. But by decentring 'belief' in my account I have tried to show that constructionist work on childhood, for all its relativism, need not be 'idealist'. 'Idealist' research in this area would accord priority and command to 'beliefs' and set them and the history of their alteration free from the domain of practice and practical problems. To understand the actions of the makers of evidence and policy principally in terms of their 'beliefs' would be to forget that they are confronted with substantial problems, and thus to deny that they operate in the temporal world. I have emphasized this theoretical point most strongly through an insistence that no matter what we believe about childhood and adulthood, we cannot pretend that the gap between past events and present evidence can be wished away. While I have written of a decrease of 'faith in the body', then, this has been to emphasize the analytic significance of the embodiment of children, makers of evidence and makers of policy.

ACKNOWLEDGEMENTS

The research behind this article was supported by Drs Rex and Wendy Stainton Rogers, and by ESRC studentship No: R00429234180. My thanks also to Dr Alan Prout, Professor Michael King and Dr Rolland Munro for their comments on earlier drafts.

9 Constructing the Bodies of Critically Ill Children: an Ethnography of Intensive Care

Bernard Place

INTRODUCTION

It is difficult not to be struck by the profound changes which occur in children who are admitted to a paediatric intensive care unit (PICU). Culturally recognizable ideas of children as being 'full of life' are dramatically transformed. In the PICU they lie, immobilized, at the boundary of life and death. This chapter outlines some processes involved in effecting this transformation. In doing so it questions the idea that human embodiment is simply concerned with issues of corporeality. Indeed, in a setting like a PICU, the definition of what exactly are the corporeal elements of a child's body are open to negotiation. The boundaries of such a body are constituted by, and contested through, the attachment of non-corporeal, technological, elements. The contesting of such bodily boundaries therefore raises questions about a conception of children's bodies simply as *naturally* occurring entities – biological and physical – and redirects attention to the notion that such entities may consist of heterogeneous elements – technological and figurative – in addition to those of a corporeal character.

The approach I shall take in this chapter is strongly influenced by social studies of scientific knowledge, specifically actor-network theory. This, Callon (1986a) suggests, is underpinned by the three principles of agnosticism (impartiality between actors engaged in controversy), generalized symmetry (the commitment to explain conflicting viewpoints in the same terms) and free association (the abandonment of all a priori distinctions between the natural and the social). The essential feature of actor-network theory is that the power of science arises from the action of both human and *non-human* actors tied together. The translation of an assembled network of heterogeneous elements into an 'immutable mobile' – a text in the form of writing, graphs, formulae, diagrams, etc. – is one strategy by which a network can be stabilized and at the same time allowing it to be moved and recombined with other such texts. Such stabilization, in the context of this chapter, is demonstrated by the production in the PICU of a vital signs observation chart – a text through which the facticity of the critically ill body is both ordered, externalized and merged with its representational form.

My approach suggests that if we wish to examine natural objects, like the body, we must attend to the processes implicated in the practices of their representation and to the sites involved in such work. The PICU is one such location where nature is fabricated through representational practice. Here intensive care nurses do work in which a natural object, a corporeal body, is represented in the form of an inscription produced in the form of a paper 'observation chart'. Such a setting therefore offer a potentially fertile sociological opportunity. If a corporeal body – the critically ill body – exists only in so far as it can be made visible then the *form* of the visibility *is* the phenomenon. Alternative representational forms of the phenomenon would constitute different phenomena. Such phenomena can, thus, be conceived of as resulting from a *situated* process of knowledge production.

THE PICU AS A LIMINAL SPACE

The following data are drawn from an ethnographic study of a paediatric intensive care unit (Place, 1996) located in a metropolitan teaching hospital. Admitting children up to 16 years old from clinical specialities such as respiratory and renal medicine, it also provided specialist services for the care of children with burns or head injuries. With seven beds or cots, 200–250 children were admitted each year. During the period of the fieldwork about one in every six of these children died. Fieldwork consisted of a nine-month period of participant observation and a series of ethnographic interviews with 18 nurses who worked on the Unit.

Every child admitted was cared for by a single nurse each shift. This enabled continuous and close scrutiny of that child in which, tellingly, they were 'looked after'. The problem presented to nurses caring for such children was that the object of their scrutiny, the corporeal body of the child, had little *intrinsic* visibility. For example, when a child was admitted with cardiac disease little information could be elicited by examining the heart in its physical, corporeal, form. Looking at the corporeal body therefore told little of its condition. The first part of this chapter therefore outlines the solution to this clinically pressing dilemma – the process whereby such a body was transformed from one with minimal visibility to one characterized by higher levels of visibility – described in the argot of the intensive care nurses, as the 'sorting out' of the child. The second part of the chapter explores the consequences which arise for in the maintenance of the visibility of this 'sorted out' body, a process involving the 'crafting of resemblance' between the child's corporeal body and its representational form in the technology into which it is, literally and figuratively, embedded.

The PICU, within Western culture at least, offers, I suggest, an unusual example of a liminal space, one betwixt and between stages in a *rite de passage* during which status is lost and gained (Van Gennep, 1960; Leach, 1976: 77; Turner, 1977). In such units, with their symbolic representations of death and rebirth, children lie enigmatically between being alive and being dead, and between being social and non-social entities. Between being human and non-human. Between being people and being things. That is, they can be conceived of as being 'quasi-objects' (Latour, 1993) – *inextricably* part-nature, part-culture, consisting of both 'soft' human flesh and 'hard' technological artefact.

The entrance to the intensive care unit signals a transition of both geographical space and conceptual classification. A *rite de passage* model suggests that at this point of entry a child being admitted to the intensive care unit will undergo a period of physical separation from his or her normal surroundings or kin. After this a period of liminality, betwixt and between, will be experienced. Potentially dangerous, as indicated already, neither dead nor alive, human or non-human activities around such a child will be hedged with ritual to give stability to its new conceptual form.

As the disorder of the corporeal (sick) body which arrives on the PICU is transformed into a more ordered shape it is, in the situated vocabulary of the intensive care nurses, 'sorted out'. The activity of admitting a child to the unit (in which the child moves physically from the world outside to the inside of the unit) is paralleled by a conceptual reversal whereby the inside of its corporeal body moves symbolically to the outside of its integumentary shell.

The disorder which characterized the corporeal form outside the PICU is, inside, transformed into an ordered corporeality. The body is literally 'sorted' – ordered, 'out' – externalized. (See also Christensen, this volume, for a discussion of the inner and outer bodies of children.)

The broad structure of any rite of passage, Turner suggests, involves, first, a period of separation (in the case of the child on the PICU moving in procession from home to hospital, being stripped of ordinary clothes and re-dressed in costumes of other worlds) followed by a period of social timelessness, a liminal state betwixt and between ordinary social structure and buttressed by highly conventionalized and unusual prescriptions concerning, for example, behaviour, food and costume. This also may involve bodily mortification and scarification. In the case of the PICU the admission of the child invariably involves the attachment of many technological artefacts – a kind of 'technodressing' – many of which require the direct, albeit for the most part temporary, mutilation of the child's body. This feature of bodily perforation is characterized by a concerted effort – by doctors in the main but assisted by nurses – of cannulation, intubation, catheterization and the insertion of artefacts into the inside and onto the surface of the corporeal body. The integrity of the body boundary is broken. Staff Nurse Jayne explains:

> BERNARD: How would you explain [to the parents] what is happening when their child is first admitted? What words would you use?
> JAYNE: I'd ask them first of all if anyone had explained about the tube if they were intubated, about the ET [endotracheal] tube . . . I'd explain that if they [their child] needed anything they could put in a drip, put a drip up. And put a tube down into their stomachs. I think that most people know what drips are from the telly. It's the one thing they know about. And if they were putting arterial or central lines in I'd explain that it was so they could continually monitor their blood pressure without continually having to do blood pressures using the machine and that they could take samples to see how much oxygen was in their blood . . .

The effect of this activity is to create a new and extended body boundary composed of both corporeal (skin) and non-corporeal (technological) elements. Once the body boundary has been physically breached, with fluids and gases both entering and exiting it, the breaches and their associated artefacts (ventilators, drips, catheters, drains, ECG leads, etc.) are connected to the surrounding technology. The body re-dressed in the clothes of the PICU, assumes a technological covering of machines, wires and tubes. The body is thus 'externalized'.

In this sense, the body is 'technomorphic' and can grow and change shape simply by the addition of further technological artefacts. The work of the nurses who work on the PICU, then, is to constantly survey, to 'look after', that revised, technological and corporeal, technomorphic body boundary. This work is directed at ensuring there are no unintended leakages of substances from its interior to its exterior; that no blood leaks out of the intravenous tubes *or* through the skin, that no oxygen leaks out of mechanical ventilator circuits *or* through the lung tissue, no urine trickles from the catheter bag onto the floor *or* from the urethra, no fluid oozes from the wound dressing *or* from the wound onto to the bed linen, no cerebrospinal fluid leaks from the CSF drain *or* from the spinal canal etc.. This technological and corporeal ('techno-social') boundary is rigorously policed and cared for with connections (both artefact/ artefact and artefact/corporeal) checked continually. The technomorphic body must remain 'intact'. The corporeal and technological elements which the nurses have assiduously kept together must not be allowed to disassociate. The child's corporeal body is connected, via tubes and wires, to the surrounding space and contextualized within that space. The broken integrity of its corporeal body has been repaired by a new, technological, boundary and the integrity of this 'technomorphic body' is maintained with the same attentiveness as that of the original, corporeal, one. The nurses are not *minding* machines and *caring* for children. *From the child's point of view*, it matters not whether they bleed to death because a technological element of this technomorphism (for example, an arterial cannula) becomes disconnected or whether exsanguination occurs as a result of a failure in a biological corollary (for example, a blood vessel rupturing). Similarly a child may stop breathing as a result of, for example, a pneumothorax (collapsed lung) or as a result of a ventilator tube becoming disconnected.

Such 'technodressing' enables the translation of aspects of the physical, corporeal, body into a conceptual analog – the generation of mathematical symbols which represent the corporeal body.

A sick body becomes a critically ill body as it is 'sorted out' into a numerical, scientific, form. At once ordered it is also visible in its mathematized form. The boundary of the technomorphic body is delineated by the mathematical rationality of the PICU. Cardiac monitors display heart *rates*, urinary catheters bags collect *amounts* of urine, mechanical ventilators deliver breaths of particular *sizes*, intravenous drips infuse various *volumes* of fluid, electronic pumps deliver specific *quantities* of drugs, temperature probes indicate varying *degrees* of heat, blood pressure transducers display varying *numbers*, etc. Such technologies transform matter from one state to another, in this case from the corporeal to the representational. If such technologies are conceived of as 'inscription devices' (Latour and Woolgar, 1986) then they have the ability to transform matter into written documents.

As I have already noted, throughout the period of admitting a child to the intensive care unit (and throughout their stay) the nursing staff are engaged in the production of representations of corporeality. Indeed it is difficult for a stranger to the paediatric intensive care unit not to be struck by the enormous effort invested by the nurses in reading symbols and signs from the medical technologies to which the children are attached and then translating them into textual form (observation charts, case notes, summary charts, laboratory result sheets). The most prominent of these documents is a large paper chart, called the 'obs chart', on which the child's 'vital signs' are recorded. Every child's body, regarded as a unique entity outside the intensive care unit is, regardless of size, age, gender, colour and illness made to 'fit' into this space.

The key feature of this document is that is has a *direct relationship* to the corporeality it represents, a relationship which is artfully constructed during the nursing care of a critically ill child. But it is not simply a process which *reveals* the underlying reality of that corporeality; it works to *constitute* that reality and in doing so works to create the impression that the 'reality' of this child's body exists independently of the means by which it is made known, that the body exists prior to its representation.

It is thus apparent that the further one gets to the *inside* of the intensive care unit, revealed here as a liminal space in which the critically ill body is constituted, the more the clinical gaze of the nurses moves away from the corporeal body of the child towards those devices which *represent* that corporeality. Such a process works to create the impression that the 'reality' of this child's body exists independently of the means by which it is made known, that the body exists prior to its representation. Thus, if a child's body is to be 'observed' then that observation must be directed at those, non-corporeal, locations – technologies and documents – where that body has been made visible.

This work has great practical utility because, in many cases, there is no visible evidence of the child's corporeal body being observably unstable and unsettled because, pharmacologically paralysed and sedated, they are incapable of movement. The identities between these (non-human) texts and the (human) body to which they relate are regarded, for the most part, unproblematically by the intensive care nurses, once the child's body is 'sorted out'.

CRAFTING RESEMBLANCE: TEXTUAL CONSTRUCTION AND THE CRITICALLY ILL BODY

Having suggested that the body is technomorphic and that, in order to 'look after' such a body its heterogeneous elements – corporeal and technological, natural and cultural, human and non-human – are handled with analytical symmetry by the nurses, how then are these elements of the critically ill body – the social and the technical – subsequently separated? How is the enduringly ambiguous relationship between the corporeal body and the technological artefacts into which that body is embedded managed? If, as suggested in this chapter, the peculiar form of the critically ill body involves a suspension of such distinctions then the relationship between exactly what is being explained, (the child's body) and the explanandum (how that body is represented) becomes pivotal. In explaining the bodies of the children they know about (to parents, to doctors and to ethnographers), nurses do not talk merely of the numbers, squiggles and traces evident on the attached technology. They talk of children's bodies. The biographical data generated by the surrounding artefacts is said not simply to *represent* a child's body but to *be* this child's body. And it is to the certainty of this identity that the chapter now turns.

I have suggested that the breaching of the body boundary and subsequent attachment of medical technologies enables a symbolic analog of the body to be generated. However the mere attachment is not enough for constitution of the critically ill body. For example, while these attachments may indeed translate the child's corporeal body into a range of representational analogs there is no certainty that these symbols accord with any conception the nurses have of what is 'really' happening to that body. The 'sorted out' body – ordered and externalized – requires verification. Only then can the nurses *separate* the heterogeneous elements they have combined in the technomorphic body.

This process of verification indicates a 'crafting of resemblance' between the two forms of the child's body – its corporeal and representational analogs. This section uses, as examples, 'the obs' (observations of bodily vital signs *made* by nurses), those phenomena of corporeality used in the PICU to subject the body to scrutiny. The argument presented suggests that these 'obs' help constitute the representation of the corporeal body within the PICU and that once this work has been accomplished the evidence of such nursing work is deleted. The result of this is that the child's body has a form which is antecedent to its representation and as a consequence the corporeal and the technological are seen as separate.

It is argued that the process of translating corporeality into representations of that corporeality – processing nature into a clearer vision – is an inherently ambiguous one because it relies on the establishment of stable networks of essentially heterogeneous elements. Should these networks disassociate any observational claims made about the body under scrutiny will undermined.

Claiming that the corporeal body, in this location, is a product of networks of heterogeneous elements enables the essentially ambiguous relationship between the human and the non-human elements in the network in the PICU to be clarified. Nurses, using inscription devices (those artefacts by which naturally occurring phenomena are translated into representations), can thus clarify the *direction* of the object/representation dyad and, in doing so, separate the elements of the network they have built into its 'human' and 'non-human' parts. The ability to make such distinctions, forming part of the daily work of intensive care nurses, provides a useful introduction to the problems of ambiguity they routinely face.

THE CRITICALLY ILL BODY – HUMAN OR NON-HUMAN?

For the most part nurses take the representations of corporeality – 'the obs' – as having an unproblematic relationship to corporeality.

Numbers generated by inscription devices reveal the corporeality.
Blood pressures, heart rates, oxyhaemoglobin saturations etc., constitute a type of 'metrological talk' which forms the stock in trade
of conversations about corporeality. Such inscriptions are said to
be aspects of the body, inscriptions which, in the day-to-day language of intensive care practitioners, simply reflect some underlying
corporeal reality. However, this relationship between 'reality' and
'representation' can, at times, be a more problematic one. With
alarms sounding continually, nurses are often be heard saying, both
to parents and to inexperienced nurses who seem uncertain of the
source or the significance of the alarm:

'Don't worry it's not him, it's the machine.'

'She's all right, it's just the ventilator.'

In such situations the constructed nature of the relationship between the corporeal and the representational is clear to experienced
nurses in a way it may not always be to those who are less experienced. The 'technomorphic body' made both of human and
non-human elements, is resolved into its constituent parts: 'him'
or 'her' *and* 'the machine'. In this case inscription devices which at
other times, unproblematically, demonstrate a corpo*reality* fail to
do so. When such a dichotomy is clear, intensive care nurses, tellingly, make reference to the concept of 'artefact' – a representation
which bears no relation to the corporeal body. Those who do not
possess the expertise to discern such categorizations can be confounded, as this extended interview fragment illustrates;

... its almost sometimes, when things have been taken off, as if
you have switched the heart off. In fact there was a baby, whose
condition had been fairly stable and mum had been down and
then gone. And about half an hour later this baby had collapsed
and died. They couldn't find the mother, even though she was
on one of the postnatal wards, she had vanished. Eventually they
found her and they found her just before the baby died and she
came down and because she saw one of the nurses switching off
the monitor, because the apex [heart rate] was so low, they felt
it was just going to distress her more seeing it go down to a
straight line and alarming. But because she had switched the
monitor off the mother went 'ape' and she [the nurse] was then

accused of having stopped the baby's heart. Because she'd switched the monitor off it was *her* fault the baby had died. Because she had switched it off she had killed the baby. She had switched the heart off. She tried explaining it, but this lady was very distressed, she was hysterical at this point. So she couldn't really explain it then, and she was just being accused constantly, which, of course, really upset her. And then the next day they were explaining this is what happened, but I don't think she ever believed that's what happened. I think she will always believe that because that monitor was switched off the baby's heart was stopped. And that was a very intelligent woman. (Staff Nurse Clare)

The relationship between the corporeal and the representational is, in these illustrations, completely inverted, highlighting further that such inscriptions are not passive reflections of corporeality. The corporeal is *constructed* through the inscription. For the most part, however, ambiguity in the relationship between what is 'human' and what is 'technology' endures:

> I think it's because they [the parents] are so used to their child, and not used to the machines, that they start believing the machines all the time and they are surrounded by machinery. Even the syringe pumps, even the temperature probes, everything is machinery and *you lose the child somewhere in between*, don't you? They are in the bed somewhere and they are surrounded by all this stuff. (Staff Nurse Marise)

How then do nurses say with such certainty 'Don't worry it's not him, it's the machine' when often 'it is *not* the machine and it *is* him'? The cost of making a mistake here about the state of a critically ill body for both a nurse and a patient is, potentially, disastrous for both. If nurses read either the representation ('the machine') or the body ('him/her') incorrectly, confusing 'the machine' for 'him', they will embark on a course of clinical action which exacerbates, rather than ameliorates, the corporeal disorder they aim to remedy. Such ambiguity forces a continual attention to the nature of the technomorphic imbroglio and is essential for a resolution of the confusion of categories as to what is human and what is non-human – what is natural and what is social – in such a setting. Such a resolution, I suggest, results in the *inversion* of the relationship whereby, instead of the natural objects under scrutiny being constituted through representational practice, those objects are seen to exist independently of those representations. That is, the construction of a relationship between the corporeal (nature) and its representational form ('the obs') through the mundane actions of intensive care practitioners is carried out in such way that any evidence that such a construction has occurred is subsequently deleted. Reality is, in this sense, *fabricated* only for the contribution of nurses who do the fabrication to subsequently be deleted.

CONSTRUCTING THE VISIBILITY OF CHILDREN'S BODIES IN THE PICU

The strikingly resonant comment in the last data extract from one of the nurses who worked on the PICU highlights the fundamental problem faced by all the nurses who worked in the Unit. They worked continually *not* to 'lose sight' of the critically ill children under their care. Many of the children are, after all, admitted 'for observation'. How then is the visibility of such bodies constructed and how is it maintained in an environment in which the visible is continually in danger of becoming opaque?

An illustration is offered here – although general features of all the observations nurses make of children's bodies can be similarly illustrated – of the manner in which a child's heart rate is observed. These data focus on mundane activities which occur everyday on the PICU which are directed at making the corporeal body visible and illustrating the gradual emergence of the child's representational form, in this case related to corporeal function.

When a child is admitted to the PICU their heart rate and rhythm is monitored. An electrocardiographic monitor is switched on, ECG pads are applied in a specific way to the child's chest, ECG wires are connected to these pads, the ECG trace is modified to show predetermined elements of a standard trace (nurses say they are looking for a 'good trace'). This oscilloscope ECG trace is translated into a number (the monitor counts the number of peaks in the trace). A nurse records this number on an observation chart. They do not however write a number on the chart but draw a small red circle, 2–3 mm in diameter in a particular place on the chart.

What is striking is how the *corporeal* heart inside the child's chest is both 'extracted' and abstracted into a series of symbols. First as an ECG trace on 'the monitor', then as a corresponding number on the screen. The small red dot corresponds to a number written on the 'obs chart', located at a particular time (time, which itself is represented on the 'obs chart'). The heart, I suggest, exists therefore along a socio-technical continuum. At one end the child's heart – a pulsating, warm, flesh and blood entity – and, at the other, a symbolic representation of the heart – a motionless, silent, cool phenomenon. At each stage in the translation some of its properties are lost and others are gained.

In this illustration, I suggest, nurses demonstrate a way of seeing one aspect of a child's corporeality. A small red dot is not a heart, neither is the number 140 and neither is the jagged green line on an oscilloscope to a person who is not a member of this PICU community. Clearly the most pertinent consideration of such actions is not 'what do we mean by representation?' but, 'what do participants, in this case, treat as representation?' In this case the small red dot, by convention, is an observation of the heart. It is, of course, only one selected feature of the heart, its rate. Other representational forms (blood pressure, core–peripheral temperature gap, skin colour, etc.) contribute to the ability to 'see' the heart. These contributory forms are also deliberately constructed in similar ways. Thus nurses are effectively and gradually 'processing' nature through a set of representational practices. This renders the child's heart in a form *progressively more external* to his corporeal body. There is, *and must be*, a link between the corporeal and its representation and whatever this link is, it is made, in a relatively unproblematic way, by combining a set of disparate and miscellaneous devices – bodies, electrical equipment, wires, pens, paper observation charts. What is less obvious, perhaps, is the repertoire of non-physical devices also combined into this omniform. For example, incorporated are a whole set of theoretical notions about a child's heart – from simple notions that it beats, to more complex theoretical ideas about where best to place the ECG pads on the child's chest, what a 'good' electrocardiographic trace is, how a two-year-old's heart should beat as opposed to children of other ages. Here observations are 'theory-laden'.[1] Additionally integrated into the omniform are conventions about how to record the heart beat on the chart with a specific shape, size and colour and in a specific place on the observation chart. The heart, a complex, pulsating, occult mass of corporeality is stabilized into a simple, still, revealed, representation – a process accomplished by putting together in one location a corporeal body, a set of technological artefacts and an assortment of texts, theories and conventions.

Such modest accomplishments – they are achieved many times each day – reveal their complexity not simply in the analysis offered here. Normally invisible, in situations where any *one* element is not arranged appropriately, this process of 'making' the heart visible becomes apparent. For example, if the electrocardiogram does not work when the child is admitted, the heart will not be visible in any form; if the ECG dots are not placed on the chest when the child arrives, the heart will remain similarly invisible; if the ECG dots are not placed appropriately, the peaks on the electrocardiogram will not be high enough to be counted by the monitor; if the heart rate is recorded in the form of a small *black* circle, it will, in the conventions of the PICU, not be the heart rate but another feature of the heart which is conventionally thus recorded. Thus, if this set of technological artefacts, corporeal body, assortment of texts, theories and conventions cannot be manipulated, then the heart rate will not appear, appear in a corrupted form, or disappear from view.

Such activities acknowledge both the local craft practices required by the nurses to make verifiable observational reports (integrating the corporeal, the technological and the textual) into an observational report which would accord with 'reality' and the importance of the different parts of the observational scenography – the corporeal, technological and textual – *interdependently* reinforcing the whole observational report. As one nurse was overheard saying to a mother anxious about a heart rate accorded the status of 'artefact' by the nurse caring for her daughter, 'it's not just the number, it's all those little things which go with it as well'. The 'little things' are those elements which have to be encompassed to make a statement 'this is how this child's body *really* is'.

By continually designing and re-designing a network of heterogeneous elements nurses *make* visible features of the child's body which are invisible to the naked eye. In short, they are constituting a material form of visibility (Lynch, 1985). This further develops the concept described earlier – that of 'sorting out' the patient, which suggested that the corporeal body was regarded as disordered in its interior milieu and ordered in its exterior environment. This is done because I suggest that the externalized and visualized corporeality constituted by the network of heterogeneous actors outlined above can, *at any time*, disassociate to recreate a disordered internality which is invisible and therefore non-manipulable in the context of intensive care nursing. For the most part this does not occur: the body remains disciplined, stabilized, controlled, manipulable.

By exploring particular aspects of the network of assembled elements it is possible to determine which actors in the network need to be reordered – the corporeal, the technological or the textual – in order to make statements about particular aspects of the child's body. For example, if the child's 'blood pressure' rises suddenly, the electrical transducer by which it is measured is examined to see if it is higher or lower in relation to the child's corporeal body. Here then technological and corporeal elements of the network are 'reflexively' tied – the one being made to be equivalent to the other. Alternatively, for example, the representation of the blood pressure on the cardiac monitor may disappear. Here the corporeal may be adjusted (the wrist rearranged to unblock an occluded arterial catheter) to reveal the blood pressure. If the 'trace' does not have a characteristic shape of peaks and troughs (either it is 'over-damped' or 'under-damped') then the 'blood pressure' will again not be 'real' and the actor-network will be manipulated to re-establish a characteristic trace, for example, by flushing the cannula with fluid or changing the position of the child's wrist. The network of heterogeneous elements in this sense is mutually reinforcing, one element is taken as validating others in the network.

How, then is the distinction between an observation of the child's body which the nurses regard as 'real' and one which they regard as 'artefact' clarified? In the process of fabricating the 'reality' of blood pressure the *direction* of the relationship between the corporeal body and its representation is crucial.

THE SEPARATION OF THE CRAFTED RESEMBLANCE

It was possible to conceive of two different relationships between naturally occurring objects and the observational reports (scientific knowledge) about those objects. On the one hand, if the corporeal body, having a status antecedent to its representation, is 'real' the network of heterogeneous actors will hold together. This however seems to be in contradistinction to what the data presented suggest happens in the observed practice of intensive care nurses. It is *because* the actor-network is *held* together that it becomes 'real'. Without the activity which holds the network together the representation is not only non-real it is non-visible. This chapter has suggested that this holding together of the network of heterogeneous elements constitutes the mundane work of intensive care nurses on the PICU and without this work the critically ill body become opaque or simply disappears.

If the interior of the body is not initially visible on an ICU then the crucial issue is not what the nurse 'sees' in a visual way but the reliability of the practices which have gone into the observational *process*. Observation then:

> becomes a question of studying a chain of surrogate phenomena via a series of manipulations and interpretations and this high-lights the fundamental ambiguity over *just what has been observed.* (Pinch, 1985: 8, emphasis in original)

Nurses caring for critically ill children cannot in any straightfor-ward way 'see' the objects of their observational intent. 'Blood pressure', 'intracranial pressure', 'tidal volume', 'core/peripheral temperature gap' can only be 'revealed' indirectly with the aid of sophisticated measuring instrumentation.

It is hard not to be struck by the attention the nurses pay to continually 'arranging' the bodies of the children they are caring for. However it is important to note that this arranging is not done for aesthetic reasons. Indeed the intensive care nurses reserve a particular type of opprobrium for nurses and intensive care units who arrange the patients *too* tidily. Peter, a senior staff nurse on the PICU, provides the *appropriate* rationale for a tidy child:

> PETER: Yes. I think with the children, you are in control of those children. You can, especially with very sick children... Rightly or wrongly on PICU if a baby cries and is unsettled you give it chloral to send it to sleep. We do it. I'm not saying if it's right or wrong.

> BERNARD: Why is that?

> PETER: I don't know. I think maybe we kind of get the feeling that if the baby's crying, it's not good for it. It's not good for its oxygen saturations or its heart rate or [blood] pressures, so it's better asleep and sedated, you know, settled.

Through the administration of sedatives the corporeal body is here tidied, to 'make' a number appear on the monitor screen, whether that be oxygen saturation, blood pressure or pulse rate. The whole corporeal body or just parts of it may be so arranged.

It is a deeply held conviction amongst nurses on the intensive care unit that nurses should, as they say, 'care for patients and not machines'. In the esteem hierarchy of PICU it is held almost as an article of faith that the child must not become objectified, an extension of the machinery to which it is attached. But in this setting both humans and non-humans (children and machines) are so inextricably linked that it is analytically unfruitful to begin with these two categories (human and non-human) as separate explanatory resources. In the technomorphic imbroglio which is the intensive care patient, however, the two elements in the heterogeneous network are separated by the nurses such that they *end up with* a clearly defined classification of what is 'human' and 'non-human'. This ambiguity, clarified through nursing care, arises from the critically ill body being technomorphic (constituted by corporeality *and* technology which the nurses handle with symmetry) *and* through a simultaneous commitment to separate and the purify these elements into their human (social) and non-human (technical) parts. To demonstrate, at the same time, an acceptance that the evidence of the body can equally be found in the technological *and* in the corporeal *but* that they must never be confused. An experienced nurse, unlike a neophyte must *never* confuse 'the machine' and 'him'.

But the direction of the link between the corporeal body and the machines to which it is connected is always regarded equivocally by intensive care nurses:

> You have to be able to read the patient as well as you can read the machines. You have to be able to link the two. Otherwise you could go all night and you don't know what state the patient is. You could read all the machines quite happily and you could have a patient who then went off rather rapidly couldn't you? (Staff Nurse Juliet)

In summary, then, the relationship between the corporeal and the technological is best conceived of as a two-way, reflexive relationship. What is 'the machine' and what is 'him/her' is not in principle discernible. Indeed it is not possible, in a setting where the construction of what is 'him/her' is of necessity a product of 'the machine' ('blood pressure', 'oxygen saturation', etc.) to conceive of a situation whereby 'what *is* him/her' and what *is* the machine could be separable.

What is 'artefact' and what is 'real' is, then, a product of an *interrelationship*, between the technological and the textual. But whilst this bodily arrangement (corporeal work) and reflexive tying of the arranged corporeality and the inscription devices (technological work) are undertaken there is still no certainty that what appears on the observation chart is, itself, anything more than a 'squiggle' on a piece of paper or 'just numbers' on a grid, or simply dots on a graph. It might quite simply be 'artefact' and not 'corporeality'. Nursing work on the textual is directed towards answering the essential ambiguity of these 'squiggles.' The corporeal in this sense is not 'revealed' by the machines, although the continual affirmation of this revelation is evidenced by the situated vocabulary of the intensive care unit. The machines are manipulated to *constitute* evidence of the internal functioning of the corporeal. Chest drains are 'milked' and 'stripped' to encourage blood and other fluids to appear in the bottle attached to the bedside – that is the 'real' drainage. That real drainage is then recorded, in numerical form, on the 'obs chart'. Tubes of all kinds are manipulated:

> Chris (PRN) was crouched at the side of the bed. She was 'measuring the urine'. To do this she lifted the drainage tube attached to the urinary catheter slowly and rhythmically up and down. Urine was 'siphoned' off. After doing this for about 15 seconds she stood up and wrote down a number on the fluid chart. (fieldnote, 22 February 1991)

What is revealed is the 'real' urine output, the 'real wound drainage, the 'real' chest drainage etc. Without these artefactual manipulations what is recorded on the 'obs chart' would be 'unreal'.

DELETING THE CRAFTED RESEMBLANCE

Throughout the process of monitoring, an underlying working assumption is that the numbers simply *reveal* an underlying reality, that there is a consonance between what the numbers say and how the child is. That is to say, a commitment to 'philosophical realism' underpins the nurse's work. However, although the 'numbers' can only be generated by the craft practices evident in the previous data fragments, the numbers are not seen by the nurses as generated by those practices. Indeed they assume an underlying reality which exists independently of the means by which the numbers are generated.

The conventional paper intensive care chart is a literary inscription. It is said to 'contain' 'facts' about the corporeal body under scrutiny in the sense that it represents bodily function. However, for the community of intensive care nurses, the *processes* of this translation are deleted. To them this is a *body* made visible and not merely a set of lines, dots and ticks. It is a network of interconnecting elements, an actor-network, which enables the statement: 'This is what is happening inside this body.' Without the assiduously constructed externality, already described, where one element in the network is used to buttress the others, the statement would be, at best, ambiguous (opaque) and, at worst, invisible. The body would *literally* disappear. The seemingly simple process of observation – 'doing the obs' – is, therefore, highly mediated. A complex interaction of nursing manipulations, technological procedures and interpretive practices help constitute those observations. It is not just a sense experience. However, in its externalized form, these aspects of the critically ill body are not regarded simply as representations. As the activities outlined in the preceding pages show they *are* the phenomena. The local practices of intensive care nurses *constitute* the corporeality that provides the focus for their work, suggesting a relationship between object and representation as follows:

representation > > > > > > > > > > > > > > > > > > child's body

However, *if the network of heterogeneous elements can be sustained*, these activities create a relationship in which the corporeal has an antecedent status, the representational practices merely *reveal* that corporeality:

child's body > > > > > > > > > > > > > > > > > > > representation

This inversion recalls a feature of scientific practice which appears to render the 'natural' world as antecedent to the activity of science which 'dis-covers' or 're-veals' such naturally occurring phenomena. Once this inversion has occurred the observational report (and in

this case the observation chart on which they are stabilized in textual form) can be said to be 'black boxed'. At this point the child's
body can be manipulated by inscription devices and all the human
(social) activities which went into the initial production of such
bodily 'facts' drop out of the scene. In the search for a parsimoni-
ous explanation for the work of an intensive care nurses one feature
of the work therefore recurs: the production of documents, literary inscriptions which provide evidence for corporeality. The simple
question is, then, if the critically ill body is actively constituted by
representational practice, how do nurses convince themselves that
the reverse is true?

The previous section suggests that, within the location of the
intensive care unit, there is little evidence of corporeality which
cannot be gathered without some non-human artefact. The child's
body in this setting is therefore a *relational* concept (Law, 1994).
The features of corporeality at the centre of the nurse's work in
the PICU would have an ephemeral existence without their technological analogs. 'Blood pressure', 'intracranial pressure' and all
the other features of corporeality are products of machines. The
body's internality is therefore given substance through its *representation*, only possible through the attachment of non-human artefacts,
a process which allows a reflexive link to be established between
the human and the non-human elements in the network. The corporeal is used to sustain the artefactual and the artefactual is used
to sustain the corporeal. Throughout this activity the integrity and
security of the connections between the human and the non-human
parts of this union need to be, and are, continually checked. It is
not surprising, then, that so much work, as I have shown, is invested in clarifying and separating 'artefact' from 'reality'. There
would be few takers amongst intensive care nurses for the proposition that the human tragedy lying attached to the plethora of
technological artefacts is nothing more than a product of discourse.
'Real' and '*not* real', 'normal' and '*not* normal', 'children' and '*not*
children', 'human' and '*non*-human' the phenomenon sits on a
conceptual boundary negotiated deftly and daily in the intensive
care unit. The phenomenon of the (human) corporeality translated
into the language of science – numbers symbols, traces – transcribed
for all to see.

But the 'success' of nurses in the PICU at constituting children's
bodies cannot be explained just because they 'reveal' a corporeality
underlying its representation. Actor-network theory suggests that
the sensual apprehension of a given natural entity is an activity

which occurs as the result of the maintenance of a stable network of heterogeneous elements. The network of both human and non-human actors is *made* so that it *can* be seen. Once the representation is *made* people can and will be convinced it is the body. The relative success or failure of technologies of visualisation can be regarded as a product of a stable network of heterogeneous elements.

The moment of inversion is signalled at the point when all the constitutive actions of the intensive care nurse drop out of the scene. When the relationship between the object and its representation is subject to dispute then the constitutive actions of the nurses are acknowledged. At this point the 'crafting of resemblance' allows the distinction between reality and what the nurses term 'artefact' to be made. In this crafting the nurses explicitly recognize the reflexive, constitutive work done in their representational practice, for example, in moving a pulse oximeter probe from one part of the body to another, or wrapping a child's feet in cotton wool gamgee when the core/peripheral temperature gap is doubted. What is 'real' and what is 'artefact' is constituted by such mundane activity, but once it is so constituted the inversion of the relationship, representation/object simultaneously signals the removal of the constitutive agent, the intensive care nurse. The achievement of antecedence is accompanied now with notions that the phenomenon is simply 'observed', 'monitored'. The technology with which, moments previously, representations were conscientiously constitut*ed* now constitute the object. Now nurses, passively, 'read' the monitors and 'record' what they observe. Having stabilized the phenomenon to be observed, the conditions whereby such phenomena were constructed are no longer referred to. The constitutor drops out of the scene. Any attempt to reinsert the constitutor back into the phenomena undermines its facticity.

The insertion of 'modalities' (Latour and Woolgar, 1979) into such statements of fact draws attention towards the *statement* about the phenomena and away from the phenomenon itself. Whilst this agonistic process is occurring, reflected in the ambivalence between 'reality' and 'artefact', the clinical conversation about the child's body is continually hedged with modalities:

'Mary, I *think* she is going off.'

'Marise *said* her blood pressure fell when she was on her left side.'

'It *seems like* her sats fall every time we turn her.'

Although these statements about corporeality are beginning to reach a stabilized form they remain 'split entities', open to challenge. Discussions ensue about these hedged observational claims in a way they do not when they are 'real'. 'Reality' is still revisable at this stage. However if, as I have suggested above, 'reality' is a *practical* matter to be crafted rather than asserted, such situations can not be used to explain why an observational report becomes a fact, since it is only *after* it has become a fact that 'reality' is obtained. Nothing will be recorded on the observation chart until these modalizers are dropped. There is no record that a nurse 'thought the patient was going off' but, on further investigation, found evidence of a poor contact between a pulse oximeter and a child's finger, or that a transducer had fallen on the floor, or that an electrocardiogram lead had become disconnected.

At the end of a process when all modalities are dropped the phenomenon which is constituted by nursing representational practice (e.g. blood pressure, intracranial pressure, etc.) becomes a 'fact' which then can underlie its representation. The constitution of corporeal facticity is a *process* not a single point in time (a process which can be reversed, of course). This is the key to the definition of the boundary – the boundary by which the critically ill body itself is constituted. In the final stage the contested body is no longer contested. It is real. Knowledge claims about what is happening in this body are, temporarily at least, resolved.

Adopting such an analytic stance therefore prevents judgements about which is 'really' the 'truth' and hence allows a focus on the *process* by which facts are *constructed* renders enduringly problematic the relationship between signs and things signified and, secondly, that the 'match' between the natural phenomenon and it's representation is *worked upon* to achieve coterminacy. Finally, this match between sign and signified (representation and naturally occurring phenomenon) is then 'inverted' because the phenomenon (illustrated in this chapter by facts about 'heart rate', 'blood pressure' and 'oxyhaemoglobin saturation') was there all the time and just waiting to be revealed. 'Reality' is thus in this sense the cause of the match. An analytic stance using actor-network theory indicates that it is more fruitful to see 'reality' not as the cause of such a match (and all such other matches between signs and things signified) but more an *effect* of the match. What is 'real' is constructed.

CONCLUSION

The data presented from this ethnographic study of a PICU indicate a process in the constitution of the object of scrutiny, a child's body, in which the phenomenon is made in such a way that it can be seen. It has no prior existence in any other form. What is natural and what is social in this phenomenon becomes blurred. It is neither social or natural, whilst at same time it is *both*. The critically ill body would not exist without instruments of visualization (it would die if not visualized). It is not possible to conceptualize such a phenomenon without the attachments of artefacts in a sociotechnical imbroglio. And yet, they *are* also separated, made to be separate social/human and technical/non-human elements.

This position, derived from actor-network theorist such as Latour (1986a, 1987) and Callon (1986a, 1986b), is radical because it unsettles our basic categories. It suggests that the categories of, for example, 'human' and 'non-human' or 'body' and 'society' appear settled because the networks of which they are the effect have been stabilized and their complex associations effaced. However, there is nothing immutable about these networks or permanent about their stability. They may at any time disassociate. It is here that the theoretical focus of the chapter lies. In the liminal 'no man's land' of the intensive care ward nurses are skilled in both combining elements and separating them into human and non-human elements. Failure in either undermines their claims to expertise. On the one hand they cannot 'see' the patient, on the other hand, they 'confuse' the categories (dehumanize the patient, concentrate on caring for the 'machines' rather than the 'patient'). Both failings disqualify claims for expertise. In this sense it is easy to see how the practical problem for the nurses of 'losing the child in between' highlights the perplexing nature of purification and mediation. It is lost in the confusion of the boundaries of what is human and what is not.

NOTE

1. That an observation is 'theory-laden' means that the separation between observational and theoretical terms has broken down. Theory-ladenness

of observations is therefore built discursively into such observational statements. To say, for example, that the heart is beating 140 times each minute is, *automatically*, to build into the statement theoretical notions of how a heart functions; that it is a pump which pulsates – theoretical notions which would, for example, be at odds with those which underpin Galenic medicine.

References

Alanen, L. (1997) 'The Politics of Growing Up', seminar paper given at Keele University, March 1997.

Allen, I. (1987) *Education in Sex and Personal Relationships*, Policy Studies Institute Research. Report No. 655, Dorset: Blackmore Press.

Anthony E.J., et al. (eds.) (1978) *The Child in his Family: Vulnerable Children*, New York: John Wiley & Sons.

Armstrong, D. (1983) *Political Anatomy of the Body: Medical Knowledge in Britain in the Twentieth Century* Cambridge: Cambridge University Press.

Armstrong, D. (1983a) 'The Invention of Infant Mortality', *Sociology of Health and Illness*, 8: 211–32.

Armstrong, D. (1987) 'Bodies of Knowledge: Foucault and the Problem of Human Anatomy', in Scambler, G. (ed.), *Sociological Theory and Medical Sociology*, London: Tavistock.

Askew, S. and Ross, C. (1988) *Boys Don't Cry*, Milton Keynes, Open University.

Backett, K. (1990) 'Studying Health in Families: a Qualitative Approach,' in Cunningham-Burley, S. and McKeganey, N.J. (eds.) *Readings in Medical Sociology*, London: Tavistock.

Backett, K. (1992a) 'Taboos and Excesses: Lay Health Moralities in Middle-class Families', *Sociology of Health and Illness*, 14, 255–74.

Backett, K. (1992b) 'The Construction of Health Knowledge in Middle-class Families', *Health Education Research: Theory and Practice*, 7, 497–507.

Backett, K., and Alexander, H. (1991) 'Talking to Young Children about Health: Methods and Findings', *Health Education Journal*, 50, 34–8.

Backett, K., and Davison, C. (1995) 'Lifecourse and Lifestyle: the Social and Cultural Location of Health Behaviours', *Social Science and Medicine*, 40, 629–38.

Barthes, R. (1977) *Image–Music–Text: Essays Selected and Translated by Stephen Heath*, London: Fontana/Collins.

Battersby, C. (1993) 'Her Body/Her Boundaries: Gender and the Metaphysics of Containment', *Journal of Philosophy and the Visual Arts*, 31–9.

Benjamin W. (1986) *Moscow Diary*, Cambridge, MA: Harvard University Press.

Benner P. (1984) *From Novice to Expert*, Menlo Park, CA: Addison-Wesley.

Benthall, J. and Polhemus, T. (1975) *The Body as a Medium of Expression*, London: Allen Lane.

Berger, J. (1972) *Ways of Seeing*, London: Penguin.

Berger, K.S. (1983) *The Developing Person through the Life Span*, New York: Worth Publishers, Inc.

Blackman, S.J. (1995) *Youth: Positions and Oppositions: Style, Sexuality and Schooling*, Aldershot: Avebury.

Bluebond-Langner, M. (1978) *The Private Worlds of Dying Children.* Princeton, NJ: Princeton University Press.

Bluebond-Langner, M. et al. (1991) 'Paediatric Cancer Patients' Peer Relationships: the Impact of an Oncology Camp Experience', *Journal of Psychosocial Oncology* 9, (2): 67–80.

Boudon, P. (1986) *Theories of Social Change: a Critical Appraisal,* Berkeley: California University Press.

Bourdieu, P. (1976) 'The School as a Conservative Force, Scholastic & Cultural in Equalities', in Dale, R., Esland, G. and Macdonald, M. (eds) *Schooling & Capitalism,* London: Routledge & Kegan Paul.

Bourdieu, P. (1977) *Outline of a Theory of Practice,* Cambridge: Cambridge University Press.

Bourdieu, P. (1986) *Distinction,* London: Routledge & Kegan Paul.

Boyden, J. (1990) 'Childhood and the Policy Makers: a Comparative Perspective on the Globalization of Childhood', in James, A. and Prout, A. (eds.) *Constructing and Reconstructing Childhood.* London: Falmer Press.

Boyne, R. (1991 [1988]) 'The Art of the Body in Discourse of Postmodernity', in Featherstone, M. et al. (eds.) *The Body: Social Process and Cultural Theory,* London: Sage.

Briggs, J.L. (1971) *Never in Anger. Portrait of an Eskimo Family,* Cambridge, MA: Harvard University Press.

Briggs, J.L. (1986) 'Living Dangerously: the Contradictory Foundations of Value in Canadian Inuit Society', In Leacock, E. and Lee, R. (eds.) *Politics and History in Band Soceities.* Cambridge: Cambridge University Press.

Brite, P.Z. (1994) *Drawing Blood,* London: Penguin.

Bronfen, E. (1992) *Over Her Dead Body: Death, Femininity and the Aesthetic,* Manchester: Manchester University Press.

Bryder (1992) 'Wonderlands of Buttercup, Clover and Daisies: Tuberculosis and the Open-air School Movement', in Cooter, R. (ed.) *In the Name of the Child: Health and Welfare, 1880–1940,* London: Routledge.

Burman, E. (1994) *Deconstructing Developmental Psychology,* London: Routledge.

Burnett, F.H. (1911) *The Secret Garden,* London: Penguin.

Burton, L. (1975) *The Family Life of Sick Children,* London: Routledge and Kegan Paul.

Butler-Sloss, E. (1988) *Report of the Inquiry into Child Abuse in Cleveland 1987,* London: HMSO.

Buytendjik, F.J. (1974) *Prolegomena to an Anthropological Physiology,* Pittsburgh: Duquesne University Press.

Callon M. (1986a) 'The Sociology of an Actor-network: the Case of the Electric Vehicle', in Callon, M., Law, J. and Rip, A. (eds.) *Mapping the Dynamics of Science and Technology,* London: Macmillan.

Callon, M. (1986b) 'Some Elements of a Sociology of Translation: Domestication of the Scallops and the Fisherman of St Brieuc Bay', in Law, J. (ed.), *Power Action and Belief: New Sociology of Knowledge?, Sociological Review Monograph 32,* London: Routledge & Kegan Paul.

Campion J. (1993) *The Piano.* London: Bloomsbury.

Canter, L. with Canter, M. (1976) *Assertive Discipline: a Take Charge*

Approach for Today's Educator, Los Angeles: Canter and Associates.

Caplow, T. (1968) *Two against One: Coalitions in Triads*, Englewood Cliffs, NJ: Prentice Hall.

Carey J. (1981) *John Donne: Life, Mind and Art*, London: Faber and Faber.

Chernin, K. (1983) *Womansize: The Tyranny of Slenderness*. London: Women's Press.

Christensen, P.H. (1993) 'The Social Construction of Help among Danish Children: the Intentional Act and Actual Content', *Sociology of Health and Illness*, 15, 4: 88–502.

Christensen, P.H. (1994) 'Vulnerable Bodies: Cultural Meanings of Child, Body and Illness'. Paper given at Children and Families: Research and Policy. XXXIth International Sociological Association (ISA) Committee on Family Research (CFR) Seminar, London.

Clair J. (ed.) (1993) *L'meau Corps: Arts et Sciences 1793–1993*, Paris: Gallimard/Electa (for Réunion des Museaux Nationaux).

Connell, R.W. (1987) *Gender and Power,* Oxford: Polity Press.

Cornwell, J. (1984) *Hard Earned Lives: Accounts of Health and Illness from East London*, London: Tavistock.

Crawford, R. (1984) 'A Cultural Account of "Health", Control, Release and the Social Body', in McKinlay J.B. (ed.) *Issues in the Political Economy of Health Care*, London: Tavistock.

Crawford, R. (1994) 'The Boundaries of the Self and the Unhealthy Other: Reflections on Health, Culture and AIDS', *Social Science and Medicine* 38, 10: 1347–65.

Csordas, T.J. (1994) *Embodiment and Experience: the Existential Ground of Culture and Self*, Cambridge: Cambridge University Press.

Cunningham-Burley, S.J., Milburn, K. and Kirk, R. (1993) 'Studying Health amongst 45–59 Year Olds', University of Edinburgh, Department of Sociology seminar series, Edinburgh.

de Jong, W. (1980) 'The Stigma of Obesity: the Consequences of Naïve Assumptions Concerning the Causes of Physical Deviance', *Journal of Health and Social Behaviour*, 21: 75–87.

Diprose, R. (1994) *The Bodies of Women. Ethic, Embodiment and Sexual Difference*, London: Routledge.

Douglas, M. ([1966] 1992) *Purity and Danger: an Analysis of the Concepts of Pollution and Taboo*, London: Routledge.

Duroche, L. (1990) 'Male Perception as a Social Construct', in Hearn, J. and Morgan, D. (eds.) *Men, Masculinities and Social Theory*, London: Hyman.

Elias, N. (1978) *The Civilising Process, Volume 1, The History of Manners*, Oxford: Blackwell.

Elias, N. (1982) *The Civilising Process, Volume 2, State Formation and Civilisation*, Oxford: Blackwell.

Ennew, J. (1986) *The Sexual Exploitation of Children*. Cambridge: Polity Press.

Ennew J. (1994) 'The Environmental Health of Working Children'. Paper given at Brunel University.

Farrell, C. (1978) *My Mother Said . . . the Way Young People Learned about Sex and Birth Control*, London: Routledge & Kegan Paul.

Featherstone, M. (1982) 'The Body in Consumer Culture', *Theory, Culture and Society* 1: 18–33.

Featherstone, M., Hepworth, M., Turner, B.S. (eds.) (1991) *The Body: Social Process and Cultural Theory*, London: Sage.

Foucault, M. (1970) *The Order of Things: an Archeology of the Human Sciences*, translated by A.M. Sheridan, New York: Pantheon.

Foucault, M. (1973) *The Birth of the Clinic: an Archeology of Medical Perception*, translated by A.M. Sheridan Smith, London: Tavistock.

Foucault, M. (1977) *Discipline and Punish: the Birth of the Prison*, London: Penguin.

Foucault, M. (1980) 'Body/Power', in Gordon, C. (ed.) *Michel Foucault: Power/Knowledge – Selected Interviews and Other Writings 1972–1977*, Hemel Hempstead: Harvester Wheatsheaf.

Fox Harding, L. (1991) *Perspectives in Child Care Policy*, London: Longman.

Frame, J. (1984) *An Angel at my Table*, London: Women's Press.

Frankenberg, R. (1978) 'Styles of Marxism; Styles of Criticism. *Wuthering Heights*: a Case Study', in Laurenson, D. (ed.) *The Sociology of Literature: Applied Studies*. Socological Review Monograph 26, University of Keele.

Frankenberg, R. (1990) Review article: 'Disease, Literature and the Body in the Era of AIDS – a Preliminary Exploration', *Sociology of Health and Illness*, 12, 3.

Frankenberg, R. (1994) 'What is Power? How is Decision? The Heart has its Reasons', in Robinson, I. (ed.), *Life and Death under High Technology Medicine*, Manchester: Manchester University Press.

Freeman, M.D.A. (1992) *Children, their Families and The Law: Working with the Children Act*, London: Macmillan.

Freund, P. (1988) 'Bringing Society into the Body: Understanding Socialised Human Nature', *Theory & Society* 17: 839–64.

Freund, P. (1990) 'The Expressive Body: a Common Ground for the Sociology of Emotions and Health and Illness', *Sociology of Health and Illness* 12 4: 452–77.

Gadow, S.M. (1980) 'Existential Advocacy: Philosophical Foundation of Nursing', in Spicker, S.F. and Gadow, S.M. (eds.) *Nursing: Images and Ideals*, New York: Springer.

Game, A. (1991) *Undoing the Social*, Milton Keynes. Open University Press.

Geertz, C. (1983) *Local Knowledge. Further Essays in Interpretive Anthropology*, New York: Basic Books.

Giddens, A. (1991) *Modernity and Self-identity. Self and Society in the Late Modern Age*, Oxford: Polity Press.

Gilborn, D. (1990) *Race, Ethnicity and Education*, London: Unwin Hyman.

Gilligan, C. (1990) 'Joining the Resistance: Psychology, Politics, Girls and Women', In Goldstein, L. (ed.) *The Female Body* (Part One), Special issue *Michigan Quarterly Review* Vol. XXIX, 4, Fall: 501–36.

Goffman, E. (1959) *The Presentation of Self in Everyday Life*. Harmondsworth: Penguin.

Goffman, E. (1968) *Stigma*, Harmondsworth: Penguin.

Goldman, R. and Goldman, J. (1982) *Children's Sexual Thinking*, London: Routledge & Kegan Paul.

Gordon, T. (1996) 'Citizenship, Difference and Marginality in Schools: Spatial and Embodied Aspects of Gender Construction', in Murphy, P.F. and Gipps, C.V. (eds.) *Equity in the Classroom: Towards Effective Pedagogy for Girls and Boys*, London: Falmer Press.

Grimshaw, J. (1993) 'Practices of Freedom', in Ramazanoglu, C. (ed.) *Up Against Foucault*, London: Routledge.

Grosz, E. (1990) 'Inscriptions and Body Maps. Representations and the Corporeal', in Threadgold, T. and Cranny Francis, A. (eds.) *Feminine, Masculine & Representation*, Sydney: Allen and Unwin.

Hallden, G. (1995) 'Gender and Generation: Self-identity in Boys' Narratives'. Paper presented at the conference 'Understanding the Social World: Towards an Integrative Approach'. University of Huddersfield, July 1995.

Hallett, C. and Birchall, E. (1995) *Working Together in Child Protection*, London: HMSO.

Halliday, J. (1971) *Sirk on Sirk*, Cinema One, No. 18, London: Martin Secker and Warburg for British Film Institute (reissued with additional material 1997).

Haraway, D.J. (1990a) *Simians, Cyborgs and Women: the Reinvention of Nature*. London: Free Association Books.

Haraway, D.J. (1990b) 'A Manifesto for Cyborgs: Science, Technology and Socialist Feminism in the 1980s', in Nicholson, L.J. (ed.) *Feminism/Postmodernism*, New York: Routledge.

Hastrup, Kirsten (1993) 'Hunger and the Hardness of Facts', *Man: The Journal of the Royal Anthropological Institute*, 28, 4: 727–39.

Hebdige, D. (1979) *Subculture: The Meaning of Style*, London: Methuen.

Herzlich, C., and Pierret, J. (1986) 'Illness: From Causes to Meaning', in Currer, C. and Stacey, M. (eds.) *Concepts of Health Illness and Disease*, Hamburg and New York: Berg Publications.

Hobbs, C. and Wynne, J. (1986) 'Buggery in Childhood – a Common Symptom of Child Abuse', *The Lancet*. II. 8510: 792–6.

Hockey, J. and James, A. (1993) *Growing Up and Growing Old. Ageing and Dependency in the Life Course*, London: Sage.

Holland, P. (1992) 'What is a child?' *Popular Images of Childhood*. London: Virago.

Home Office and Department of Health (1992) *Memorandum of Good Practice on Video-Recorded Interviews with Child Witnesses for Criminal Proceedings*, London: HMSO.

Hutchby, I., and Moran-Ellis, J. (eds) (1998) *Children and Social Competence: Arenas of Action*, London: Falmer Press.

Isern, P. (1993) 'Levi's og det autentiske. Jagten På en moderne erfaring', *Samtiden*, 5: 45–53.

James, A. (1986) 'Leaning to Belong: the Boundaries of Adolescence', In Cohen, A.P. (ed.) *Symbolising Boundaries: Identity and Diversity in British Cultures*, Manchester: Manchester University Press.

James, A. (1993) *Childhood Identities: Self and Social Relationships in the Experience of the Child*, Edinburgh: Edinburgh University Press.

James, A. (1995) 'On Being a Child: the Self, the Group and the Category', in Cohen, A.P. and Rapport, N. (eds.) *Questions of Consciousness*, London: Routledge.

James, A. (1998) 'Imaging Children "at Home", "in the Family" and "at School": Movement between the Spatial and Temporal Markers of Childhood Identity in Britain', in Rapport, N. and Dawson, A. (eds.) *Migrants of Identity*, Oxford: Berg.

James, A., Jenks, C., and Prout, A. (1998) *Theorizing Childhood*, Cambridge: Polity Press.

James, A. and Prout, A. (1990) 'Re-presenting Childhood: Time and Transition in the Study of Childhood', in James, A. and Prout, A. (eds.) *Constructing and Reconstructing Childhood*, Basingstoke: Falmer Press.

Jenks, C. (1982) *The Sociology of Childhood: Essential Readings*, London: Batsford.

Jenks, C. (1994) 'Child Abuse in the Post-modern Context: an Issue of Social Identity', *Childhood*, 2(4): 111–21.

Jenks, C. (1996) *Childhood*, London: Routledge.

Johnson, M. (1987) *The Body in the Mind. The Bodily Basis of Meaning, Imagination and Reason*, Chicago: University of Chicago Press.

Keat, R. (1986) 'The Human Body in Social Theory: Reich, Foucault and the Repressive Hypothesis', *Radical Philosophy*, 24.

Kempe, C.H., Silverman, F., Steele, B., Droegmuller, W. and Silver, H. (1962) 'The Battered Child Syndrome', *Journal of the American Medical Association*, 181, 17–24.

Knorr-Cetina, K.D. (1981) *The Manufacture of Knowledge – An Essay on the Constructivist and Contextual Nature of Science*, Oxford: Pergamon Press.

Kopelson, K. (1996) *Beethoven's Kiss: Pianism, Perversion, and the Mystery of Desire*, Stanford, CA: Stanford University Press.

La Fontaine, J. (1985) *Initiation. Ritual Drama and Secret Knowledge Across the World*, London: Penguin.

Lakoff, G. and Johnson, M. (1980) *Metaphors We Live By*, Chicago: Chicago University Press.

Lakoff G. and Turner, M. (1989) *More than Cool Reason: A Field Guide to Poetic Metaphor*, Chicago: University of Chicago Press.

Latour, B. (1986a) 'Visualization and Cognition: Thinking with Eyes and Hands', *Knowledge and Society: Studies in the Sociology of Culture, Past and Present*, 6: 1–40.

Latour, B. (1986b) 'The Powers of Association', in Law, J. (ed.) (1986) *Power Action and Belief: a New Sociology of Knowledge*, London: Routledge & Kegan Paul.

Latour, B. (1987) *Science in Action – How to Follow Scientists and Engineers Through Society*, Cambridge, MA: Harvard University Press.

Latour, B. (1991) 'Technology is Society Made Durable', in Law, J. (ed.) *A Sociology of Monsters: Essays on Power, Technology and Domination, Sociological Review Monograph 38*, London: Routledge.

Latour, B. (1993) *We Have Never Been Modern*, Hemel Hempstead: Harvester Wheatsheaf.

Latour, B., and Woolgar, S. (1979 [1986]) *Laboratory Life: the Construction of Scientific Facts*, 2nd edition, Princeton, NJ: Princeton University Press.

Law, J. (1986a) 'Laboratories and Texts', in Callon, M., Law, J. and Rip, A. (1986) (eds.) *Mapping the Dynamics of Science and Technology –*

Sociology of Science in the Real World, London: Macmillan.

Law, J. (1986b) 'On power and its Tactics: a View from the Sociology of Science', *Sociological Review*, 34(1): 1–38.

Law, J. (1994) *Organizing Modernity*, Oxford: Blackwell.

Laws, S. (1991) 'Male Power and Menstrual Etiquette', in Homans, H. (ed.) *The Sexual Politics of Reproduction*, London: Gower.

Leach, E. (1976) *Culture and Communication – the Logic by which Symbols Are Connected*, Cambridge: Cambridge University Press.

Leavis, Q.D. (1969), 'A Fresh Approach to *Wuthering Heights*', in Leavis. Q.D. and Leavis, F.R., *Lectures in America*, London: Chatto & Windus.

Leppert, R. (1993) *The Sight of Sound: Music, Representation and the History of the Body*, Berkeley, CA: University of California Press.

Lesko, N. (1988) 'The Curriculum of the Body: Lessons from a Catholic High School', in Roman et al. (eds.) *Becoming Feminine: The Politics of Popular Culture*, London: Falmer Press.

Lewis, M. and Brooks, J. (1978) 'Self-knowledge and Emotional Development', in Lewis, M. and Rosenblum, L.A. (eds.), *The Development of Affect*, New York: Plenum.

Lynch, M. (1985) 'Discipline and the Material Form of Images: an Analysis of Scientific Visibility', *Social Studies of Science*, 15(1): 37–66.

Lyon, M.L. and Barbalet, J.M. (1994) 'Society's Body: Emotion and the "Somatization" of Social Theory', in Csordas, T.J. (ed.) *Embodiment and Experience: the Existential Ground of Culture and Self*, Cambridge: Cambridge University Press.

Martin, E. (1989) *The Woman in the Body*, Milton Keynes: Open University Press.

Mascia-Lees F.E. and Sharpe, P. (1995) 'Piano Lessons', *American Anthropologist*, 97, 4: 763–7.

Mauss, M. (1950) 'Les Techniques du Corps', *Sociologie et Anthropologie*, Paris: Presses Universitaires de France.

Mauss, M. (1973) 'Techniques of the Body', *Economy and Society*. 2,1: 70–88.

Mayall, B. (ed.) (1994) *Children's Childhoods: Observed and Experienced*, London: Falmer Press.

Mayall, B. (1996) *Children, Health and the Social Order*, Milton Keynes: Open University Press.

McNay, L. (1994) *Foucault: a Critical Introduction*, Cambridge: Polity Press.

McRobbie, A. and Garber, J. (1976) 'Girls and Subcultures', in Hall, S. and Jefferson, T. (eds.) *Resistance through Rituals: Youth Subcultures in Post-war Britain*, London: Hutchinson.

Mead, M. (1955) 'Theoretical Setting', in Mead, M. and Wolfstein, M. (eds.) *Childhood in Contemporary Culture*, Chicago: University of Chicago Press.

Mead, M. (1962) *Male and Female*, London: Pelican.

Merleau-Ponty, M. (1962) *Phenomenology of Perception* translated by C. Smith) London: Routledge & Kegan Paul.

Merleau-Ponty, M. (1988) *In Praise of Philosophy and Other Essays*, translated by Wild, J., Edie, J. and O'Neill, J. Evanston: Northwestern University Press.

Merton, R.K. (1973) *The Sociology of Science: Theoretical and Empirical Observations*. Chicago: Chicago University Press.

Milburn, K. (1995) 'Never Mind the Quality, Investigate the Depth!,' *British Food Journal*, 97: 36–8.

Morrison, T. (1990) *The Bluest Eye*, London: Picador.

Morss, J.R. (1996) *Growing Critical: Alternatives to Developmental Psychology*. London: Routledge.

Moss, D. (1989) 'Brain, Body and World. Body Image and the Psychology of the Body', In Valle, R.S. and Halling, S. (eds.) *Existential-Phenomenological Perspectives in Psychology. Exploring the Breadth of Human Experience*, New York: Plenum Press.

Nichter, M. and Cartwright, E. (1991) 'Saving the Children for the Tobacco Industry', *Medical Anthropology Quarterly*, 5, 3: 236–56.

Neill, S. and Caswell, C. (1993) *Body Language for Competent Teachers*, London: Routledge.

Nielsen, H.B. and Rudberg, M. (1994) *Psychological Gender and Modernity*, Oslo: Scandinavian University Press.

Oakley, A., Bendelow, G., Barnes, J., Buchanan, M. and Hussain, O. (1995) 'Health and Cancer Prevention: Knowledge and Beliefs of Children and Young People', *British Medical Journal*, 310: 1029–33.

O'Brien, M. (1989) *Reproducing the World*, Boulder, CO: Westview Press.

Okely, J. (1978) 'Privileged, Schooled and Finished: Boarding Education for Girls', in Ardener, S. (ed.) *Defining Females: the Nature of Women in Society*, London: Croom Helm.

Olesen, V.L. (1992) 'Extraordinary Events and Mundane Ailments', in Ellis, C. and Flaherty, M. (eds.) *Investigating Subjectivity. Research on Lived Experience*, London: Sage.

Open University (1985) *Birth to Old Age: Health in Transition*, Milton Keynes: The Open University Press.

Orbach, S. (1988) *Fat is a Feminist Issue*, London: Arrow Books.

Parkin D. (ed.) (1982) *Semantic Anthropology*, ASA Monograph 22, London: Academic Press.

Parsons, T. (1951) *The Social System*, London: Routledge & Kegan Paul.

Pinch, T. (1985) 'Towards an Analysis of Scientific Observation: the Externality and Evidential Significance of Observational Reports in Physics', *Social Studies of Science* 15(1): February, 3–36.

Place, B.J. (1994) 'The Constructing of Bodies of Critically Ill Children: an Ethnography of Intensive Care'. Paper to the ESRC Childhood and Society Seminar on Childhood and the Body, Keele University, December, 1994.

Place, B.J. (1996) 'Constructing the Critically Ill Body'. Unpublished PhD Thesis, South Bank University, London.

Pointon, M. (1990) *Naked Authority: the Body in Western Painting 1830–1908*, Cambridge: Cambridge University Press.

Prendergast, S. (1992) *'This is the Time to Grow Up': Girls' Experiences of Menstruation in School*, Cambridge: The Health Promotion Trust.

Prendergast, S. (1994) *'This is the Time to Grow Up'. Girls Experience of Menstruation in School*, London: FPA (second edition).

Prendergast, S. (1995) 'Learning the Body in the Mind', in Holland, J.

and Blair, M. (eds.) *Debates and Issues in Feminist Research and Peda-gogy*, Milton Keynes: Open University Press.

Prendergast, S. (1996) 'Throwing Like a Girl . . . but Catching Like a Boy: Some Thoughts on Everyday Embodiment in Secondary School', *Working Papers on Childhood and the Study of Children* No. 12, Papers from the Conference '*Children, Health and the Body*', Dept of Child Studies, Lindkoping University, Sweden, April 1996.

Prendergast, S. and Forrest, S. (1997a) '"Shorties, Low-lifers, Hard nuts and Kings". Boys and the Transformation of Emotions', in Bendelow, G. and Williams, S. (eds.) *Emotions in Social Life: Social Theories and Contemporary Issues*, London: Routledge.

Prendergast, S. and Forrest, S. (1997b) 'Gendered Groups and the Nego-tiation of Heterosexuality in School', In Segal, L. (ed.) *New Sexual Agendas*, London: Macmillan.

Preston, P. (1994) *Mother Father Deaf*, Cambridge, MA: Harvard Univer-sity Press.

Proust, M. (1983) *Remembrance of Things Past*, Vol. II, translated by Scott-Moncrieff and Kilmartin, Harmondsworth: Penguin Books.

Prout, A. (1986) '"Wet Children" and "Little Actresses": Going Sick in Primary School', *Sociology of Health and Illness*, 8, 765–89.

Prout, A. (1989) 'Sickness as a Dominant Symbol in Life Course Transi-tions: an Illustrated Theoretical Framework', *Sociology of Health and Illness*, 11, 4: 336–59.

Prout, A. and James, A. (1990) 'A New Paradigm for the Sociology of Childhood? Provenance, Promise and Problems', In James, A. and Prout, A. (eds.) *Constructing and Reconstructing Childhood*, Basingtoke: Falmer Press.

Qvortrup, J. et al. (eds.) (1994) *Childhood Matters: Social Theory, Practice and Policy*, Aldershot: Avebury.

Roberts, D.K., (ed.) (1938) *The Centuries' Poetry 4: Hood to Hardy*, Harmondsworth: Pelican Books.

Rudberg, M. (1995) 'A Bloody Story? On the Construction of Bodily Gender for Girls', *Nora* (Nordic Journal of Women's Studies), 1: 32–44, Scandinavian University Press.

Salmond, A. (1982) 'Theoretical Landscapes. On a Cross-cultural Conception of Knowledge', in Parkin, D. (ed.) *Semantic Anthropology*, ASA Monograph 22, London: Academic Press.

Sarbin, T. (1966) 'Role Enactment', in Biddle, B. and Thomas, E. (eds.) *Role Theory Concepts and Research*, New York: Wiley.

Sarris, A. (1971) *Confessions of a Cultist: On The Cinema 1955/1969*, New York: Simon and Schuster.

Scheper-Hughes, N. (1989) *Child Survival: Anthropological Perspectives on the Treatment and Maltreatment of Children*, Dordrecht: Reidel.

Scheper-Hughes, N. and Lock, M. (1987) 'The Mindful Body: a Prolegomenon to Future Work in Medical Anthropology', *Medical Anthropology Quarterly*, 1, 1: 16–41.

Scott, P. (1991) 'Levers and Counterweights: a Laboratory that Failed to Raise the World', *Social Studies Of Science*, 21, 1: 7–35.

Shapin, S. (1985) 'Following Scientists Around', *Social Studies of Science* 18, 3: 533–50.

Shilling, C. (1993) *The Body and Social Theory*, London: Sage.

Scholem, G. (1991) 'Walter Benjamin and his Angel', in Smith, G. (ed.) *On Walter Benjamin: Critical Essays and Reflections*, Cambridge, MA: MIT Press.

Shrum, W. (1988) 'Review Essay – The Labyrinth of Science', *American Journal of Sociology*, 94(2): 396–403.

Simmel G. (1902) 'The Number of Members as Determining the Sociological Form of the Group', *American Journal of Sociology*, 8, 1: 1–46, 158–96.

Simmons, R.G. and Blyth, D.A. (1988) *Moving into Adolescence*. New York: Aldine and De Gruyte.

Smart, B. (1985) *Michel Foucault*, London, Routledge.

Solberg, A. (1990) 'Negotiating Childhood: Changing Constructions of Age for Norwegian children', in James, A. and Prout, A. (eds.) *Constructing and Reconstructing Childhood*, Basingtoke: Falmer Press.

Spender, D. (1989) *Invisible Women: the Schooling Scandal*, London: Women's Press.

Spicker S.F. and Gadow S. (eds.) (1980) *Nursing: Images and Ideals. Opening Dialogue with the Humanities*, New York: Springer.

Stafford, C. (1995) *Learning and the Process of Childhod in China*, Cambridge: Cambridge University Press.

Stainton Rogers, W. and Roche, J. (1994) *Children's Welfare and Children's Rights: a Practical Guide to the Law*, London: Hodder and Stoughton.

Star, S.L. and Griesemer, J.R. (1989) 'Institutional Ecology, "Translations" and Boundary Objects: Amateurs and Professionals in Berkeley's Museum of Vertebrate Zoology, 1907–39', *Social Studies of Science*, 19(3): 387–420.

Steedman, C. (1990) *Childhood, Culture and Class in Britain: Margaret McMillan 1860–1931*, London: Virago.

Steedman, C. (1992) 'Bodies, Figures and Physiology: Margaret McMillan and the Late Nineteenth-century Remaking of Working-class Childhood', In Cooter, R. (ed.) *In the Name of the Child: Health and Welfare, 1880–1940*, London: Routledge.

Steedman, C. (1995) *Strange Dislocations: Childhood and the Idea of Human Interiority 1780–1930*, London: Virago.

Swann, A. (1993) 'Recognition of Abuse', in Owen, H. And Pritchard, J. (eds.) *Good Practice in Child Protection: a Manual for Professionals*, London: Jessica Kingsley Publishers.

Tattum, D.P. and Lane, D.A. (eds.) (1989) *Bullying in Schools*. Stoke-on-Trent: Trentham Books.

Thomson, R. and Scott, S. (1991) *Learning about Sex. Young Women and the Social Construction of Sexual Identity*, London: Tufnell Press.

Thornburg, H.D. (1981) 'Adolescent Sources of Information on Sex', *J. School Health*, April: 274–7.

Truffaut, F. 1968 (1962) *Jules and Jim,* London: Lorimer.

Turner, B.S. (1984) *The Body and Society: Explorations in Social Theory*, Oxford: Blackwell.

Turner, B.S. (1992) *Regulating Bodies: Essays in Medical Sociology*, London: Routledge.

Turner, T.S. (1980) 'The Social Skin', in Cherfas, J. and Lewin, R. (eds), *Not Work Alone: Cross-cultural View of Activities Superfluous to Survival*, London: Temple Smith.

Turner, T. (1994) 'Bodies and anti-Bodies: Flesh and Fetish in Contemporary Social Theory', in Csordas, T.J. (ed.) *Embodiment and Experience: the Existential Ground of Culture and Self*, Cambridge: Cambridge University Press.

Turner, V.W. (1977) 'Process, System and Symbol: a New Anthropological Synthesis', *Daedalus*, 106 (3), Summer, 61–80.

Urwin, K. and Sharland, E. (1992) 'From Bodies to Minds in Childcare Literature: Advice to Parents in Inter-war Britain', in Cooter, R. (ed.) *In the Name of the Child: Health and Welfare, 1880–1940*, London: Routledge.

Vaihinger, H. (1924) *The Philosophy of 'as if'*, London: Routledge & Kegan Paul.

Van Gennep, A. (1960) *The Rites of Passage*, translated by M.B. Vizedom and G.L. Caffte, London: Routledge & Kegan Paul.

Vendler, Z. (1984) 'Understanding People', in Sweder, R.A. and Levin, R.A. (eds.) *Culture Theory: Essays on Mind, Self and Emotion*, Cambridge: Cambridge University Press.

Walker Perry, N. and Wrightsman, L.S. (1991) *The Child Witness: Legal Issues and Dilemmas*, London: Sage.

Watson, J., Cunningham-Burley, S., Watson, S. and Milburn, K. (1986) 'Lay Theorising about the "Body" and Implications for Health Promotion', *Health Education Research Theory and Practice*, 11, (2), 116–72.

Wattam, C. (1992) *Making a Case in Child Protection*, Longman: Harlow.

Wiltshire. J. (1992) *Jane Austen and the Body*, Cambridge: Cambridge University Press.

Woodroffe, C. et al. (1993) *Children, Teenagers and Health: the Key Data*, Milton Keynes: Open University Press.

Woolgar, S. (1988) *Science – the Very Idea*, London: Routledge.

Woolgar, S. and Pawluch, D. (1985) 'Ontological Gerrymandering: the Anatomy of Social Problems Explanations', *Social Problems*, 32(3): 214–27.

Wright, E. (1990) 'New Representationalism', *Journal for the Theory of Social Behaviour*, 20(1): 65–92.

Index